CYBERSELFISH

CYBERSELFISH

AN CRITICAL ROMP THROUGH THE TERRIBLY LIBERTARIAN CULTURE OF HIGH TECH

Paulina Borsook

zer0 books

Winchester, UK
Washington, USA

First published by Zero Books, 2026
Zero Books is an imprint of Watkins Books.

For distributor details and how to order please visit the 'Ordering' section on our website.

ISBN: 978-1-80695-184-0
978-1-80695-185-7 (ebook)
Library of Congress Control Number is available

A CIP catalogue record for this book is available from the British Library.

Design: Matthew Greenfield

UK: Printed and bound by CPI Group (UK) Ltd, Croydon, CR0 4YY
Printed in North America by CPI GPS partners

CONTENTS

FOREWORD

Reading Paulina Borsook's *Cyberselfish* from here in 2026 creates an unexpected sensation: of stasis; of the salt marsh; of a halt having been declared. That's not down to the book's cutting-and-slashing tone — such a bittersweet reminder of a lost culture of irreverent critique. The sense of abeyance instead comes from the uncanny realization that so little has changed among the people Borsook writes about.

Despite Silicon Valley's supposed preoccupation with innovation and change, the core "technolibertarian" ideas and identities that Borsook skewered so perceptively in 2001 have barely shifted in the interceding twenty-five years. This is just one insight that makes the current reprint so critical: from hypothetical cryogenics to contractual polyamory, you will immediately recognize the compulsions of a specific subset of California technologist. These may seem novel as they and their ideas surge into wider public consciousness under the banner of firms like FTX, Palantir, OpenAI, and SpaceX. But the truth Borsook's early document reveals is that in our time they are already fossils, frozen in amber — or at best, badly shopworn.

Like any such compulsion, this fixated repetition — not a body of inquiry but "an animist religion [made] out of PCs" — is rooted in deep psychological wounds and frailties. In part thanks to her outsider's viewpoint as a woman surrounded by men far less impressive than they appeared,[1] Borsook saw this, too, far before most. Her lampooning of the childishness of the technolibertarians' cry for the abolition of bedtime is

1 Another notable early warning against techno-authoritarianism was written by a woman: El Sandifer's *Neoreaction: A Basilisk.*

no less spot-on now that these man-children have successfully seized the reins of human civilization: technolibertarianism "cuts through all that messy icky maddening complexity that's the Real World: It's a comfort to believe everything does best if left alone."

What has changed (or at least is changing) is a broadening awareness of these strange and off-putting Silicon Valley beliefs. The public is now well aware of the techno-futurists backing far-right politics and fostering an AI industry with bizarrely anti-human public messaging, as well as their strange commitment to nakedly anti-social "innovations" like prediction markets.

The enduring emotional core of the technolibertarian theory of progress, too, remains the same: as Borsook puts it, "Magical thinking: If you think good thoughts about the future, it will be a good future!" But as this Panglossian vision begins to more overtly vampirize the health and prosperity of the society that nurtured it, the pitch is losing its glamour.

In the decades after *Cyberselfish* first appeared, figures like Elon Musk and Mark Zuckerberg positioned themselves as essentially squishy liberals, working to connect humanity and solve climate change. I count myself among the many misled, to one degree or another, by this deceptively pro-social marketing effort. Innumerable lesser lights, too, spent the decade after the Great Financial Crisis declaring their goal to "do well by doing good," while Peter Thiel could have been understood as a conventional right-wing libertarian. Only Donald Trump's arrival and its consequences created the conditions in which Musk and Thiel's technolibertarianism could openly reveal its true and final form: an exterminationist logic viscerally repulsed by human life itself.

As a student radio nerd and music writer in the early 2000s, I was seduced by the frontier rhetoric of the file-sharing revolution, and a huge portion of my career as a journalist has involved writing about cryptocurrency. Both technologies were products of the "cypherpunk" ethos Borsook here properly classifies under technolibertarianism. That movement had an alluringly populist and anti-authoritarian sheen, but again Borsook sees the deeper truth. She reads much of cypherpunk aesthetics and politics as differing little from the adoption of "militia" language, identity, and affect as a compensation for growing up as a bullied nerd. (Take Palmer Luckey, head of major defense contractor Anduril, who looks like he'd be of more use at a Magic: The Gathering tournament than anywhere near the Pentagon — much less a battlefield.)

And now, with AI and crypto, we have seen the reality that comes after the end of copyright protection for artists, the end of anti-money laundering protections, the end (at least in the US) of law itself. The promise of total freedom is starting to look a lot more like total chaos. One must ask whether that was the real goal all along.

Borsook's chosen term offers a menu of Venn Diagram partners. Technolibertarianism is recognizable in Richard Barbrook and Andy Cameron's contemporaneous "The California Ideology." Émile Torres and Timnit Gebru's recent, more academic acronym "TESCREAL" breaks the ideological complex down into its many variations and branches, including Cosmism — a pre–Silicon Valley Russian breed of techno-fantasia — and Effective Altruism, which Silicon Valley has transmuted from a modest idea about wealth disparity into a billionaire-flattering ideology of econometric charity and Malthusian tradeoffs. In my own work, I use the term "techno-utopianism" to highlight how these ideas focus on the far future at the expense of the present. But it's ultimately a bit simpler than that: technolibertarism boils down to a theory of society rooted in social Darwinist conceptions of nature and the Austrian School economics of Friedrich Hayek. It cashes out to hardline deregulatory free marketeering, deeply influenced by Ayn Rand's hyperindividualist "objectivism."

Hayek's core premises include the idea that any attempt to make the productive forces of industry work for the improvement of all mankind is a "road to serfdom" that inevitably impoverishes entire societies. The suffering of the poor and marginalized is, seen through a Hayekian lens, unfortunate but inevitable. Any attempt to help the huddling masses through the power of social organization risks disrupting the just-so signals that guide Adam Smith's Invisible Hand of the market, and so destroying the very prosperity the do-gooders aim to share.

Paramount for the Hayekians is the belief that market data is not just one source of feedback for social organization, but the *definitive and unfailing* North Star of economic and social life. As Borsook writes, "These guys believe that Real Soon Now, in an era of digital, untraceable, anonymous cash, capitalism will have triumphed in its purest global form," in large part by capturing more and more granular detail in its market data — that is, by being able to put a price on everything.[2]

In the place of governance of any kind, the technolibertarian posits everything as trending towards a naturally occurring equilibrium that produces the best possible outcome. But the brutal reality is that the "free" market fails again and again, while its self-interested defenders use power to create the illusion of "natural" balance.

This uncertainty — the possibility that the market is *not* the source of all truth and value — is the nightmare of the Hayekian technolibertarian. Intellectual work produces massive external

2 As I write, we are seeing the apotheosis of these ideas in the rise of Polymarket and Kalshi, "prediction markets" developed by staunch technolibertarian Robin Hanson in the early 2000s, in conjunction with a new market-driven theory of governance dubbed "futarchy." Hanson's funding, as with so many of these anti-government ideas, came from the government.

benefits not captured in economic terms by the likes of social critics or fraud investigators; hence the technolibertarian devalues criticism and education, and seeks to delegitimize them broadly. It doesn't seem a stretch that the staunch refusal of billionaires like Elon Musk to fund cultural institutions in the manner of previous oligarchs is a matter of fragile ego: the technolibertarian worldview is built *for* men who don't understand art, to protect them from the threatening suggestion that they should ever be brought to try.

As Borsook sums it all up: "In high tech, political libertarianism takes the shape of a convenient obliviousness to the value of social contract and governance, however imperfectly and stupidly enacted." It is the belief that, in fact, some men *are* islands. Mostly engineers ,it turns out.

The most fascinating claim in *Cyberselfish*, one that I've rarely if ever heard articulated elsewhere, is that Silicon Valley was turned against the idea of democratic oversight specifically by "the US Government's mostly awful handling of free speech and privacy as these relate to technology." The US first started aggressively trying to limit the spread of digital encryption methods in the 1970s, but the recent passage of anti-encryption and anti-privacy measures in the UK shows the continuing sway of the absurd censor's impulse: if nothing else, encryption is a practical necessity for the security of the modern internet.

It seems a deep cruelty that the mishandling of encryption in the 1990s should lead, in our own time, to so much callow libertarian destructiveness.

As I write this, peer-reviewed analysis has concluded that Elon Musk's DOGE mania, in which he and a crew of white thugs with street names like "Big Balls" ripped the copper wire out of critical government programs, has led directly to the deaths of more than 1 million people worldwide. His response has been a denialist tantrum for the ages. The idea that any government program has ever had a positive impact, or that removing one would have real-world consequences, seems simply alien to him and his ilk. Borsook brutally dismantled this element of Musk's character long before Elon himself came into the limelight: "The most virulent form of philosophical technolibertarianism is a kind of scary, psychologically brittle, pre-political autism...an inability to reconcile the demands of being individual with the demands of participating in society."[3]

At an even more systematic level, Borsook points out that the wealth of Silicon Valley was rooted in a robust, publicly funded California school system, prior to the libertarian Proposition 13 undermining the state's ability to collect taxes. The stupidity and avarice rife in the tech sector today are the visible fruit of that hollowing out of education: a product the market is particularly bad at producing without government help.

One price of all those unpaid taxes may be the looming collapse of the AI bubble meant to become the Valley's Next Big Thing. Inflated by the same self-satisfied hopium Borsook saw twenty-five years ago, the technolibertarian dream metastasized, in the form of AI, into a delusion of Godhood, a premature promise that "tech" would cure cancer, solve climate change, and replace all human workers. Many fortunes have been committed or deployed to achieving this dream of pure capital, but the returns in efficiency or profit haven't yet manifested, creating a looming crisis of confidence. As Borsook wrote when Sam Altman was about fifteen years old, "Virtuality means using computers to overcome boundaries of time and space and physical limitations" — but not necessarily successfully.

3 "Pre-political" certainly describes the variety of technolibertarianism I have studied the most, Effective Altruism, whose theory of politics, for all its supposed novelty, boils down to a tired familiarity: letting the richest run things.

The Valley has been seduced from the start by its own Silicon, ever-more inclined to mistake representation in 1s and 0s for the thing itself. But the return of the Real is inevitable. The only question is exactly how, not whether, it will upend our delusions of certainty.

David Z. Morris

INTRODUCTION

I LIVE IN SANTA CRUZ, a college and surfer town about seventy-five miles down the coast from San Francisco, historically known for its boardwalk. Until the resident University of California campus (UCSC) was built there in the 1960s, it was a small town largely settled by farmers and fisherfolks and enjoyed by retirees and vacationers. UCSC changed the tone of the place to that of earth-muffin and sunny good vibes: What else could be expected from a school that has as its mascot the banana slug? UCSC's History of Consciousness graduate program (not mickeymouse but as rarefied as you'd think) is highly regarded among humanities geeks. Its pioneering programs in organic gardening and agroecology are world famous, as is its music department with its strength in Javanese gamelan.

But in recent years, this nuclear-free, vegan-friendly, lesbian/feminist-sympathetic, New Age–tolerant town has become a southern satellite extension of Silicon Valley. Twenty miles through the coastal mountains over nasty tortuous Highway 17, Santa Cruz is taking on a new identity, that of a bedroom community for one of the greatest and growing concentrations of new money, technology workers, and corporations that the United States — and the world — has ever seen.

Surveying the personal ads in free weekly alternative papers is always a good way to key into what matters locally: for example, in Washington, DC, GS grades are specified. So it didn't surprise me when, maybe for the tenth time during the four years or so since I had moved to Santa Cruz, I saw listed in the personals a particular kind of notice for a man looking for a woman. It didn't say he was buffed or liked walks along the beach or motorcycle trips to Big Sur or was into caring and sharing or, more *mode de jour*, that he was dominant but respected limits or was predominantly attracted to Asian women. Instead, "Ayn Rand enthusiast is seeking libertarian-oriented female for great conversation and romance. I am a very bright and attractive high-tech entrepreneur."

This juxtaposition of Ayn Rand enthusiasm and high tech entrepreneurship might seem as random an association as eye color with birthdate, for when people think about high tech, they may not think about politics or culture or the values carried with it. All they may know of high tech are its advertised appeals: the charisma of Apple Computer and Steve Jobs, the quirky pleasures of Web surfing, the scads of instant millionaires it creates, the way email so readily puts grandparents in touch with their grandchildren or long-lost childhood sweethearts.

People who are rightfully glad to be participating in a mailing list for migraine sufferers or to be using laptop computers to work from home most likely haven't thought about the corporations, institutions, and people that have made doing so possible. People not intimate with technology may be thrilled by how holdings in high tech stocks have enhanced the value of their retirement portfolios, pleased by the ease of online shopping (furniture.com! i-drycleaning! e-gravel!), concerned that their children may not be Web savvy enough to have a lucrative career as a knowledge worker, bemused when they spot a blimp flying over a sporting event carrying signage for a tire company's Web site.

But high tech, like any human artifact, is not culturally tasteless, odorless, colorless. It contains attitude, mind-set, philosophy; and with geeks, the attitude, mind-set, and philosophy is libertarianism, in many-blossomed efflorescence. The libertarian-technology axis has been solidly in place long enough that the phrase "a self-described neopagan libertarian who enjoys shooting automatic weapons" required no further explanation when it appeared as part of a technology news feature in an April 1998 issue of the online magazine *Salon*. A

Wall Street Journal front-page feature by Gerald Seib in June 1998 described how, "by wading into the world of computers, federal trustbusters also have waded into the country's foremost hotbed of libertarian political activism." Northern California's high tech community is a libertarian psychographic hot zone, and this guy's mate-quest had to be the Real Deal.

Yet high tech's dominant libertarian mind-set is less well known than the obvious wealth and new ways of living and working it keeps spinning off — and, upon close inspection, it's also far less appealing. It's a pervasive *weltanschauung*, ranging from the classic eighteenth-century liberal-philosophy that-which-governs-best-governs-least love of laissez-faire free-market economics to social Darwinism, anarcho-capitalism, and beyond. It manifests itself in everything from a rebel-outsider posture common in high tech (I program, I attend raves, and I practice targetshooting with the combat shotgun on weekends) to an embarrassing lack of philanthropy (unless it involves the giving away of computers). The technolibertarian stance can be well thought out or merely a kind of reflexive guild membership (all my geek friends and coworkers think like this, so why not join the fun?).

STRANGERS IN THE NIGHT

My fascination, mongoose-to-cobra style, with the romance between libertarianism and high tech has existed for quite a while. I was first startled by what I've come to call technolibertarianism when I started knocking around high tech in the early 1980s. In the San Francisco Bay Area, where I have spent most of my adult life, most liberal-arts flakes ineluctably end up working with computers, because that's where the jobs are. So it was for me back in 1981, a few years out of UC-Berkeley with a degree in psycholinguistics, a smattering of acting classes, a lot of waitressing, and a few crabbed little published poems to my name.

Initially, the geekworld I was running into seemed peopled with characters very like the familiar Cal Tech/Jet Propulsion Lab/ Southern California aerospace guys I fondly recollected from my childhood in Pasadena. There, the engineers and scientists more likely than not shared a vaguely New Deal mentality. They were of a generation that had seen what good things the government could do, from winning World War II to putting a man on the moon. And even if some were strong on anticommunism, conservative rather than liberal, they believed that the government could do great and good things. The unspoken cultural assumption was that progress in our shared civilization was helped along by government programs supporting scientific research, public health, education, and the bringing of electricity and telephony to rural areas. And if quizzed, these technologists would probably all have agreed that there was a shared civilization worth fostering, for geek and nongeek, rich and poor.

On first inspection, the 1980s and 1990s nerds *as people* didn't appear that different from the ones I'd known as a kid. But I came to realize that their values, politics, and orientation to the world were very very different from those of the benign guys in my childhood who, yes, actually had carried slide rules and worn pocket protectors, as no one in high tech actually does now. It took many years of personal observation — while I moved from technical-writer positions at software firms to staff positions at computer magazines to, starting in 1989, freelance gigs for high tech corporations and for the glossy, glamourous high tech style sheet *Wired* — to piece together a picture of an emergent social and political subculture, one that can seem dangerously naive and, at its worst, downright scary.

Attending technical conferences and trade shows, getting to know and making friends with computerists, eavesdropping and reading, I was trying to make sense of the libertarianism I found all around. The belief systems I ran into were confusing, for this passionate libertarian population has for the most part only experienced good things, and not bad, from government. And they were disturbing, for beneath them I sensed nastiness, narcissism, and lack of human warmth, qualities that surely don't need to be hardwired into the fields of computing and communications.

In light of the peculiar mind-set I had been encountering all around, this lonely-hearts ad in that Santa Cruz alternative weekly did not register as an anomaly. Nor should I have been taken aback (though in the nicest possible way) by the volume of email generated by a humor piece I wrote for www.suck.com, the *Spy* magazine of the World Wide Web. I had conceived of the satire as "The Cosmo Girl's Guide to Dating Technolibertarians," and the Sucksters retitled it "Sex and the Single URL." It was full of helpful dos and don'ts ("do say how you've never gotten over Ayn Rand, whom you first read when you were seventeen"; "don't talk about your friend the urban planner who uses HUD money to develop low-income housing"). More remarkable, but inadvertently so, was what the emailers were saying. Guys felt certain we'd met (we hadn't). Guys were positive that I had been writing about them, or about someone they knew (I hadn't written about anyone in particular). Guys wanted to meet me for coffee, as I was obviously their dream girl (it was a joke, guys, and no, thank you). At last! A woman who understands me! No, more modestly, I was just someone who had been paying attention.

An essay I wrote for *Mother Jones* magazine in July 1996 articulated more directly my unease with technolibertarianism and focused on the aggressive lack of philanthropy in high tech and the contempt for government when government had been so verrry verrry good to high tech. As I wailed,

> Without government, there would be no Internet... Further there would be no microprocessor industry, the fount of Silicon Valley's prosperity (early computers sprang out of government-funded electronics research). There would also be no

> major research universities cranking out qualified tech workers: Stanford, Berkeley, MIT, and Carnegie-Mellon get access to state-of-the-art equipment plus R&D, courtesy of tax-reduced academic-industrial consortia and taxpayer-funded grants and fellowships.

High tech's animosity toward government and regulation goes beyond the animosity that exists in most of the general population, and is stridently opposed to other views.

"Cyberselfish," the essay, is tied for first place on my life list in terms of the amount of email generated by something I've written. It seemed to have externalized the dismay other folks have felt with this high tech political culture. It flew around the Internet and got me interviews on radio and speaking gigs at conferences — yet was also the first thing I have ever written that got me flamed (Netspeak for being the object of electronic vituperation.) "Cyberselfish" achieved a modest amount of net-fame; two Usenet groups (the Internet's public electronic chat forums) devoted themselves to trashing the piece and questioned my personal and professional integrity, which only shows the state folks get themselves into when their religion, masquerading as politics, gets attacked. Libertarianism on the Net, in spite of more than twenty years of government support for the Net's creation and development, is a seed culture that continues to self-propagate for intellectual generation after generation.

OTOH (Internet acronym for On The Other Hand), that same *Mother Jones* essay got me responses from young people working in what's known as South Park,[1] saying they had never heard this counterversion of reality before. It seemed to address the vague disquiet they had been feeling about the grim fairy tales of Big Bad Government versus the unlimited free market. Prosperity, goodness, and health were supposed to be everyone's

1 The name comes from the eponymous San Francisco urban green around which Web startups, e-commerce companies, *Wired* magazine, and every other go-go Netnew Net venture is, or wants to be, located.

destiny once Toffler Second-Wave old-and-in-the-way Machine Age bureaucrats got out of the way. These South Parkers had been wondering if what they had been promised would turn out to be Potemkin villages for a new age, and, to mix metaphors (though not countries), if that *Mother Jones* essay was samizdat, Voice of America broadcast, circa 1957. It's as if naming the demon — technolibertarianism — drained it of some of its power, much as in psychotherapy the first step toward solving a problem consists of observing it and describing it.

And the demon does have plenty of power. It was the inspiriting force behind *Wired* under its original owners, when it was the *Playboy/Rolling Stone/Vogue* for twenty-first-century digital boys (in spirit, if not the flesh), tastemaker/marker of this culture. Part of the magazine's transgressive sexiness historically stemmed from its sassy, enraged libertarianism: What adolescent male (in thought, if not biological fact), the original target in sensibility (bratty, precocious) for the magazine, doesn't want to rebel against nannies, even in the form of the Nanny State?

When I have run into liberal elder statesmen and women of high tech — meaning people over the age of thirty — they sigh with only a small amount of hope and a great deal of resignation when I say I am trying to document high tech's default political culture of libertarianism. Like weary Resistance fighters too long without succor, they have almost given up speaking out against the consensus reality in which they live and work. Libertarianism is a computer-culture badge of belonging, and libertarians are the most vocal political thinkers and talkers in high tech.

WHO GOES THERE?

In talking about the connection between computer folks and libertarianism, I don't mean only registered members of the official Libertarian Party. This is the party that routinely nominates Harry Browne as its presidential candidate (though there has always been a big overlap between the Libertarian Party and technologists). Classic libertarianism combines the traditional conservative right's aversion to government, with regard to laws, entitlements, and services, with the traditional left's insistence on individual liberty. But the ubiquitous free-form libertarianism of high tech is as much a lens through which to view the world as it is a political philosophy. This worldview shape-shifts into all manner of beasts, varying in form from socially conservative belief systems that would do Gary Bauer proud to those that look fondly on anarchy in personal and economic affairs. The Silicon Valley worldview contains within it all different colors of free-market/anti-regulation/social Darwinist/aphilanthropic/guerrilla/neo-pseudo-biological/atomistic threads.

Technolibertarians could be your brothers or cousins who are computer science graduate students, pretty much in any school in the country. One might be the guy you call to fix your computer, whether you work at home or in an office. They are likely to be present among those who staff your Internet Service Provider (ISP). They could be numerous among the computer professionals attending a Star Trek or science-fiction convention or among the local practitioners of Wicca who have day jobs working with or on computers. Both the male history major turned Web designer who sports surfer baggies and his female colleague who sports a baby T-shirt are, more likely than not (and whether or not they identify with the word), technolibertarian. A game-designer who telecommutes from the Mother Lode country of the foothills of the Sierra Nevadas and the people who get all mushy around the word "entrepreneur" are libertarian. Pretty much wherever you go, where there are two or more computer people gathered, from Salt Lake City to Gainesville, Florida, whether online or off — in computer science departments, high tech startups, or anywhere on the Internet — there is libertarianism.

Technolibertarians can also be the suits — that is, business types — who have swarmed into high tech as never before. They are the newly graduated MBAs who have made San Francisco once again the financial center of the West, as it was for decades after the nineteenth-century forty-niners came to town. Investors both institutional and individual, marketers, analysts, consultants, newsletter-writers, commentators, pundits, and theorists, and all the other aspirants and carpetbaggers attracted to the wads of money being made in Silicon Valley: their libertarian number is legion. If they aren't libertarian before they get here, they sure catch on real quick.

It's gotten to the point where spammers (those despised untouchables of the Net who violate netiquette by clogging people's email inboxes with commercial junk mail) celebrate themselves as free-market wealth-creating entrepreneurial heroes. They decry those who protest against spam as Stalinist big babies who would stand in the way of progress. Yet spam itself points to contradictory tensions inherent in the technolibertarian notion of property rights über alles: How do you resolve the conflict between the rights freedom marketers should inalienably have to flog their wares (usually silly or seamy-seeming propositions, such as multi-level marketing schemes or invitations to visit porn sites) and the annoyance-tending-toward-rage their intrusive consumption of network resources causes for most folks? Whose rights trump whose? Ah, that's politics, and despite libertarian wishes for it to be otherwise, it ain't and has never been easy.

Perhaps it's overly broad to dump all these folks into the same large libertarian Venn diagram, but "libertarian" is the best word I can come up with to describe such a deep, broad, but inevitably ambiguous cultural current. I know of no other obvious term of art, and "libertarian," used in this sociological sense, is no vaguer than, say, "democratic," or "hierarchical." Consider the word as placed in its religious and cultural, and not strictly political, semantic fields.

VARIETIES OF RELIGIOUS EXPERIENCE

Much as there are two forms of the plague — bubonic (less contagious and not necessarily lethal) and pneumonic (violently infectious and almost always fatal) — technolibertarianism manifests in two forms: political and philosophical.

Political libertarianism, logically enough, asserts an overt anti-regulatory / pro-market bias. It is tempting to argue that this is the position of folks who are pro-business everywhere — but in high tech, the antigovernment stance isn't usually combined with the common business hypocrisy that's called corporate welfare (that is, business people who hate the government until they need a bailout or a subsidy). Instead, in high tech, political libertarianism takes the shape of a convenient obliviousness to the value of social contract and governance, however imperfectly and stupidly enacted.

Still, the relationship with government is complex, for these high tech workers may have voted or raised money for Clinton, in spite of his administration's alienating stands against strong protections for free speech and privacy. Elected state and federal representatives from Silicon Valley are split between Democrat and Republican. With some exceptions, most people in high tech aren't comfortable with the reactionary social agenda of the radical right wing of the Republican Party. It's bad for business, the Republican backward-gazing vision to a 1950s or nineteenth-century America that never was, because high tech always believes the future will have to be better! Yet people in area codes 650 and 408 might have voted for Tom Campbell, the socially moderate (and pro-choice), fiscally conservative Republican representative from Silicon Valley.

These *political* technolibertarians in character seem not so different from other members of their age, education, and income cohort, believing that government may be more broken than not, but that it is not the Great Satan. In that sense, technolibertarianism is far more of a political way of being in the world than an actual voting pattern. Many libertarians within high tech may be registered as Democrats, Republicans, Greens, Libertarians, or as independents, or may not have voted in years — yet on any test that could be designed to assess "how libertarian are you?", would score high high high.

It is for these reasons that political scientists who study the demographics of the Net do not find voting patterns that differ much from those of the world outside. A quick Web search of proceedings of recent meetings of academic political science associations lists nothing on libertarianism or high tech, much less their intersection. As a friend who is a liberal political science professor at Stanford remarked: Why would political scientists pay any attention to a movement that basically says conventional notions of politics are bunk? Because of their conceptual dismissal of government, technolibertarians typically can't be bothered to engage in conventional political maneuvers — and so as political entities are largely rendered invisible. And because they are invisible, they know little about affecting government.

High tech mostly remains distant and unfamiliar to much of the mainstream political class of the United States. It doesn't matter if it's Cokie Roberts writing embarrassingly ill-informed commentary on the dangers of netizen mobocracy[2] or former San Francisco mayor Dianne Feinstein, now a California senator, voting *for* the now declared unconstitutional Communications Decency Act, a would-be, though impossible to implement, damper on free speech on the Net.

High tech, with its wealth and attitudes, has tended to fly both over and under the radar of conventional politics and those who pontificate about it. Although, heading into the presidential election of 2000, both Republican and Democratic candidates

---

2 In an April 5, 1997, column cowritten with her husband, she complained that because of the ease of access email gives, "representative government is under attack."

came a courtin' because there is now so *much* money to be creamed off.

A backhanded testimony to the presence of *political* technolibertarianism does come from academic political science — though in a roundabout way. Terry Christensen, a professor of political science at California State University-San Jose since 1970, where he is now the department chair, specializes in local politics. San Jose, the market town of Santa Clara County, high tech's epicenter, has a population roughly equal to that of San Francisco — and has become the site for downtown growth and redevelopment (museums, fancy hotels, convention center).

Apricot orchards and canning are long gone from Santa Clara County, once called the Valley of Heart's Delight. Through accidents of geography and geology, it had been some of the best land for farming since agriculture began (topsoil in the hundreds of feet). Now gone forever, California Pastoral has been irretrievably displaced by high tech — with its grab of agricultural lands for housing and industrial parks, its congested roads and highways filled with commuter traffic. These are *political* events, though it might be more pleasant to pretend otherwise.

With a few exceptions (Applied Materials, Adobe), high tech companies have been and mostly remain absent from local politics[3] — odd, given how much they now shape the *local* economy and the demands their presence places on the local community. And it was only in late 1999, when gridlock and astoundingly poor planning for housing (Let's zone light-industrial! So what if people have to drive two hours in each direction in order to live in a house they can afford!) somewhat threatened the Valley's ability to recruit, that *local* politics came to seem relevant to Valley movers and shakers.

Christensen says that until recently, high tech didn't even

3 Hewlett-Packard, the company, and the Hewlett and Packard foundations set up by its two founders, remain the glorious Silicon Valley exceptions, in all respects, with regard to corporate citizenship and community activism.

make political donations for local issues and candidates. Only in the late 1990s did it begin to make its presence even lightly felt. Over the decades that he's watched the local scene, there have been only a few issues where high tech interest made itself known: IBM demanding to locate its facility outside where San Jose zoning said it could; a consortium of high tech companies acting to clean up aquifers contaminated by high tech manufacturing; and later, the same group successfully lobbying to have a county sales tax assessed to support mass transit.

It's not a lot for more than twenty-five years of radical growth and change in the community. The local level is where most people feel the presence of politics (has the proposed Santa Cruz no-smoking-while-waiting-on-line-outside-at-the-movies ordinance gone too far?), and feel also that they can influence politics. High tech's absence as a political actor from the community where it so affects the light and air around it is strange, given how strong a socioeconomic reagent it is: Christensen arrived at CSU-SJ at a time when he could look forward to buying a house. Now, not only are most newly arrived professors unable to buy a house, they may not even be able to afford to *rent* in the communities where they teach.

But "Silicon Valley" companies and executives and workers may identify themselves not with where they actually live and work and go to movies and send their kids to school but, more saliently, as members of a high tech archipelago. This virtual territory extends from Sebastopol, home of O'Reilly Associates, esteemed publishers of highly technical computer books and boosters of Open Source Software,[4] way north of Marin County (which is itself north of the Golden Gate Bridge); way east over the East Bay hills in Contra Costa County to Pleasanton, home of HRIS (human resources information systems) gargantua PeopleSoft; west to the Silicon Valley-San Francisco transit — itself

4 Open Source Software is a sort of worldwide communal product-response to Microsoft's hegemony.

a seventy-five-mile arc; and south over the hill to Santa Cruz, with its ever-growing population of software companies and geek houses, equipped with high-speed T1 communications lines and residents who have odd pets (lizards allowed to hibernate in refrigerators, for example), and in many cases, even odder sexual habits. On a good day, it would take more than four hours to circumnavigate this "Silicon Valley," which, as Christensen rightly points out, maps onto no known geopolitical districting or governing body and spreads out over at least eight counties.

In a more typical city-with-suburbs setup, such as that surrounding New York City, people identify themselves as belonging in part to New York City, even though they might live or work on Long Island or in New Jersey or Connecticut. Tri-state authorities exist for transit and a multitude of other matters for which commuters pay taxes.

Defying conventional boundaries is just how high tech likes it. Perhaps *the* most prominent, hyperlinked, and mediagenic venture capitalist (VC), John Doerr (if you hadn't been explicitly informed otherwise, you'd think he was running for office) explained in an interview in a November 2, 1997, issue of the *San Francisco Examiner*,

> When I look at a map of the world... I don't visualize it in terms of miles or even countries. Instead I see Internet packages of E-mail messages flowing between various points. If you drew the kind of map that I'm talking about, you'd find that Boston, Massachusetts, is adjacent to Palo Alto, California — the amount of electronic traffic between those two points is just incredible.

The desire to slip the surly bonds of earth, which runs through much of technolibertarian thinking, might be called virtuality. Meaning "virtue" not in the sense of Plato or chastity before marriage but in the sense of "virtual reality." In the positive sense, virtuality means using computers to overcome boundaries of time and space and physical limitations: It's about email and flight simulators. In the negative sense, it means the same thing, but with the blinding consequences of ignoring the ways, good and real, that we are all grounded in time and space and the realm of the senses. Local politics is all about really being there.

RAVERS AND GILDERS

In this more discorporated realm where techies like to dwell lies *philosophical* technolibertarianism, which goes far deeper than mere politics or economics. Returning to the plague metaphor, philosophical technolibertarianism is the pneumonic strain, which takes down all in its path. It's harder to describe, for if a worldview is pervasive, persuasive, and just part of the air that you breathe, it's harder to cast into visible relief. If you were born in twelfth-century France, you might have been only half-aware of the ways that Christianity influenced every move that you made — and so it is with the philosophical libertarianism in high tech. I can't count the number of times I've gotten into a discussion with a thoughtful, sweet high tech guy about something where he will snort disdainfully about how he's not a libertarian (meaning, he's not like those crazy people over there) and then will come right out with a classic libertarian statement about el stewpido government or the wonders of market disciplines or whatever. It's rather like women who say, "I'm not a feminist but I do believe in equal pay for equal work."

In any event, the most virulent form of philosophical technolibertarianism is a kind of scary, psychologically brittle, prepolitical autism. It bespeaks a lack of human connection and a discomfort with the core of what many of us consider it means to be human. It's an inability to reconcile the demands of being individual with the demands of participating in society, which coincides beautifully with a preference for, and glorification of, being the solo commander of one's computer in lieu of any other economically viable behavior. Computers are so much more rule-based, controllable, fixable, and comprehensible than any human will ever be. As many political schools of thought do, these technolibertarians make a philosophy out of a personality defect.

But beyond the extreme frightening margins, philosophical technolibertarianism self-organizes into different clusters,[5] most fundamentally devolving to whether you are raver or a gilder. These are shorthand for the two main cultural moieties, or perhaps sects, of technolibertarianism.

Ravers are neohippies whose antigovernment stance is more hedonic than moral, more lifestyle choice than policy position. Keep your laws off my body: Let's hear it for drugs, sex, and rock 'n' roll! People who cluster around this technolibertarian locus might want to believe there is a one-world community a-buildin', where through the wonders of the Net we will all communicate and love one another and sing whatever the cyberspace version of "Kumbaya" is, without the repressive parental influence of nasty old governments to interfere in this freelovefest.

Emblem of the ravers is former Grateful Dead lyricist and Electronic Frontier Foundation[6] cofounder John Perry Barlow. Barlow wrote the notorious "Declaration of Independence of Cyberspace," which, in language longing to evoke Henry David Thoreau in "Civil Disobedience" and the Jefferson Airplane's late '60s revolutionary call-to-arms "Volunteers of America," cries out that you are old and sick and tired and tyrannical and we are beautiful and free and loving and of the future. Posted

5 Self-organization, chaos, and complexity theory are indeed much beloved by technolibertarians, for these branches of natural science, aside from being trendy, appeal to engineers' physics envy and also imply that all would beautifully work out if natural laws were allowed to run their course. Take your pick: Rousseau's noble savage or the deism of God as Divine Clockmaker.

6 The EFF is a nonprofit organization dedicated to protecting First and Fourth Amendment rights in the realm of computers and communications

Net-wide, his "Declaration" is perhaps the best-known expression of this kind of technolibertarianism. It's no coincidence that the last fad that Timothy Leary embraced before his death was the Net and that he was taken on as a kind of Jove figure by Barlow and other cyberhippie utopians.

The world-famous "Burning Man" camp-out/festival/artpark that takes place in the Nevada desert every Labor Day weekend is much loved by raver technolibertarians. Their faithful attendance there signals that even though they may have come to spend more time day-to-day thinking about upside earnings potential and mezzanine financing than the wired worlds to come, they can still rave on.

They stand in contrast to what might be called the gilders, social conservatives who would find common ground with former Reagan speechwriter and loopy antifeminist George Gilder, who is in love with the spirit of enterprise and the spirituality of the microchip. Gilder has raised paeans, in countless books and articles, to the wonders of both, puts on conferences, and in some circles is considered high tech's Supreme Intellect. Gilders are most similar to those of the conservative branch of the Republican Party and are suspicious of the government for many of the same reasons. Former *Wired* magazine executive editor Kevin Kelly, an evangelical Christian, might be characterized as a gilder. Gilders aren't necessarily religious in the conventional sense, but many of them are.

MAGIC: THE GATHERING

And just as there can be Chinese Baptists and African American Baptists as well as Jimmy Carter–type Baptists, and Chinese Americans and African Americans and WASP Americans, so there are both raver and gilder philosophical and political technolibertarians who have other group identities as well. Since most trumpet the value of individualism, they would be horrified to consider that they could be sorted into tribes — but I'll do it anyway. For political technolibertarians (for example, the Catos and the cypherpunks — rather analogous to 1968's McGovern Democrats and SDS activists) and philosophical libertarians can all undergo a raver/gilder spectroscopic analysis. And biological thinking appeals to them all.

Mainstream Cato technolibertarians are named in homage to the powerful and longtime Washington, DC, libertarian think tank the Cato Institute (which coincidentally also got its start in San Francisco). To them, government is fine for dealing with the anachronism of nation states (foreign policy, defense, import-export hassles) but is irrelevant to all else and should just get out of our way. This is a belief system common among high tech executives and VCs — ravers and gilders alike.

Contrast the Catos with the group that consists of the anarcho-capitalists and cypherpunks (radical pro-privacy computer activists). These guys believe that Real Soon Now, in an era of digital, untraceable, anonymous cash, capitalism will have triumphed in its purest global form. "Borders ain't nothing but speedbumps along the information superhighway," as Tim May, perhaps one of the most famous, brilliant, cranky, and vociferous of the original cypherpunks, put it. The members of this group indulge in a wicked excitement about the withering away of states and the possibility of the Hobbesian war of all against all that would result. In a perverse way, cypherpunk fascination with the globalization of capital is reminiscent of the Marxist dream of the eventual triumph of world socialism: The state will wither away into a proletarian workers' paradise.

Is it a good thing or a naughty thing to dream of a time when corporations will rule the world? Dark satanic mills or heaven in hell's despair? Discuss.

If it's a hell, it's one like that imagined by cyberpunk sci-fi writer William Gibson. Cyberpunk is the label applied to gritty, mostly urban, just-lurking-around-the-corner-near-future science fiction, replete with global settings and the long shadows cast everywhere by transnational corporations. Gibson's *Neuromancer* remains the first and best of the genre's source documents.[7] Cypherpunks seem to take gleeful pleasure in imagining this hell, just as teenage boys love the dark, ghoulish, and apocalyptic and revel in a world of heavy metal music, Goth aesthetics, and action thrillers with lots of explosions and car crashes. In cypherpunk cyberpunk dreams, everything consensual / contractual / privatized ensues (any two individuals can arrange anything they want among themselves with no busybody intrusion of third parties such as government or fellow feeling), although chaos, improvidently, is loosed upon most.

At their most wacko, cypherpunks have some commonality with the paranoia, self-importance, and displaced anger of militia people. With their love of what they imagine anarchy to be, cypherpunks are ravers more likely than not, though some have quaintly Heinleinesque, "Starship Troopers" notions of women betraying a streak of social conservatism more akin to the gilders. One curiously retro alternative model for females is Lara Croft, the buffed and cut video-game heroine, who encapsulates a Navy SEAL brain in a bimbo body and has the powers of Superman but with a distribution of subcutaneous body fat more aesthetically pleasing to adolescent males of all ages. The other extreme alternative view of women considers them a totally alien species of Other / Second Sex that's just too subjective and airy-fairy to understand. Subscribers to this view display a discomfort with the feminine in the Jungian sense — that is, with all things subjective, emotionally gooey, and more concerned with kith and kin than scoring points (just what was the valuation

7 *It's not for nothing that Mike Godwin, online counsel for the EFF, takes as his online handle "mnemonic," after Johnny Mnemonic, the protagonist of the short story proleptic of *Neuromancer*, later made into a disastrous Keanu Reeves vehicle.

on your founder's stock when your employer got acquired?). So in spite of the orgiastic raver notions some cypherpunks have about drugs and sex, they still can harbor not-so-secret gilder tendencies. These really come out with their sociobiologically deterministic explanations for all kinds of stuff: for instance, why men are so disproportionately more interested in cypherpunk carryings-on than women. It's because they're modern-day warriors! Women just don't want to trouble their pretty little heads about the fate of nations. It's a mind-set less well articulated but still palpably present in more moderate geek subcultures.

The tribal circle of raver technolibertarians also takes in extropians. These are self-described radical optimists who believe in space colonization, cryonics, happy cyborg person-machine enhancements, uploading brains into computers, and other jolly onward-and-upward notions. Also part of this circle are many parts of the neopagan and alternative sexuality communities in which certain members of high tech are very heavily represented — consensual S-M, for one, and polyamory, what in another era was called swinging or open marriage, for another.

An infatuation with would-be biological thinking cuts across most technolibertarian axes. In the narrowest sense, it's an infatuation with a model of economic behavior that borrows explicitly from biology and implicitly from the Austrian free-market economist Friedrich Hayek. It marvels at ant behaviors and is much taken with adaptation, economy as ecology, and the survival of the fittest, all as models of organisms using simple rules to run complex organizations.

But in the broader sense, you hear this new language of biology all over Silicon Valley. It's talk of ecological niches, small fleet mammals (plucky little startups) winning out over large lumbering dinosaurs (machine-age large corporations), and low-hanging fruit (easy market pickings). These ideas equate innovation with evolution. With its economic as opposed to cultural/cult appeal, this line of thinking is probably more gilder than raver, though it has adherents all over the moral and cultural high tech map. Like most technolibertarians, sympathizers with biological-economic thinking (and Bionomicians in particular) tend to be white, affluent, and male — and singularly unconscious of all the privilege that accrues from that placement on the socioeconomic spectrum. Members of a soon to be extinct species of toad would probably not see their demise as an implicit and essential part of progress, however.

WHAT'S WRONG WITH THIS PICTURE?

Political libertarianism simply ignores time-honored ongoing government funding for work-study jobs and for land grant universities. Indirect government subsidy (defense electronics contracts) created and nurtured the microelectronics industry and its companion infrastructure (middle-class home-mortgage guarantees and deductions for its laborers). Federal and state institutions provide an operable legal system (imperfect, but better than most others you could live under), which ensures that the courts can remedy disputes over intellectual-property squabbles and corporate espionage. Local, state, and federal governments make provisions, more or less, for air and water quality, vehicle and pharmaceutical safety, and most other consumer protections.

One tiny example of the unexamined linkage between government and high tech is the effect of tax-revolt Proposition 13. The consequences of this cap on property taxes began to take hold in the late 1970s, at a time when California, for decades, had public schools consistently ranked among the best in the country. These schools in turn provided qualified workers from feeder secondary schools, local junior colleges, and state universities who helped form the dense-pack critical mass of electronics skill that made Silicon Valley — the business Dream Landscape — possible. Now Silicon Valley complains that it can't find enough skilled workers in-state and must go abroad to find the people it needs. Yet somehow the connection doesn't seem to get made between the twenty-five years of shameful K-12 per-student spending in California (hovering for years somewhere around the bottom percentiles in the United States, putting California in the company with catfish-farm-poor, historically disadvantaged states such as Mississippi) and the lack of local talent.

Quiz: Where would *you* want to do business in 2000? In Russia, where there's no regulation, no central government, no rule of law; or in Northern California, where the roads are mostly well paved and well patrolled and trucks and airplanes are safer than not, where the power grid is usually intact and the banking system is mostly fraud-free and mostly works, where construction of new buildings is inspected to make sure they are basically safe and sound, where people mostly don't have to pay protection money, and the majority of law enforcement personnel are not terribly corrupt or brutal? If gangs steal computer chips from factories, these thefts are investigated and the perps prosecuted. And government, through subsidy and regulation and supervision, is the Not-So-Bad-Actor/invisible hand behind this relatively peaceful, mostly prosperous scene, making wealth creation possible.

That government has had anything positive to do with any of these structures, checks, and balances that influence so much of how we all live and work (and how high tech so flourishes) is *invisible* to technolibertarians. Yet political technolibertarians driving their Hummers home to pricey mansionettes off Woodside Road derive as much benefit from these government interventions as do the poor schnooks driving their Ford LTDs to so-passé factory jobs within commuting distance of Kankakee.

Philosophical technolibertarianism gives one pause because it colors, deeply and widely and mostly unconsciously, a zillion personal and institutional decisions. The notion that because one is rich one must be smart, however fallacious, is deeply embedded: People can equate piles of money — or the promise of it — with good sense, wisdom, and savoir faire. Santa Clara County (probably targeted by the former Soviet Union as ground zero of the Northern California, and hence the US, high tech industry) is now the county with the highest per-capita income in the United States, and — by the screwy assumption that whatever leads to money is good and motivated by wisdom — is now the philosophical heart of the heart of the country. It's a notion that's particularly risible when applied to high tech, which is proudly apolitical and ahistorical.

Many many people have bought into the idea that the future is high tech and those who run high tech know best how to create the future. The limo driver who took me to and from LAX for a taping of a 1995 daytime TV talkshow whose subject was online romance told me in earnest he was going to make his fortune using the Net to sell stuff. He hardly knew what the Net was — but he'd picked up on the buzz and wanted to be part of the action, and was no doubt ready to swallow whatever ideology was being handed out with the promise of getrichkwik.com.

My LAX driver was not so different from the Manhattan cabdriver ten years earlier who gave me a ride a few months after the breakup of the Bell System and the major deregulation of the US telephone market. That driver said he was going to make his fortune starting an independent telecommunications company. How many of those hath deregulation wrought? Hasn't Pacific Bell's merger into Southwestern Bell (rather, SBC Communications), which is yet again merging with Ameritech, demonstrated the tendency toward monopoly that deregulated industry slips into? How about AT&T buying cable giant TCI? Or MCI Worldcomm and Sprint? But that 1984 cabdriver had been ready to believe — as are all kinds of people in this decade who want to participate in the zippy new aeon, the Internet one, where the future's so bright you gotta wear shades.

And emissaries from that future — a fascinating, not utterly foreign land — are arriving daily. To get to know this country they come from, you might want to first get a sense of its language (Bionomics in Your Daily Life — Chapter 1), its military elite (Cypherpunks, Digital Cash, and Anarcho-Capitalism, Oh My — Chapter 2), its main propagandists and theorists (*Wired*: Guiding

the Perplexed-Chapter 3), its social programs (Cybergenerous — Chapter 4), and its creation myths (But How Did This Happen? — Chapter 5).

And when you are in the process of discovering a new country, it's important to understand its geographic dimensions.

KNOWN SIGHTINGS

Although the contemporary world of people and companies involved with computers and communications is riddled everywhere with libertarianism, Northern California / the San Francisco Bay Area / Silicon Valley is perhaps where it is most prominent.

Boston, its Route 128 hightechlandia boomtown from the 1970s now way eclipsed by Silicon Valley, is less inclined toward this mode of thought and action. This original high tech sector is less libertarian perhaps because of the strong historic ties between Cambridge-based MIT and the US government, particularly as a Department of Defense contractor.

Similarly, the huge high tech industry that has grown up around Washington, DC, began with "beltway bandits" servicing major government information-technology contracts, spook spin-offs providing network-security solutions. In addition, third-party subcontractors aiding these endeavors feed at the public trough. The physical proximity to the seat of national government constantly reminds the participants in the Northern Virginia Silicon Valley–analog of all the operations government performs: funding basic research; maintaining rule of law, which they understand to be essential to commerce; and subsidizing education — all to the benefit of high tech.

Government was the source of the goodies that created the critical mass of infrastructure, people, and expertise that generated, in the 1990s, high tech companies that no longer had direct government ties. These include many many major Internet companies: America Online (AOL), Middle America's Internet Service Provider (ISP); and UUNET, one of the very first and still one of the largest ISPs. Since commercial as opposed to federal accounts feed these companies, you can bet libertarianism will come to be The Way Things Work And How We Think Around Here.

And as for the way things work, people who aren't that familiar with high tech, but who do know something about geeks on the loose, know Microsoft. And that it's in Seattle.

NORTHERN EXPOSURE

Seattle, though, is a more like a company town, such as Hershey, Pennsylvania, than a high tech ecosystem seething with varieties, big and small, of entrepreneurial programmer-newts and coder-flamingos. Once dominated by its timber, shipping, and salmon industries, Seattle went through its Boeing era. Now, Seattle — with the penumbra Microsoft casts over it — is generally envisioned as Bill Gates's feudal estate of Microserfs. To only mildly exaggerate in order to make the point, Microsoft is generally regarded as a Borg[8] monoculture that resembles only itself, or perhaps IBM at the height of its computer-industry hegemony in the 1970s, and is not so very much like the rest of high tech.

So although Microsoft is the biggest and best-known high tech entity in the world, Silicon Valley is still where most high tech innovation — in culture or technology — springs from.

8 "Borg" refers to an enemy culture on Star Trek: The Next Generation. Borg are insect-like in their obliteration of individuality, and emphasize becoming part of the hive (or, as they call it, the Collective). Their catchphrase is "Resistance is futile. You will become assimilated."

The rest of high tech fears and loathes Microsoft for the most part, even as much as it is in the habit of passionately hating the government. Writhing in cognitive dissonance as it watches the Department of Justice's antitrust lawsuit with Microsoft, where both government agency and megacorporation hoot and huff over territory, high tech opinion lurches from toeing the libertarian freemarketer line ("Why is the government going after one of the most successful examples of American free enterprise? Fools and madmen!") to being appropriately perturbed at Microsoft's anticompetitive tactics, market strangleholds, and bars to innovation.

Yet even Microsoft itself isn't immune to the libertarian specter stalking high tech. Witness an email forwarded to me by a good geek friend in the summer of 1997, when the Department of Justice was already engaging in some of its antitrust investigations into Microsoft's acquisition of Web TV (a startup that was meant to make World Wide Web use as easy as TV use). The email was said to have been written by someone at Microsoft; that may be apocryphal, as much on the Net is — though no less telling for being so.

The DOJ email reader is sarcastically addressed as "highly trained" and "overpaid," although it is extremely unlikely that the government email *reader* was paid nearly as well as the Microsoft email *writer*. In the body of the email, the writer mocks the government employee for having no life, and presumes the government must be anxious because it can't figure out how to regulate software and can't stomach the notion that people might be able to succeed without government help. There's some slams at the email reader's likely sexual incompetence (the implication being the government drone is an impotent male), followed by proclamations that those with intelligence and drive will drag "the rest of you luddites kicking and screaming into a better tomorrow," whether or not the DOJ sanctions it. What concludes this lovely screed is gun-talk implying that it's only the concern that Microserfs not get shot at by evil, sexually inadequate government agents à la Waco, Ruby Ridge, or a DEA bust gone bad that is making them cooperate. It's only the government's threat of superior armed forces that gives it any power anyway.

This mimicking of militia language is not a coincidence; it's a style that pervades much of technolibertarianism. The people who wrote the Lone Gunmen geek conspiracy-theorist characters into *The X Files* did not need to look very far for real-life inspiration. These technolibertarians wearing camo-gear of the mind are definitely Out There.

Because jokes reveal truth about a culture more than almost anything else, it's valuable to mention another bit of email humor which I first received in April 1998. It came my way just as the head-butting between Microsoft and the DOJ was really hotting up and the *Los Angeles Times* had broken a story that Microsoft was seeking to plant fake third-party/concerned citizen letters of support in major media. Written by Jim Allard, a Massachusetts engineer, the joke letter later won honorable mention in "21st Challenge," the technoculture humor contest run by the online publication *Salon*. The object of the game was to manufacture some fine fake vox populi Microsquish support letters:

> To the editors of *Soldier of Fortune magazine/Washington Times,*
>
> I am incensed by the unconstitutional persecution by Janet Reno's jack-booted thugs of the followers of Bill Gates' religion, the Branch Microsoftians. All the residents of Seatliwaco, Washington, know their neighbors in the secluded campus/compound as quiet, law abiding citizens who keep to themselves and indulge in their harmless hobbies of...stifling competition and stockpiling large calibre weaponry taped to the bottoms of their cubicle desks. In honor of Patriot's Day, I say it's high time for every red-blooded American to stand up to the governmental agents of the international socialist

> vegetarian Linux-GNU-Apache-Java-Netscape conspiracy, and lock-and-load for Bill!

Allard obviously knows his technolibertarians, particularly of the Tough Boy/Insurgent kind.[9]

When I was a young hippie, I learned that the personal is the political, and to think globally but act locally. High tech, as located in the San Francisco Bay Area, is offered as proof of today's best-case Yankee melting-pot can-do know-how straddling the globe. It creates the products that are touted as the epitome of the American good life that everyone everywhere must desire; and its values, however unconscious, seem to spread with the wealth and cultural visibility they acquire.

So technolibertarians matter, much as the New Left and the counterculture of the '60s mattered and continues to matter: both as extreme instantiation of a cultural shift and as a social trend with the potential for long-lived consequences. And much as the causes — and effects — of the cultural change known as the '60s are muddied and complex, so it is with this complicated, multiply sited culture of engineers and money-guys. However imperfectly, it's worth trying to tease out what these mostly American, mostly West Coast inventors and programmer-droids and plutocrats are up to — for they have the big bucks, and cultural juice, that will be affecting us all as we head into the next millennium.

9 Linux-GNU-Apache-Java-Netscape are all non-Microsoft kinds of software platforms. And with the exception of Java (which, though a commercial product in the conventional sense, enables programmers to create software that works across different kinds of computers), they are specifically the opposite of monopolistic in their distribution: they are more or less given away for geeks to bang on and build on, with revenue coming from support and tweaks.

CHAPTER ONE

BIONOMICS IN YOUR DAILY LIFE

EARLY ONE EVENING IN MID-1993, I was having dinner with a friend, Dan Lynch, at San Francisco's Embarcadero Center. Created in the 1960s to be the Rockefeller Center of the west, the Embarcadero Center is a nouveau prestigious white-collar address close to the Financial District (the City's equivalent to Wall Street / midtown Manhattan) and to the wharves, San Francisco's ancestral source of commerce. The happy background thrum of knowledge-worker money aside, the setting for our meal was fitting because the Embarcadero Center's particular form of celebratory Christmas decoration every year — outlining the buildings with electronic lighting devices — makes them look from across the Bay in Berkeley like CAD/CAM schematics for skyscrapers.

My dinner companion was one of the real fixer/handler/macher/know-it-alls of Silicon Valley, who had been one of those old-time SRI/Arpanet/Internet forefathers. Although he hadn't yet in 1993 cashed out for the second time, he was the founder of Interop (the first trade show devoted to the commercialization of the Net), the cofounder of Cybercash (an early electronic commerce venture), and board member of the Santa Fe Institute (complexity, chaos, and all that jazz). This varsity-string I-get-around high tech guy was sort of a double alpha in brains and dominance (and wit, too), who dressed like the manager of a lumberyard. The only way you'd have known he was worth kazillions of dollars would be from the newish Lexus he always drove and the casual mention he made of the places he owned in Los Altos Hills, Napa, and Tahoe.

Among the responses he gave to the question I asked him of what he was up to next (once you stop having to work for survival, you have to figure out what to do with your life that provides meaning) was his modest mention of an interest in economics. I found this curious, for I wasn't in the habit of thinking that powernerds, even one as broadly thoughtful as this one, cared much about larger social issues, or about slippery, badly defined philosophical attempts to understand human behavior, particularly a subject that notoriously suffers from physics envy and a lack of hard replicable data. In other words, most guys for whom the system of startup and cash-out works really well don't usually spend lots of time thinking about that system. It's losers of the game, or maybe those who are outside observers of it, who usually have the time or interest to Go Analytical/Meta.

It was Bionomics that Dan Lynch was talking about. He sent me a copy the very next day of Michael Rothschild's eponymous book (*Bionomics: Economy as Ecosystem*) and invited me to attend the first Bionomics conference a couple of months hence in San Francisco. Rothschild's original subtitle for his *Bionomics* was *The Inevitability of Capitalism*, and the beginning of the book's ascent into larger view came from a favorable review in the August 19, 1991, issue of the *Wall Street Journal*. After this, folks from Newt Gingrich to the editorial staffs of *Fortune* and *Forbes* became similarly entranced.

John Baden, a free-market environmentalist, wrote in the *Wall Street Journal*:

> Occasionally a book signals a fundamental shift in the way people should think about economics. Such a book integrates important and disparate findings into a new perspective... Mr. Rothschild...offers a fascinating and highly creative alternative to the way conventional economics views the world... The paradigm laid out in Bionomics harmonizes liberty, prosperity, and integrity... Mr. Rothschild has it right.

Baden, though, was both sorta right and sorta wrong about *Bionomics*. It turns out that many mainstream economists, Nobelists among them, have been operating for years on the assumptions that devotees and new readers of *Bionomics* believed were new and unique. Concepts such as the importance of technological change in driving economic growth has been central to the work of Robert Solow, and there's even an entire branch of economics, called evolutionary economics, where, according to MIT professor Paul Krugman, economic theory has looked like evolutionary theory for a very long time. But then, popularizers, like blondes, maybe do get to have more fun: Thomas Moore (*Care of the Soul*) got a lot more celebrity and return on his investment than his mentor, James Hillman, who had been cranking out his sensible, slightly dysphoric small-press Jungianism for decades before Moore wrote his bestsellers.

But Baden was right in that *Bionomics* was the right book for the right time. The ideas and metaphors of *Bionomics* were supremely adapted to high tech culture and were most timely as geeks and Net entrepreneurs were coming into cultural dominance as never before. We all want better ways to understand ourselves and to better articulate what we believe we are doing.

BIOLOGY IS DESTINY

Bionomics borrows from biology as opposed to Newtonian mechanics to explain economic behavior, describing the way the world works in terms of learning, adaptation, intelligence, selection, and ecological niches. It favors decentralization and trial and error and local control and simple rules and letting things be. Bionomics pays homage to Friedrich Hayek, one of the residents in the traditional libertarian pantheon, who believed that only free markets can lead to freedom (been to China lately?) and that command and control (all government intervention of course irresistibly leading to Stalinesque collectivization of farms) leads to serfdom.

Bionomics, reduced to a bumper sticker, which, yes, you could occasionally actually see on cars when driving around the Bay Area, states that "the economy is a rain forest." The Bionomics argument goes that a rain forest ecosystem is far more complicated than any machine that could be designed — the idea being that machines, and machine-age thinking, are the markers of Bad Old Economic Thinking. No one can manage or engineer a rain forest, and rain forests are happiest when they are left alone to evolve, which will then benefit all the happy monkeys, pretty butterflies, and funny tapirs that live in them. In our capitalist rain forest, organizations and industries are the species and organisms. Although, if a corporation is the analog for, say, an individual tapir, then what is the rain forest analog for an individual person? A mitochondria?

What about the fact that actual rain forests are now being destroyed because of the free market?

To extend the metaphor, economic life flourishes when technology marches on, accelerated by competition. Here, innovation equals genetic mutation, and competition equals natural selection. So, of course, government regulation *must* equal messing with the rain forest's natural progress. Never mind that people have been messing with ecology (acting like big bad government) since forever: controlled burning to increase forest health or, oh, even doing things like farming. And that, actually, many *healthy* ecosystems remain in a fine state of balance and relative stasis, organisms having for the most part maximally optimized their environments, with relatively small amounts of oscillation, churn, and evolution — until something drastic happens. The dinosaurs did have a pretty good, and varied, run, you know? At least until the death-star comet hit…

Regardless, the intersection between Rothschild's libertarian economic theories and high tech turns out not to be as random as

I had thought that night over dinner in San Francisco's Financial District — nor its spreading out into the larger world so magical. In spite of his de rigueur East Coast establishment credentials (MBA and law degree from Harvard, stint with the Boston Consulting Group), Rothschild had been involved back in the late '70s and early '80s with an early software success, Micropro (which brought you that early success/early obsolescence word-processing program Wordstar). There, (1) he saw that people were madly rushing to pay for elusive, information-based intangible goods, that is, revisions (revs) to software, and (2) he came to the attention of the venture capitalists (VCs) on the board of the Marin County startup, in particular, Arthur Patterson. Patterson, part of longtime VC powerhouse Accel Partners, was instrumental in handing out Rothschild's book as the 1990 VC firm's Christmas gift to the folks they thought mattered.

Lynch read the book, glommed onto Rothschild when he was a speaker at a Sand Hill Road meeting of the Western Association of Venture Capitalists a few months later — and the Bionomics Institute was born, along with its annual conference, its Web site, its "Vitamin B: Your Daily Dose of Bionomics" (a daily bit of inspiration, whether a quote from elsewhere or an original in-house observation, was made available on the Bionomics Institute Web site or delivered fresh to your email address), and its software startup, Applied Bionomics, Inc. (now called Maxager). Lots, though not all, of the conference attendees and speakers have been associated with high tech: They perhaps make up the single biggest chunk of adherents.

A typical Vitamin B:

> Evolving slowly in relatively protected isolation, Hawaii's flora and fauna are reminiscent of traditional industries: heavily protected by tariffs, regulations, old-guard owners and other well-entrenched interests. Archaic technologies and business processes abound, similar to the unique life forms that inhabit the Hawaiian islands. Unlike Hawaii, however, traditional

> industries are not scenes of pastoral richness. More often, they exhibit class divisions and crusty resistance to anything that threatens the established owners. Yet the path of their establishment, and the dynamics of their demise, are strikingly similar.
>
> (James Moore, December 1995, *Upside* [a monthly magazine targeted to Silicon Valley's business elite])

You can argue the biological metaphor both ways: If shelter creates unique beauty in nature, there also might be examples in economics. *Sports Illustrated* didn't turn a profit for Time, Inc. for years, but because it was sheltered by its parent corporation, it was given an opportunity to flourish — and is now doing very nicely, thank you.

Or you can argue that removing shelter in nature does bad things: rats that escaped from ships starting in the nineteenth century have wreaked havoc on Hawaii's bird population, which had not evolved defenses against such predators. There is also the matter of how indigenous peoples of the Western Hemisphere sublimed almost out of existence once they were exposed to microbes (smallpox, influenza) they had been sheltered from. In terms of shelter in the business world, Wal-Mart, with its predatory pricing, can run locally owned businesses out of the shelter of their own home towns, thus creating a more uniform retail monoculture worldwide. Or you can agree with Moore up to a point, by saying shelter in nature can be good but sometimes bad and sheltering companies can be bad but sometimes good; yet they can both end up on the ash heap of history — and so your point is? This Vitamin B, like so much of the Bionomics argument, sounds great but tastes lighter and lighter the more you look at it.

Lynch says that the fit between Bionomics and high tech is intuitively obvious, for "computers embody learning mechanisms. There's the great belief in trial and error. You see it in rev after rev of software. You don't have to wait for evolution: you see it." Rothschild would agree, for in high tech, what he calls "super-accelerated capitalism, you see in two years what you might see [in other venues] in 20 or 30 years."

Evolution of product lines, competitors driving each other from market niches — these metaphors conform to day-to-day high tech reality. Thomas Kuhn (who popularized the notion of paradigm shifts in *The Structure of Scientific Revolutions*) has argued that the same idea occurs to lots of folks more or less at the same time (was it a Russian, a German, or a Frenchman, precisely, who invented the internal combustion machine? Was Wallace or Darwin more properly the dad of evolutionary theories of natural selection?). It might be argued that if Bionomics hadn't existed, someone else would have had to invent it.

The notion of "memes," and how they spread, might provide a handy explanation. A concept created by British sociobiologist Richard "selfish gene" Dawkins, a meme signifies an intellectual construct, paradigm, or cultural commonplace that propagates like brushfire or sexually transmitted diseases (STDs) or fashions in footwear. Virus transmission is often invoked as a metaphor to explain the spread of memes. "Information wants to be free" is the first part of a famous remark made by Whole Earth Catalogue founder/Global Business Network totem Stewart Brand, where he also added, "and information wants to be expensive." The comment has been misunderstood and mutated into the meme that might be stated, "information has a way of getting out there in spite of attempts to contain it — and of getting reproduced for free" — a ubiquitous idea much beloved by raver technolibertarians. Even more fundamentally, the meme that models human thought processes on computing (the brain is a big computer, with different kinds of storage and processing capacities) is an example of how the meme of computation has entered into contemporary thought streams. The appeal of the Bionomics meme is that it cuts through all that messy icky maddening complexity that's the Real World: It's a comfort to believe everything does best if left alone.

So Lynch himself contributed to the spread of the Bionomics idea by buying and handing out enough copies of Rothschild's book that the publisher finally decided to go into a second printing (new cover — in the greater Bionomics community there is prestige in having a copy of the book with the *earliest* cover). He says with pride that the fact that so many people now take Bionomics ideas for granted is proof of his success as a popularizer.

In a case of parallel evolution, former *Wired* executive editor Kevin Kelly produced a 1995 book, *Out of Control: The New Biology of Machines, Social Systems, and the Economic World,* about a similarly Bionomics-esque cosmology — and theoretically totally independent of Rothschild's work. Kelly argued that economic life has grown too large and too complex to be managed, and that borrowing from biological thought, through such naturally occurring models as genetic algorithms and flocking behaviors of geese, would provide more useful tools to organize economic and social activity. Kelly was smitten with many of the concepts of Bionomics and was fascinated with notions of evolution and the beauties of decentralization. Like many of the speakers at Bionomics conferences, Kelly dwelled on outcomes of actions made by particles, molecules, cellular automata, and Internet routers. Kelly's view of the ideal world to come is scarily de-individualized and overautomated, a view that lurks beneath much Bionomic and technolibertarian speculation. In any event, as these things tend to work (great minds thinking in the same channels, small minds thinking alike), Kelly ended up as the keynoter at the Third Bionomics Conference.

RED IN TOOTH AND NAIL

One of Bionomics' libertarian catchphrases is "simple rules, complex behaviors." As Steve Gibson, former executive director of the Bionomics Institute (TBI), put it, "Tinkering with monetary policy to affect the economy is an example of machine-age thinking. Global liquidity flows make financial markets respond instantly and viciously." To bionomicians, all the foofaraw about what the Fed is going to do next is beside the point.

Bionomics is a great system for the top percentiles, the endlessly entrepreneurial, the happily workaholic. But where in this ecosystem is there room for other kinds of species? What about the vulnerable, the ones who weren't able to cash out, those whose skillset or native endowment doesn't fit well into the shiny happy new information economy? Here I think of my sister: biology degree from Stanford, plus a master's in public health, one of those divorced-in-her-forties-with-two-teenagers-to-raise-while-trying-to-reenter-the-workforce sad stories, who grasps after any kind of health education job she can find. She has at times had to resort to selling flowers at BART stations to prevent her house from being foreclosed. In other words, she has precisely the skillset (teaching, community service, environmental consciousness) that has little bionomic value in our fabu hyperaccelerated crashboombang economy. These jobs have gone away, or hardly pay a living wage. And I hate thinking about the skilled blue-collar workers I know (for the foreseeable future, unglamorous but necessary functions such as installing sound electrical wiring and plumbing still need to be performed) who struggle to support their families. It's hard to see what adaptation or evolution functions here: Although you might develop new ways to better teach first-generation immigrants about prenatal care, the need to teach prenatal care, and the substance of it, will not suddenly evolve into something else.

One of my total-doll hypernerd friends — who jokingly says, "I'm a computer scientist. How can I help?" and it's only half a joke, for he truly would dash to the assistance of anyone who asked — has gone from elite science/technology establishment to elite science/technology establishment. He's the sort of Big

Brain whose friends tend to get to choose between professorates and executive positions at startups. As compassionate and considerate a human being as you could ever hope to find, when we were arguing about age discrimination in high tech, he made a comment that went something along the lines that if there really were value in old COBOL programmers (COBOL being the programming language of the mainframe era), then obviously there was a niche there and the natural dynamics would take care of it and soon there would be a startup that would venture this. High tech, of course, doesn't generally value experience and age; my friend was missing the point that an old COBOL programmer might be capable of programming in newer languages or might bring wisdom to contemporary technology problems.

His idea was as logical, but as preposterous, as asserting that since baby boomers, the biggest blip in consumer-demo models, are aging, then fashion designers are going to suddenly start creating haut couture for, and feature models disporting, bodies that in another era would have majorly relied on girdles. True, there was some flare-up in demand for older programmers because of Y2K problems. Even so, Y2K didn't create a full-employment act for older programmers, whether or not they knew COBOL.

For my hypernerd, honey-bunny-baby of a centurion of high tech, who has tons of friends who in their middle thirties can decide to cash out and never work again, who has friends who do have their very own private residential helicopter pad, and who himself chooses to live a life of voluntary poverty and simplicity (a studio apartment and no car, with a salary that could comfortably support a family of four anywhere outside Boston, New York, or San Francisco) but could opt for big bucks any time he wanted — for him, thinking biologically makes sense. It's rather like the picture you'd have of the wondrously efficient meritocracy of the music biz if all the musicians you knew, or you yourself, were the sort of players who got featured at Tanglewood or were asked to sit in on sessions with Brian Eno.

Everyone would seem to be doing well, and some stupendously so; you simply wouldn't see or know the equally talented but obscure musicians who had to consider themselves lucky if they had steady gigs playing in the cocktail lounges of airport Holiday Inns. And as for the street musicians you sometimes walked past, who were *really good,* you just might be inclined to think there was something somewhat defective about them.

In the rarefied heights of my friend's high tech alpine meadow community, the glacial melt makes for enough clear drinking water to go around, and the pica population lives in harmony with the bluebells.

Contrast my sweet computer scientist friend with the son of the man my mother employed as a gardener for years, someone not so biologically fit in high tech's ecosystem. Offspring of a tight-knit hard-working immigrant family, he miraculously went off to college (California State University-Los Angeles, though; not Carnegie Mellon), where he earned an undergraduate degree in computer science. Alas, he could not find work in his chosen field — Cal State-LA not being one of the prestige schools that high tech so heavily recruits from — so went to work in his father's gardening business. Not that there's anything less than honorable about gardening, or going into the family business. However, high tech propounds the myth that if you become One of Us, then prosperity and ease necessarily await, and what's more, that everyone is equally moldable into what high tech demands — which is like saying everyone can be a wizard chess player.

Flatlanders, or the less elite, are, then, not so ecologically favored. Their choices are more limited, or are made for them by others — though maybe that's always the definition of the hidden injuries (if you are not found bionomically fit) and entitlements (if you are) of class. Bionomic fitness might also simply be an expression of nothing more than the growing gap between rich and poor in the United States and worldwide, as that gap reveals itself among the computation-intensive class.

As another member of the international high tech elite conspiracy (well, not a conspiracy, but a loose consortium of like-minded folks) said in an interview with anthropologists from California State University-San Jose (what you might call field notes from the belly of the beast):

> If I can get more done I can make more money by working more; that's OK because you've made the choice to do that and the purpose is that maybe some day you'll be able to do something with that money. But that's a free choice and some people consider work entertaining. Those who want to play more can work less because they'll get their work done faster, so they can have more free time to do things they feel are more worthwhile than working.

In actuality, though, this kind of Milton Friedman–esque choice is something most people in high tech don't have: Most can either string themselves out with work (but maybe they can't if in addition to quant skills, they are not endowed with tons of stamina and little need for down time, either physical or psychological), which can be exhilarating in the short term, deadening in the long term, or find themselves not very employable. Some, true, do have the option to knock themselves out for the duration of a contract and then, say, take off for a tour of Bhutan, Mustang, and the archeological treasures of Turkey. But that's an elite Young Person's option, the option of no need for constancy, some steadiness in your life. It doesn't work well with family life, or with wanting *balance* in your life.

EUGENICS

What's tacit in much of this biological-economic language (and I don't mean in only that which is officially sanctioned by the Bionomics Institute, but in the similar-sounding patois that is uttered throughout high tech) is, as in any culture, a bias toward certain kinds of genotypes/phenotypes.

The entrepreneur personality — which needs little downtime, which must be narrowly focused and not prone to self-doubt, which will do all and anything to succeed, which tirelessly and compulsively must act like the greatest salesman in the world, which by definition is workaholic, which risks (and maybe devalues) family life and health — thrives in this ecosystem. "Succeeding in technology is like being a 911 operator or a doctor in a triage unit," said Jon Carter, a recruiter at the Palo Alto headhunting firm Egon Zehnder International, quoted in a May 7, 1998, *Wired News* story. It brings to mind Yeats's "Second Coming": "The best lack all conviction/The worst are full of passionate intensity."

In the realm of *people*, the Bionomics worldview evokes a question I had as I watched the hostile-takeover world of the 1980s: Why is it *not* okay for a company that's doing fine by its customers, employees, community, and stockholders simply to be left alone? So *what* if it merely performs well but not optimally? Where is the place for the non-high-end/non-best-of-class/but-maybe-with-quiet-virtues-of-its-own company? For the company that doesn't optimize for fleeting shareholder value but for other qualities? Say for creating goods that last, for treating both employees and customers well? In economic life, perhaps it's a laughable question, whether aggressive buyers of corporations should leave good-enough companies alone, but what happens when this same Darwinian logic is applied to kinds of people as well as kinds of companies?

Where the biological logic really falls apart is that often what's maladaptive in one circumstance is supremely adaptive in another (sickle-cell anemia, not useful to the organism in North America, was quite valuable in Africa for providing partial resistance to malaria). If you maximize all the time for what's biologically fit at the moment, you lose out in the long run. For example, those inclined to mood disorders (depressives and manic-depressives) famously abuse substances, themselves, and others, blow opportunities that come their way, and don't go for the main chance. The culture of optimism that *Wired* and other technology business-porn magazines have promoted suggests its opposite: the medieval Christian sin of accidie and anomie. If you're dysphoric and critical, lack that Coué-like / W. Clement Stone positive mental attitude, you're a morally blighted enemy of progress. It's magical thinking: If you think good thoughts about the future, it will be a good future! Clap your hands if you believe in faeries!

Yet so often the downers are the folks who create and perform that which over time we come to value most: from the printmaking / natural history pioneering of John James Audubon to the writing of Virginia Woolf to the politicking of Lincoln. The hypersensitive maladaptive no-commercial-potential individuals, the runts of the litter, and the defective members of the species can — because as humans and not plenaria we can value things not just of momentary food / shelter / mate-status-enhancing enticement — create the best of what makes us uniquely human. Creative endeavors of all kinds don't necessarily stem from being efficient economic units / agents.

Artists (I use the term broadly, regardless of mode of expression: words, images, sounds) suffer from depression at up to eight times the rate of the general population; scientists seem to suffer from it at half the rate. It's not that I am arguing with sniffy superiority for the delicate sensibilities of People Wearing Black over People Wearing T-Shirts that read, "In this era of digital Darwinism, some of us are ones. You're a zero." It's that the bionomic worldview presents a reverse discrimination that says the not functionally optimized (up and productive and making economic sense at the moment) are invisible or useless. It's not that this is stated anywhere; it's just that it's implied everywhere.

Every once in a while you come across something that allows you to acquire some of the knowledge you would have been looking for if you could have been the fly on the wall you've always wanted to be. It might be listening in on the deliberations of the membership committee of an exclusive club (Skull and Bones? Or The Jonathan Club? Santa Monica's ultra WASP exclusive beach club) so that you could actually come to understand how it decides who to accept and who to reject. It could be the discovery of the documentation depicting how the Pentagon was lying about the effectiveness of the military operations in Vietnam. It could take the form of finding the articulation of a prejudice you had long suspected, just as Henry Ford was sure he had found proof of the perfidy of the international Jewish banking conspiracy when he came across "The Protocols of the Elders of Zion," the phoney-baloney document that's been floating around forever that demonstrates conclusively how those nasty miserly Jewish international bankers control the lives of decent, Christian, god-fearing folk.

In my incarnation as a fly, I found a comely wall to land on when I came across in the January/February 1998 *Cato Policy Report* an excerpt from the essay "Why Do Intellectuals Oppose Capitalism?" (which first appeared in 1986 in *The Future of Private Enterprise* [Georgia State University Press]; reprinted in *Socratic Puzzles* [Harvard University Press, 1997]), the triumphant confirmation of my libertarian fears. Written by primo libertarian Harvard philosophy professor Robert Nozick, the piece gives his explanation of why who he calls intellectual wordsmiths are so often disgruntled, resentful, envious anticapitalists. He asserts, rightfully, that poets and journalists and many academics and those of similar ilk are really ticked that "a capitalist society rewards people only insofar as they serve the market-expressed needs of others; it rewards in accordance with economic contribution, not personal value."

Yes! The libertarians-know-the-price-of-everything-but-the-value-of-nothing argument writ large! I would disagree with Nozick's contentions that workers in visual media don't share these discontents (performing artists aren't even mentioned in his essay), for although many visual artists, whether cynically or sincerely, promote and market themselves, I've never met any who would take the philosophical position that the market efficiently recognizes aesthetic value. Perhaps it can over time, but that time period can in some places be centuries (Mendelssohn rehabilitated the reputation of Bach, T. S. Eliot the Metaphysical Poets — a delay of several hundred years in the value chain). What sells and what doesn't, and for how much and when, is precisely as irrational as notions of taste and beauty and as marginally predictable as the luck of a blackjack player. True, some artists have a gift for being famous or a genius for self-promotion. But that's not the point.

I would affirm that yes indeedybob there are values the market can't compute or dictate (why else do people want to work for relatively little money at places they consider cool, whether at a non-profit or at MTV?). I don't think it is just wordsmiths who hold this position (I think of scientists who work for love of the beauty of what they discover, for far less than what they could earn in the private sector); but it's probably true that those more versed in dealing with the unquantifiable say there can be value in the immeasurable — or, at least, immeasurable by obvious market means.

The "Communist Manifesto" has it right: What it calls bourgeois capitalism "has resolved personal worth into exchange value and, in place of the numberless indefeasible chartered freedoms, has set up that single, unconscionable freedom — Free Trade." Marx and his pal Engels had other relevant things to say about the spread of global capitalism (much more accurate for the description of what is happening at the end of our own century than at the end of his). That crew was far better at analysis of how capitalism works than at coming up with policy-wonk recommendations. But, then, Marx was yet another member of Nozick's resentful underpaid wordsmith class.

In any event, Nozick's essay blames it all on school and goes on to explain that verbal sorts who did well there just can't get over the fact that other kinds of people get better rewarded by society, such as

> those with substantial (but not overwhelming) bookish skills along with social grace, strong motivation to please, friendliness, winning ways, and an ability to play by (and to seem to be following) the rules. Such pupils...will be highly regarded and rewarded...and they will do extremely well in the wider society, as well.

In other words, your future sales manager is likely to be more capitalism-friendly than, say, Pauline Kael in training might have been (given all the fine things that '80s- and-'90s-style capitalism has done for the movies, that wouldn't be too surprising). But, then, student body presidents, whether as kids or when all grown up and having left that honor behind, probably have different internal markers of success than those less other-directed. And Nozick ignores the plethora of writers and pundits who do whatever it is they do for the money, for that success in wider society. But whether what they do is work they are proud of, or whether it is work of lasting value, is not factored into the libertarian equation.

Nozick further posits that numbersmiths, "quantitatively bright children,...do not receive the same...attention and approval...as do verbally bright children...and it is apparently these rewards that especially shape [the wordsmith's] sense of entitlement." And so, numbersmiths tend to be far less anticapitalist. I can't speak for conventionally recognized verbal acuity leading to a sense of entitlement, nor for the wiseasses who are not rewarded for their verbal felicities. Certainly, lots of smart talkers get ahead and become well-placed lawyers, businesspeople, and college professors (like Nozick himself). But I think that even if the letter of his argument is wrong, the spirit of it may be right: humanities geeks are more likely to be squishy liberals and snail darters. It's like the argument for wilderness: it has value precisely because you can't put a dollar value on it.

Chances are most technolibertarians haven't heard of Robert Nozick, much less read him. But chances are also good that most would agree with his bias toward valuing people who acquire MBAs and away from people who write little novels of the emotions. Money is something you can count; the value of human subjectivity you can't. Technolibertarians wouldn't really know how to grok a less quantitative/algorithmic weltanschauung. It's C. P. Snow's two cultures antipathy taking a form he hadn't quite imagined.

And many technolibertarians would probably concur with Nozick's conclusion that poetasters are nothing more than sore losers. I've heard it myself from technolibertarians on the Net who, engaging in schadenfreude, claim I am only annoyed with them because of my own sour grapes. No, it's not that I denigrate their success; it's mean-spiritedness and hypocrisy and cognitive blinders I can't abide. Which Bionomicians as *people* are no more guilty of than anyone else; but they may be guilty as ideologues...

CHANGE IS GOOD

What does make sense to technolibertarians, instead of a world where money is poorly correlated with value, is a delta-world (change of a certain kind defines certain units of scientific measurement) that maps onto engineering reality (you fix the bug, improve the product, bring out a new model). The delta-world is one of management by quarterly reports, Web Weeks, and day-trading. Whether this maps well onto all aspects of human breathing or striving is something else.

Virginia Postrel, longtime editor in chief of *Reason* magazine, sort of the *Nation / New Republic / Atlantic Monthly* of libertarianism, gets at this delta-world ideal in her "Dynamism, Diversity, and Division in American Politics" speech, which she delivered at the Fifth Annual Bionomics Conference in 1996 — and which was subsumed in her 1998 book *The Future and Its Enemies: The Growing Conflict on Creativity, Enterprise, and Progress.* She made good points about how the Jeremy Rifkins and Patrick Buchanans of the world have more in common with each other than, say, with their more obvious political allies. She sees folks like Rifkin and Buchanan as agents of stasis who either long for a fantasy past or want to plan (code for control-freaking / bureaucratizing / anti-individualist acting) for a better future; on the other hand, agents of dynamism believe in

> the complex ecology of human beings...preferring decentralized choice... They are open-ended... Nobody — no individual, no governing group — knows enough about a society to manage it in detail... Dynamism is harder to understand than stasis... It is the product of millions of unplanned choices directed by no central person or organization... Popular culture...religion...the family...they are complex systems that do not stay put, spontaneous orders subject to no one's control... Dynamic systems not only accommodate diversity; their flexibility allows them to accommodate external change. They are resilient. When the world changes, they permit many small-scale experiments, increasing the chances of success and decreasing the consequences of failure. They allow fine-tuning.

It sounds great. Who would not want to be on the side of dynamism? *Wired* magazine celebrated its sixth anniversary with an entire issue devoted to the proposition that "Change Is Good" (emblazoned on the front cover). Myself, I'm so *glad* that I live in an era of photocopiers, laptops, call-waiting, Telfa pads, Advil, and narrow-spectrum antibiotics.

But I don't think all change is good, or without cost. I *am* a Luddite — in the true sense of the word. The followers of Ned Ludd were rightfully concerned that rapid industrialization was ruining their traditional artisanal workways and villages, creating nineteenth-century local environmental disasters and horror-show factory working (and living) conditions for family members of all ages. For decades, the displacements of the Industrial Revolution sent hundreds of thousands of people to lives of penury, starvation, disease, and despair in the slums of big cities. The Luddites were early labor and ecology activists, upset not so much with technology per se but with technology's destructive effects on their bodies, on their children, on the places where they lived, on their ability to make a sane living. And, in a sense, they were early protesters of de-skilling.

De-skilling is not a purely late-twentieth-century phenom (where reliance on computers means that people with less skill and knowledge — who can be paid far less — perform previously more-skilled jobs). Considering the failure of so many modern buildings (in design, execution, defect of materials, workmanship), isn't it worth questioning whether kids straight out of an architecture program, slaved to CAD/CAM workstations and paid relatively little, are doing as good a job as the senior architect they displaced, who has knowledge not so containable in commercial software? So the Luddites smashed mechanical looms, the symbols and agents of their oppression, and have had an unfair bad rap ever since as loons and barbarians. Not to romanticize the agrarian past, but much of urban and small-factory-town life of the Industrial Revolution was very much like that of Blake's dark Satanic mills. Technology and trade marched on and global empires were created; monopolies arose; it all sounds familiar.

Yes, a middle class sprang from this industrialization, and it certainly made possible the improved standard of living a century later for North Americans and Western Europeans; but that dynamism of the nineteenth century was hardly without grievous cost. In this model of how the world works or should work, there's the spirit of Lenin: in regard to revolution, you have to break eggs to make an omelet. Or maybe the model is biological: nature has her own cycles of creation and destruction, and who are we to argue?

Like the Luddites, I am not so sure most change benefits most people. Postrel's spectrum from stasis to dynamism (with sense and sensibility heavily weighted on one side of that spectrum) ignores all the largely invisible stable societal structures (just to name two: (1) public investment in sanitation, education, and public waterways; (2) changes in common law that made it legal for women to vote and own property) that make all this dynamism productive and possible. Contrast this with the lack of centralized authority that was so dreadfully inconveniencing in the recent unpleasantness in the Balkans. The changing world Postrel refers to often changes for the better because its governments change.

Which brings up a subject/object confusion that percolates throughout much of the discourse of high tech: the misapprehension that *because* computers and communications technologies change quickly (at least in terms of speeds and feeds, bits and bytes; whether they *actually* work faster, given their increasing overbuilt complexity, is another matter entirely), and because most white-collar and some blue-collar work now makes use of them in one form or another, the erroneous conclusion is drawn that this same white-collar and blue-collar work, and the enterprises and industries they are part of, must also be changing as rapidly. Wrong. It's like saying that, since today's automobiles weigh less than the ones built in the 1970s and contain lots more electronics than the ones built in the 1970s, they must routinely travel much faster than 1970s cars — say, 120 mph, not 60 mph — or routinely get 60 miles per gallon, instead of 30, which we know not to be the case. They may have more microprocessor-based gizmos in them, but that by its lonesome is not that big of a change over previous generations of automobiles.

The computer-productivity paradox, as it is commonly called, describes the very disconcerting finding that with all the paradigm-shifting empowerment of the individual / middle-management genocide that distributed data processing has rained down on us all, by most measures there hasn't been a productivity gain. Yes, people can now do, but may also be expected to do as part of their job, things they couldn't before, but that's too long a side issue to get into...

In Paul Krugman's terrific January 22, 1998, column for the Microsoft-owned online publication *Slate,* called "Entertainment Values / Will Capitalism Go Hollywood?", he explains that

> yesterday every industry was going to look like automobiles, and every company like General Motors; today every industry is going to look like software, and every company like Microsoft... Even though information technology may well be the driving force behind future economic growth, it's very unlikely that the information-technology industry is ever going to be more than a fairly small share of the economy. In its day electricity changed everything, too, but there was never a time when most people worked for electric utilities or even for employers who looked anything like electric utilities.

Nevertheless, Kevin Kelly's *New Rules for the New Economy,* first appearing as an article in the September 1997 issue of *Wired,* came out as a book in the fall of 1998. These rules rely on a whole bunch of biological metaphors as belly-flopped onto the scripture of high tech business. Aside from bobbing requisite curtsies in the direction of Peter Drucker and Alvin Toffler, Rules Boy Kelly describes the circumference of what he calls the Network Economy — which looks a lot like an exploded version of the electronics industry. The rules, in turn, are a lot like his "Nine Laws of God," with which he concluded *Out of Control* (his previous book), and are guides for his idea of what neobiological civilization ought to be. Kelly has a bad case of the delta blues.

Which means I must bring up another of my friends, this time a libertarian eco-warrior. With multiple degrees in chemistry from Good Schools, he's made a career of working for the good (an internationally respected nature organization, a public-interest law firm filing claims on behalf of atomic radiation survivors, etc.). And he struggles and struggles to reconcile his anarchistic, government-despising political impulses with the global depletion and degradation he is familiar with *factually* as a scientist. For what he sees is that transnational corporations are beholden to no communities but their stockholders; and the work he and others try to do on behalf of the environment doesn't fit for the most part with the libertarian worldview he holds. If corporations have no obligation to conform to the dictates of a governing body, most can't be bothered to do well by doing good. He hates this contradiction, as he must. My friend is also a secular humanist with a tinge of the woo-woo; in other words, he has no religious faith in the conventional sense.

Compare my friend, who is a practicing biologist, but an agnostic, with Kelly, a lapsed Catholic, born-again Evangelical, who can operate on faith when facts don't support him. My friend would much prefer to hold onto a worldview as espoused by people like Kelly, but his real-world day-to-day experience of the intersection between the natural world and the corporate one gets in the way.

It's not surprising that Kelly is an admirer of the late Julian Simon, the libertarian right's stalwart against what they believe is environmental alarmism — in other words, the "false" environmental concerns about overpopulation, habitat destruction, and catastrophic trashing of complex ecological cycles, which stand counter to the blooming, buzzing, budding, dynamic, don't-mess-it-up-by-touching-it, economic models. And when you read through Kelly's works, if you are, like me, not a professing

Christian, you begin to feel you are running up against a universe bounded by a faith you may not share, particularly in his brushing aside of environmental issues as so much noise. I am not a theologian, but it seems to me that in Kelly's change-is-good/all-is-well thinking about the world (he has very much taken to heart the words of his mentor, Stewart Brand, editor of the *Whole Earth Catalogue*: "We are as gods and might as well get good at it"), there is a Christian belief in the bounty of the Lord's Creation and that the Creator will provide and that nothing bad can happen without there being a Divine Providence behind it, though we, as poor mortals, may not understand.

True, the Black Death resulted in a major reforestation of Europe and helped bring about the demise of the feudal system, but not before a lot of collateral damage. And a bit earlier, the mass extinctions 65 million years ago in the age of dinosaurs seemed to help along the development of mammalian species. But I don't think these are scenarios most of us would look to as exemplars of how we want our world to work.

To enjoy listening to Kelly's gospel-influenced delta blues, you may have to buy into some leaps of faith you hadn't bargained for. Biology as metaphor can take under its wing credos that are as backward-turning as they are forward-looking.

DON'T KNOW MUCH ABOUT BIOLOGY

The best part of the Bionomics philosophy is that much of it is syncretic synergistically nifty-cool: It is *fun* to admire the action of an invisible hand (or paw) in biological systems, observe how nature sorts things out, and wonder how well that might map onto our own ant-hill scurrying behaviors. We can learn from artificial life, for example, in seeing how organisms built out of software interact with their synthetic, within-the-computer environments in lifelike ways. And it's diverting to learn how local control and decentralized computing can help US Forest

Service employees, who are on the side of the angels, combat their ecosystem-destroying, selling-timber-below-market-rates institutional culture. What an interdisciplinary gas!

Yet as with any overarching grand unified theory of everything, Bionomics leaves some important pesky bits out. Like how, even in high tech, if you're being historically and intellectually honest, you can't claim that the best technology, the best marketing, the best management, the best company, the best people, the best — *anything* — necessarily triumphs in the marketplace.

I got to know one of TBI's summer interns: She was bright and outgoing and poised, someone anyone would call a good kid. She and I chatted about how fiercely impossible teenage boys can be, and then she admired the portable printer I had hooked up to my laptop. This Diconix printer has a footprint smaller than a shoe box and weighs about as much as that same shoe box would weigh when containing only one pair of Arche boots. For more than twelve years, I have wrapped my trusty printer in a sweater, thrown it in my suitcase, and taken it everywhere. It takes standard cartridges that are easy to install and cheap to use, its correspondence quality is pretty damned good for inkjet (it can print graphics off the Web well enough), and it has several different built-in fonts to choose from. It uses the most standard of cables, ports, and interfaces, and loads pin-feed paper with ease. If you have ever printed something out in a library from a database, chances are it was with a Diconix printer: The wee beasties last forever, take up little room, and are quiet enough for library use, whether when printing or simply sitting there at the ready (compare that to the resting-state hum of a LaserJet). If you ever see one for sale, grab it; owners of Diconix printers seldom let them go, much as was the case with the Swiss-made Hermes typewriters of the 1960s and 1970s. In all the years I've owned my Diconix, all it has needed is a $1 fuse and the occasional cleaning (I do it myself) with rubbing alcohol and a Q-Tip. In short, it inspires computer lust and admiration in everyone who sees it.

When I explained to this Bright Young Thing that there is nothing like it available on the market now, she was aghast. Good student that she was, she had learned only about the evolution of product lines and the efficiency of the marketplace. She had never heard about its inefficiencies. She was surprised that an information-technology product so wonderful could be thirteen years old. It's hard to say where the shortcomings of my Diconix lay; perhaps it was too well engineered so that it lasted too long and customers didn't need to keep buying new ones. Maybe it's because the Diconix parent company, Kodak, didn't have the marketing clout of Hewlett-Packard, the dominant player in the printer market. I don't really know. But the undeserved fate of Diconix printers (so sad, all gone away now) is hardly the only such sad story in high tech.

Most technologists would assert that CP/M or DR/DOS were better operating systems than the market-triumphant MS-DOS, and that Unix (in one of its many flavors/variants, perhaps such as Linux) is certainly more sturdy than Windows NT — if not better all the way around. People who used Amiga computers felt their machine came equipped with features and functions far in advance of what was available on the Macintoshes and PCs of their day (the 1980s); and as the bumper sticker you see on cars driving on Sunnyvale/Cupertino off- and on-ramps to Highway 85 says, "Macintosh 89 = Windows 95."

Sometimes technological superiority does make the difference: The simplicity and bulletproofness of TCP/IP (Transmission Control Protocol/Internet Protocol), the basic set of network software that undergirds the Internet, won geek hearts and minds over from more tetchy, complicated, and proprietary communications protocols. Yet in the 1980s, venture capitalists didn't want to fund a startup called Cisco (now the communications giant that among other things makes much of the gear that runs the Internet and at the end of its fiscal year in July 1999 had $12.15 billion in revenues) because the company's core competence was based on publicly available, nonproprietary intellectual property developed by a bunch of geeks largely funded (though indirectly) by government money — that is, TCP/IP. Cisco founders bootstrapped/self-funded the company — and now who can possibly accurately gauge the size of Net-based/Net-related/Net-affected business? And VCs now fund companies using technologies that have publicly proven their superior soundness over time, such as one of the Net's email protocols and Linux, a version of Unix.

But the VCs hadn't been entirely self-deluded in turning down Cisco; they had to have been aware that *marketing* can determine what lives and what dies, not an ideal of evolutionary technology virtue. For the Silicon Valley liturgy goes thus: The Apple Macintosh marketed/commercialized what Xerox PARC (Palo Alto Research Park) invented but failed to market properly; the Macintosh took off only because of the creation and growth of desktop publishing (another market creation); and it's only because Apple egregiously made one self-centered, self-destructive, bad business decision after another that Microsoft was able to come along years later and somewhat poorly catch up with Apple's applied technology lead. Microsoft was also better able to convince developers that going their way was the better *business* decision, although most technologists would say Apple had far better technology, developed years before Microsoft would palely imitate it, too. The rest we know. The Darwinian struggle isn't necessarily about the triumph of the best, but the survival of the most marketable.

As has been talked about a lot in the 1997, 1998, and 1999 fussing about Microsoft and antitrust, it's a dirty little secret in high tech that superior marketing and inferior technology will beat out superior technology and inferior marketing every time, and that other factors, aside from Darwinian fitness, determine which technologies, and which companies, thrive or perish.

Increasing returns is one of these factors, a notion that economists have been writing about for twenty-five years. It's the idea that a good becomes cheaper as more of it is produced. It also becomes more useful as more people use it — a concept that applies really well to communications technologies such as telephones, facsimile machines, and email. As the production cost of the good decreases, it is valued more by its consumers — which makes for a tidy growth curve.

Linked with increasing returns is the companion notion that the companies/technologies that get to market first can lock in consumers — what in the computer industry tends to be called the installed base (of users). Economists call this "path dependence," and it refers to the situation where, for example, people have already bought and trained themselves on the quiddities of WordPerfect for Lawyers or Windows 95 or AutoCad, and the prospect of completely changing over to something else represents such a loss of investment and hassle and incompatibility with the rest of the world that they just won't do it. Or at least not very easily.

This is not to say that people never switch over to entirely newer technologies; of course they do from time to time, and it hasn't killed them or their MIS departments (though they might have felt like they would have preferred to die during the weeks and months of the transition). But, contrary to the vicious evolutionary model trumpeted by many in high tech, natural selection isn't entirely what's operating in that marketplace — or any other human endeavor. Monopolies do result, as they have throughout recorded history, and not necessarily through merit.

As Krugman also wrote in his January 22, 1998, *Slate* column,

> A world in which increasing returns are prevalent is one in which markets are likely to get it wrong. Products that should be developed never get off the ground, or do so much later than they should, because everyone is waiting for other people to move (I'll buy a fax machine only when enough other people

> have them to make it worthwhile). Industries can get locked into the wrong technology (Macintosh is better than DOS, but everyone uses DOS because everyone else uses DOS). Waste occurs because of coordination failures (in the early days of railroad each line had a different gauge). Indeed, increasing returns have traditionally been used as arguments *against* free marketers, *for* government intervention.

Another pesky bit that Bionomics leaves out is that sometimes you really do need to bring in the Feds (or some other centrally organized force) to redress local problems like, say, a tendency toward lynching. Ditto for unfair business practices. Ditto for emissions levels and crash safety of automobiles. There is also the reality that you can't always go off and start a company of your own if you are, say, being sexually harassed where you work and you are a cancer researcher or a plasma physicist, because the job requires an institution and not a storefront. And what's more, you may have the skills of a scientist and not those of a businessperson, and so wouldn't be doing yourself, or your family, or society any good if you were forced from the work that you were born best to do, which is basic science, not applied marketing. It also really is a good thing that federal protection is provided to whistle-blowers and that regulation can create *better*, more level playing fields for businesses to evolve on (something most mainstream free-market economists have no problem with). What many high tech thoughtleaders ignore is that sometimes, when you're dealing with irreconcilable differences, interests, forces, and personalities, no win-win-win solution is obtainable: Complex rules of law are the way to go.

At bottom, Bionomics steps around the fact that technology creates as many problems as it solves, and that assessing the market value of things such as basic research, fine art, clean water, or a whole bunch of other negligibly fungible stuff is not easy, fun, or maybe even possible.

LITTLE SHOP OF HORRORS

When I emerged from the first two-day Bionomics Conference, which Lynch had encouraged me to attend, at that hotel on Fisherman's Wharf, I was exhilarated and horrified. Exhilarated, because I sensed I had stumbled onto Something Seminal at Its Beginning and was amazed at the caliber of high tech presence there: Gil Amelio, then head of National Semiconductor, now booted-out CEO of Apple; Carver Mead, then a Cal Tech prof who's now gone entirely to the private sector, remaining a big cheese in neural networks and Very Large Scale Integration (how you keep packing more power onto chips); Michael Riordan, CEO of biotech giant Gilead Sciences. Much of what Bionomics is about in its largest sense is great intellectual fun — seeing relationships between patterns in nature and patterns in computation or economics, thinking in interdisciplinary ways, and applying technology in exuberant and other than its obvious bean-counter, accounts-payable ways — and for that reason, I had a blast.

But my second response, horror, had to do with seeing, writ large as only a confab of True Believers can do, technolibertarianism. Lynch says that TBI has somewhat steered clear of pure-form libertarians (whether merely self-identified or of the Libertarian Party), because Bionomics is about dynamism: throwing stuff out, learning from it, and moving on in real-world ways, and not about ideological purity. To *me*, however, the way Bionomics thinking and talking has spread out into high tech and beyond is part of the default libertarian culture of the Net, and of high tech.

On hand at Bionomics conferences there were usually representatives from libertarian and conservative outposts in the real world: local libertarian bookstores, folks promulgating tax evasion/shield-your-money-offshore schemes, and outspoken, culturally conservative Catholics. Although some of the speakers were hardly in the camp of the culturally conservative, I almost never spotted any neoliberals, much less ecofeminists, or any others of a more lefty, though equally offbeat/chaos-loving character among those setting up shop at the conferences or in the audience. Typical "Vitamin Bs" extol the usual libertarian things (pro: nuclear power, school choice, computers in schools, workers being made ever more unattached to an office or a workplace, HMOs as models of economic efficiency and choice; anti: global-warming alarmists, Microsoft trust-busting, federal clean-air regulations), often with a digital thrust. Whether this suited its self-concept or not, Bionomics has mostly been allied with traditional conservative causes and people.

So I wasn't terribly surprised that George Gilder, a sort of culturally retro techno-evangelical, had been one of the featured speakers at the First Bionomics Conference. Gilder often shows up playing the part of a Jonathan Edwards–type theologian where high tech philosophizing is at hand. For example, he had been one of the keynoters at the 1994 Atlanta conference "Cyberspace and the American Dream." Sponsored in part by the Committee for American Progress and the now-faded-away Progress and Freedom Foundation (with close ties to Contract with America boosters), the Atlanta conference had in its declaration of principle that "cyberspace has the potential to create almost unimaginable freedom and prosperity for all Americans... Yet we find ourselves burdened with a system of government with a bias: when in doubt, regulate." Gilder's appearance at that first Bionomics conference was a marker indicating future conferences were to be a playing field for the technolibertarian powers that be.

In what was one of the high/low points of the conference, Gilder, the parson of what *Wired* magazine has called the "digerati," labeled the homeless the true economic parasites, because they occupy some of the most expensive real estate in the world (Union Square in San Francisco, all over Manhattan) for free. Right, George; there are lots of symbolic manipulator/knowledge-worker jobs for chronic schizophrenics, who are the way they are because of their lack of moral fiber and who have been scamming Big Government spending programs.

The seriously mentally ill seem to have always been among us: Schizophrenics appear in every time and place, in roughly the same percentage of the population. How a society deals with these people is a measure of its civility. Do we incarcerate them in pits? Chain them to walls? Let them wander the streets? Hope some church-run or other private charity can figure out what to do with their addled neurotransmitters? Never mind that there are waiting lists for drug rehab programs and laughably inadequate funding for halfway houses and treatment programs for those with certifiably bad brain chemistry, or that low-income housing has gone away through the beauty of gentrification. Nah, it's too much regulation that's to blame for making these parasites (a strange echo of Maoist rhetoric, where *capitalists* were the parasites).

Other inadvertent lessons about the technolibertarian dark side were ready to be had at the Second Bionomics Conference, the following year.

CULTURE OF COMPLAINT

It was there, six months before the Oklahoma City bombing, someone first darkly warned me of how fed up people in this country were becoming with the Feds and that armed insurrection could not be long in coming. It was more confirmation that in spite of seeing itself as ecumenical, Bionomics attracted — and fit well with — the fringe of the right rather than the left.

Although the *speakers* could be varied (Web designers and editors; record-company execs; centrist Democrats), I had that same infiltrating-a-political-cell impostor feeling I'd had when staying (because it was the only place on the island left with vacancies) at a resort in the Straits of Juan de Fuca owned by an obscure New Age cult. Everyone assumed you were there because you too believed in the One True Way; why else would you be? On Orcas Island it was energy balancing and high colonies that were the Light and the True Path; at the San Francisco Marriott it was the goodness that refinements in technology and decentralization would bring.

In keeping with cult qualities, there was also something of the idolatry directed toward Rothschild himself. People at the conference spoke with reverence and affection toward Michael (rather like Madonna, no last name was needed), just as I remember EST-holes speaking of EST founder Werner Erhard (encyclopedia-salesman-turned-Messianic-multimillionaire) in the '70s. There was gratitude in the air for the one who had brought Revelation: how right that the effort of human innovation in toolmaking should make obsolete old bad ways and bring about new good things, hosanna hosanna! And, of course, much of this is true; innovations in technology (better stirrups, new printing presses, faster micro-processors) should be praised, as should be the wondrous human tendency toward innovation, particularly when given room to move. All power to it. But *what* was that you were saying about the miseries of the Industrial Revolution? Of saving money by lopping headcounts in customer support by putting your clients through voicemail hell?

These Bionomics conferences were clearly in part about bringing together the Best and the Brightest (or perhaps, most notorious) in the technolibertarian world. As with Gilder at the first conference, there was at this second conference the man who best typifies another important piece of bandwidth on the technolibertarian spectrum — though at the opposite end from Gilder — John Perry Barlow, the quintessential raver.

Glamour is a severely underrated driver in human affairs, and it was one of the secrets of the success of *Wired* — giving nerds and money managers the chance to see themselves as the stars of their own MTV video. (I'm not an office droid! I'm Tom

Paine! Captain Jack Aubrey! Mick Jagger! Hasn't it been the appeal of consumer goods and pop-culture icons, rather than civil liberties, that made capitalism ultimately so alluring to former communist countries?) And so it is with Barlow, who has iconic stature, though in another part of the forest from Gilder. I was struck by how the guys in the room were captivated by a kind of charisma that's often in short supply in high tech (how else could Steve Jobs have gotten away with his shenanigans or obtained his celebrity?). A kind of imaginative transference was taking place as Barlow spoke: In buying his chiliastic we-can-be-together / up-against-the-wall-mother rap (that is, the adherents to the technolibertarian future versus the bad guys in Washington), they too were imagining they would have some of his rockstar-once-removed ability to work a crowd and acquire his verging-on-legendary priapic success scoring with nubile females. What a vision for those whose lives and presentation of self are so far from such possibilities. It's not that Barlow's a looker or that what he has to say is other than rather vague but lofty-sounding exhortation. It's that he's got the *moves*.

In any event, at that same Bionomics conference, Barlow also, discreetly, had JFK jr. (yes, that one, late lamented) in tow. Once again, all the claims that technolibertarians make of being outside the dominant power structure ain't necessarily so. Barlow is himself a graduate of elite private schools — not that there's anything wrong with that, obviously, but this pedigree is simply at odds with his cowboy-outsider persona.

At the more general level, the Second Bionomics Conference brought home the scare at seeing yet another manifestation of the *celebration* of the winner-take-all, casino society, which is steadily moving us toward being the Argentina of the North. I'm sure this isn't the intention of the folks at TBI — but it may be the unintended consequence of it. The "I've got mine (or certainly intend to if the god-damned bureaucrats don't get in my way), so screw you" mentality certainly seemed to characterize much of the community I saw forming around TBI.

While milling around during the breaks, I was beset and clung to by a lot of educated, disgruntled, white, libertarian guys; not too many women are terrifically attracted to these ideas, perhaps because, as difference feminists such as Carol Gilligan hold, women tend to worry more about interrelationships and compassion and less about looking after their own self-interest. This second conference was held in a hotel where, as in many big cities, well-heeled conventioneers rub up against what used to be called in another era Skid Row residents. Yet it was the guys inside the hotel, and not the ones hanging out on the Market Street sidewalks, who were being aggressive in their pose of disenfranchisement and badly-done-by-ness and embattlement. They were affluent by practically any measure you could devise; they were educated and held commanding positions in the industrial and technological upheavals that have occurred since downsizing, automation, outsourcing, and computerization have taken over work life. Yet it was the Bionomics attendees who seemed to be forming a revolutionary cadre — and not the hopelessly bypassed-by-postmodernism lumpen outside on Market Street.

It's a fish-barrel-gun cliché of a speech-act to pick on rich white guys when their less-privileged brothers are very close by, out in the cold. But it's still simply worth pointing out that it's usually the hungry and disadvantaged who romantically are thought to feed revolutions — not those who have had a good pick of education, jobs, residences, and recreational choices. The attitude of disgruntlement bordering on victimhood is simply a cast of mind I've kept running into throughout my travels in technolibertarian land: Why do the petty restraints of regulation, often irrational but not majorly in the way of most of these folks, get them so livid?

A hint came when one of these technolibertarians started courting me with earnest email. After about a week of increasingly amazing dialogue (engaged on his side, horrified but fascinated on mine), I emailed him some notes toward an initial critique of libertarianism and high tech. He was enraged, of course; but the most revealing thing he said was, "I bet your article will make you look good with your arty friends." Voila: the ancient nerd-rage at being slighted by the (to him) attractive art student who would have nothing to do with him, his feeling excluded and subtly damned by the strangely impenetrable community of shared subjective values of humanities geeks. High tech libertarians can be as suspicious of the notion of a shared pool of humanist values (and the judgments that spring from them) as the worst, politically correct, dead-white-male-decrying ethnic studies major. Damn, it's Nozick's envious wordsmiths acting up again!

BLOCK BY BLOCK

At the Third Bionomics Conference in 1995, I was struck forcibly by another trait I have come to associate with much technolibertarian culture: its edge-city/urban-avoiding aspects. The event took place at a ghastly Redwood Shores business hotel, adjacent to the big and much-feared Oracle Corp.[10] I heard from my TBI friends afterward that most attendees *loved* the conference site, smack in the middle of nowheresville dismal office park suburban Silicon Valley — as opposed to when it had been held twenty miles north in San Francisco. It's ugly! There's no place decent to eat! There's nothing to do outside the hotel! Although New York, Los Angeles, and, in particular, San Francisco are where many of the high-visibility Net companies are — particularly those

10 The 500-pound-gorilla database company Oracle and its CEO, Larry Ellison, are considered in high tech to be simply a smaller-scale version of Microsoft and Bill Gates.

involved with e-commerce and what's called content creation (you know, the stuff people read and look at, as opposed to the technical infrastructure / programmer tools / corns complexities) — high tech has historically had a city-loathing / urban-problem-avoiding bias. Which matters as far as playing into a certain philistinism and ignoring how the Other Half (make it the Other Vast Majority) lives. Which is a little odd, because cities tend to have business ecosystem diversity the ways suburbs do not.

END OF AN ERA

The last pure-form Bionomics conference took place in October of 1996. I attended, as I had the previous three conferences, because the conference had become my private hunting preserve for ideas and sources. But that year, the conference received a full-page mention in *Wired*. In the past, Bionomics had been a for-my-eyes-only personal view into the zeitgeist. Prodromal enough, the keynoter was the president of the Washington, DC–based Cato Institute, the first among equals of libertarian think tanks.

By this point, perhaps not so surprisingly, Bionomics-type language had spread everywhere in Northern California high tech, though most who deployed it had no idea that there was a think tank located between San Quentin Prison and the Bay that was the single greatest fountainhead of the meme.

As for charting the spread of the meme, the Bionomics Institute's board of directors decided from very early on in the organization's life that one way to track the success of the organization was to see how much biological thinking began to shape the terms of argument in discussions of economics and technology. Members of the Bionomics community would send in mentions in print wherever they found the language of economy-as-ecosystem. At first, these were rare, prized sightings, along the lines of spotting a white buffalo. By 1996, they had become Too Numerous to Count, like the term the medical community uses to describe the number, say, of white blood cells or pathogens present at the site of an infection.

For example, Intel chief (and *Time* magazine's 1997 Man of the Year) Andy Grove said in the February 26, 1996, *Forbes ASAP*: "Remember, the PC is not a thing. It is an organic phenomenon like a river, it flows. It constantly adapts to underlying technology changes, user demands, even market surprises." This may have been a surprise to those who don't make an animist religion out of PCs, but there it is. What can you do, as volunteers at the Hunger Project (Erhard Seminar Training's affiliated do-gooder non-profit) used to say, in unconscious homage to Victor Hugo, about the force of an idea whose time has come?

Or there's Evan Schwartz, a former *Business Week* reporter, who came out with a book called *Webonomics* in 1997, which he later updated as *Digital Darwinism* in 1999. Both books borrowed from biology to create simplistic rules for e-commerce success.

The examples are endless.

But then you have to inquire how much you believe in which version of the Whorf hypothesis: How much does language shape thought? How much does thought shape language? Does the proliferation of Bionomics Moments really mean people in the popular press get it? Does the reliance on a new set of metaphors (remember "Information SuperHighway" and all the bad puns and lame infographics it generated a few years back? Gone away now, praise Buddha) imply more than the general laziness/desperation/tendency toward imitation that most people who write fall into? I think of how, since the '60s, people have been tossing around language that *sounds* like "the personal is the political" or "we are all downstream"; but I can't really say that, thirty years later, I really believe that most folks understand how power relations and intrapsychic personality demons are intertwined, or how if you want the doors to stores in a Tucson shopping center to open automatically, as opposed to manually, you are contributing to the smog over the Grand Canyon.

You can argue that the spread of the Bionomics meme is: (a) an idea whose time has come, much like recreational drug use fit with the emphasis on individuality and pleasure-seeking and rebellion in the '60s; (b) the mark of the fine puppetmaster hand of the VC community, the true freemasons of our era, who influence far more than the lumpen-rest-of-us comprehend about what happens where, when, and which new-fangled notions get credence and which get ignored; (c) an externalization of the swing in fashion toward libertarianism, which is enjoying a vogue throughout American life right now with everyone from militia wackos to *New York Times* columnists; (d) a manifestation of the romanticization of nature, at a time when nature is disappearing like never before; (e) a divine accident.

And whenever a trend goes mainstream, you know it's on the verge of becoming invisible as a trend per se.

What happens when outsiders become dispensers of the Conventional Wisdom? What becomes of a once-esoteric subculture that every dweeb now unconsciously pays homage to daily? Easy: Sell out to the Big Guns, very possibly from the East Coast. This is a model eerily similar to the path taken by many a startup: create something of interest; attract the attention of a Traditional Moneyed Entity; and sell out when you get bored with your own creation.

In the 1980s, IBM took over ROLM, the Silicon Valley startup that pretty much developed digital telephony — a technology involved in today's highly automated telephone exchanges and stuff like fancy voicemail at your desk. IBM, the Old Guard, saw the fine thing/new market ROLM had created, bought it, but could not help but absorb it into IBM Big Blue bland corporate culture — where ROLM never did much nor was heard from much again. What was left of ROLM was eventually sold off to Siemens, the German electronics giant.

ROLM's founders moved on to other new ventures, as is done in these parts.

This is exactly the process that unfolded around TBI: The 1996 conference no longer attracted the with-it cool cabal of high tech power brokers. I certainly didn't intersect with the kinds of folks I'd met at previous conferences — private-rocket entrepreneurs and very senior longtime staff scientists at Apple and the like. There were far more women in attendance, who, when they spoke up and out, mostly did not have nice things to say (hate to say it, but the sociologists know it seems to be true: once women start infiltrating an organization or profession or just about anything, it is perceived to lose status. Think of the profession of "physician" in the former Soviet Union). There were far more critics in the audience. Clearly the event had lost the neophyte edginess it had once had; and between the spreading out of bionomic-like language into the language of high tech at large and the far more fun prospect of making money/running a startup, it was decided that there would be no more Bionomics conferences, and TBI was put into suspended animation.

Bue that's where things get really interesting. The events that followed demonstrated the unanticipated reach of these ideas. By the spring of 1997, the Cato Institute had agreed to take over the conference. Cato, with its menhir of a HQ smack in the middle of DC, is among the sleekest and most fearsome of the right-wing, free-market, think-tank conquistadors. Hugely funded since the lace 1960s and early 1970s, it has colonized political discourse in the United States. Cato as an institution has the kind of corporate sponsorship and bland East Coast establishment persona that gives it an authority inside DC politics that such a mavericky West Coast high techy institution such as TBI could never have. Yet Cato wouldn't be taking over the TBI conferences purely out of a spirit of philos. Nope, it's gotta be that realization that Northern California high tech has got the money — and large candidate pools of the politically naive and libertarian-predisposed — to make it an untapped and potentially rewarding (to use the language of free-marketers) market for Cato. Think of the great Dutch merchant-traders of the seventeenth century, dominating European markets (translation: East Coast establishment mindshare), and their joy in discovering and then getting to colonize a Spice Islands of CEOs, potential donors, and sympathizers. And renaming them the Dutch/Cato East Indies.

STRANGE BEDFELLOWS

This friendly takeover brought, in the fall of 1997, a joint Cato/Bionomics conference to San Francisco, with a program far more Cato-ish than Bionomics-ish. Which meant far more pure-form libertarian hoo-hah and far less on offbeat or life-mimicking uses of technology. The Cato folks, in spite of their despising of so much of The Government, sure seem to a Left Coaster a lot like the other self-serious folks inside the Beltway.

The spookiest interlude (one of terror, and no pity) came when Peter Huber gave the luncheon keynote. Huber, former MIT engineering professor and top-drawer lawyer (Harvard degree, Circuit and Supreme Court clerkships) has been knocking around libertarian technology policy, with one of his foci the deregulation of telecommunications, for at least a decade. Again, he is a guy more Cato-ish than bionomic. Choosing a telecommunications sharpshooter to rally the troops made sense, given that Cato, as of 1998, had as board members folks such as Rupert Murdoch and big-shot donors such as TCI's John Malone, as well as people from Viacom, and various RBOCs (Regional Bell Operating Companies).

Huber had burst with a flash into the communications-policy world back in the mid-1980s with a report he wrote for the US Department of Justice, commissioned by Judge Harold Greene (the guy who oversaw the breakup of the old Bell System starting in 1984). Borrowing a term from Buckminster Fuller, the "Geodesic Network" advised that in the realm of communications, everything would interconnect and self-heal and route most efficiently if left on its own without the Great Satan of regulation and the devil would take the hindmost and, as I think it was said by a terror of the Counter Reformation, "God will sort them out." During the St. Bartholomew's Day Massacre, both adherents to the Apostolic Catholic Faith and the miscreant Huguenots were slaughtered; if Mistakes Were Made, the Great Customer Service Rep in The Sky would handle it. Deregulation teleology asserts something along the same lines: If the good (in the corporate or maybe even the community sense) is snuffed out along with the bad in the course of the magnificent music-making of the free market, it's not so bad if it's in the service of a Bigger Goal. Which I guess for Huber is mostly the making of money.

In other words, Huber's take on the aftermath of the divestiture of AT&T was pure technolibertarian. The sin of this divestiture was that entrepreneurs such as Craig McCaw (wireless telephony CEO whose business was bought out by AT&T — another Seattle zillionaire) had been prevented from performing their magic of wealth creation earlier on in our century because our regulatory structure before 1984 didn't allow for it. Thus was Huber marked a hell-fire and damnation preacher of a kind that Max Weber in his *Protestant Ethic and the Spirit of Capitalism* would have recognized.

But the sinister part of his presentation really came with the quivery not-really-bothering-to-suppress-it rage directed at Janet Reno and the obeisance paid to old English common law. Hatred of a Democratic attorney general and raising paeans to common law are old-time reactionary gestures, not just libertarian ones. But most alarming was his repeatedly expressed disgust with what's on TV. This rant was odd for someone who has devoted so much of his professional life to telecommunications deregulation. If you don't like government intervention in the lives of communications businesses, how can you be upset with whatever it is they choose to communicate? Or allow to be communicated, given the proper exchange of money for bandwidth? Now I may share Huber's disaffection for the idiot box — *Wiseguy* is the only television show as an adult I've been loyal to — but when people start railing about "filth" in any medium, as Huber did several times that day when he talked about television, I get very nervous. A worldview that equates Godhead with money but damns mass entertainment as impure (unexalted ribaldry has been around at least as long, it seems, as there have been written records, probably even longer; every era has its penny dreadfuls and its porn) — well, that's more the political and economic culture of a Singapore with maybe only slightly better movies, or of a China (prisoners make for a lean, disciplined, productive, nonunion workforce — and such entrepreneurial opportunities!) than the United States of Walt Whitman, John Huston, or REM.

Paradoxically, back when the FCC *was* regulating the broadcast industry more, much of what Huber found objectionable wasn't on the air — and there was more insistence on public affairs programming. Some of the change is of course the general loosening of moral tone in the last few decades (you can routinely have at least fratboy sex-and-scatological humor on TV, if nothing else) — but maybe that can be blamed on the Nanny State, too. If those single welfare mothers hadn't gotten food stamps in the 1960s, then we would have had no *Ellen* or *In Living Color*!

A Grand Inquisitor, Huber was a Savonarola, riling up his audience — except there wasn't a Botticelli in those rooms to be led into throwing his paintings into a bonfire. Still, folks at their luncheon tables nodded and laughed and cheered and booed at the right places.

As fascinating and frightening as Huber's monster-hiding-under-the-bed choler was to someone who worries more about monopolies than decaying moral fiber, he is not a Silicon Valley guy, so it's not exactly fair to make him out to be their spokesman. But he has much common ground with them; he has helped to frame the anti-regulatory communications environment (I wonder how he and his pals will feel when newly, proudly deregulated Telecommunications-Act-of-1996-empowered communications companies start trying to erect transmitters in their residential neighborhoods. No local red tape in the way!); and he is a member of the Gilder cohort. And with that, he fit right in.

And Cato itself, among the top-five-most-quoted think tanks in the US news media, originally funded by the likes of the Ken Starr–sympathetic Scaife Foundation, will continue to forge alliances with Silicon Valley. Its April 27, 1998, Briefing Paper No. 37, "Silicon Valley Versus Corporate Welfare," written by Cypress Semiconductor CEO T. J. Rodgers and signed by more than fifty Silicon Valley luminaries (Scott Cook/Intuit/Quicken, VC superstar John Doerr/Kleiner Perkins Caufield & Byers), is typical of the entente between West Coast technologists and East Coast libertarians. The "Declaration of Independence" from corporate subsidy is a principled, if reductive, technolibertarian manifesto against congressional pork for high tech industries and for the savings so obtained to be "devoted to reducing corporate income taxes, the capital gains tax, or the personal income tax."

In November 1998, there was a "Cato West" conference (scrapping the Bionomics positioning/branding) — in Silicon Valley, without the noise and irrelevance of San Francisco and the biological meme. Renamed "The Annual Cato Institute/ *Forbes ASAP* Conference on Technology and Society," with the predictable theme "Washington, DC, versus Silicon Valley," it was set at the San Jose Fairmont Hotel. Aside from a session where three science-fiction writers spoke (though not writers of the dystopian/cyberpunk persuasion), the quirkiness and sass of the original Bionomics was all gone. What remained were heavyweights in the libertarian world (libertarian law professors and

Cato staffers) side by side with heavyweights in the technology sector (Larry Ellison, Scott Cook) and heavyweights from the corporate world (Alfred R. Berkeley III, president of NASDAQ). Keynoter was Milton Friedman, and Microsoft was one of the sponsors. In November 1999, it was pretty much more of the same: "Technology and Society 1999/The Evolution of the New Economy." Assimilation has been completed. And in a way, it's all very sad.

But what happened to TBI and to the original Mr. Bionomics himself, Michael Rothschild?

FROM THEORY TO PRAXIS

What would possibly make *more* sense for a West Coast technolibertarian think tank than for it to turn its energy into the creation of a software startup? Stemming from consulting work Rothschild did to help with profit-maximizing decision-support factory-automation software for a division of National Semiconductor (the bionomic idea being that if you make real-time data available to folks working at line jobs, pushing decision-making down and away from Control Central, i.e., Mahogany Row — then people will be able to make better decisions and productivity will go up and errors down and quality will improve and factories can be more responsive to changing conditions in the material world), Maxager, nee Applied Bionomics, was formed.

Maxager presents in small form a concatenation of characteristics that define one of the technolibertarian gestalts — meaning that Maxager can be viewed as a test case for all that Bionomics advocates. It also serves as the technolibertarian crown of creation: the startup.

In applying his considerable energy and intelligence to Maxager, Rothschild's focus has gone from the theoretical to the applied; but whether Maxager succeeds or fails will be interesting ideologically. If Maxager fails through no true fault of its own (as many, if not most, startups do, due to cash-flow probs or unpredictable technical glitches or vagaries in market or client situations or a zillion and one perfectly unblameworthy and acausal reasons), it will be interesting to see how it will be interpreted by Bionomics sympathizers and freemarketers. That Bionomics made real doesn't work? That the market isn't always the marker for true value? And if Maxager succeeds (for reasons that may have less to do with whatever merits its software has and something to do with all the contacts TBI / Rothschild has in the VC / private-angel-money / high-tech-insider world), will this support the superiority of an idea, or will it be seen as the usual mystery-mix of time, place, luck, and contacts that can make one company flourish where one goes sclerotic? As Napoleon said of one of his generals, "But is he lucky?"

The philosopher Karl Popper uses the term "falsifiability." Maybe, it's simpler to talk instead of what a tautology is — that is, in order for something to prove itself *true*, it has to be capable of being proved false. What are the conditions and outcomes that could prove the application of Bionomics true or false? Will what happens with Maxager be proof of bionomic theory? If it succeeds, fails, gets bought out, limps along — what will any of it mean?

For now, the peculiar locus of fake-o biology, technology, and libertarianism represented by Bionomics shows no signs of going away. I can't begin to speculate if it is a harbinger of social Darwinist horrors to come, or if it will come to be seen as a societal trend that was very much a product of its decade and will recede into background with time, as has been the fate of management-by-walking-around or the deployment of macrame plant-holders in interior design. It's just too soon to tell. But the next time you hear economics talked about in terms of niches and predators and evolution, know that what you're mostly hearing is the language of the free market, and not very much Mother Nature.

CHAPTER TWO

THE CRYPTO WARS: CYPHERPUNKS, DIGITAL CASH, AND ANARCHO-CAPITALISM, OH MY

IN EARLY SEPTEMBER 1996, because as unlikely as it might sound, I *knew* there would be many moments of high entertainment value, I attended a conference sponsored by Apple Computer on cryptography, the science of codes. For decades mostly the concern of government spook agencies and a few mathematicians, crypto (as it is commonly abbreviated) has emerged as both a necessary and a practical component of the way computers and communications now operate. Cryptography has also long been a rallying point in the ideological conflict between high tech and Big Government.

You or your employer or someone you do business with or buy from probably has been using crypto for years without anyone necessarily knowing it. Every time you use an ATM, for example, the communication between you and your bank is encrypted to ensure the safety and privacy of the interchange. Crypto is routinely used in any kind of electronic funds transfer (direct deposit of your paycheck; electronic IRS refund). An automobile manufacturer might encrypt communications with its branch offices and suppliers all over the world to prevent industrial espionage, just as a sporting-goods manufacturer might routinely encrypt the plans for its upcoming product lines to keep them safe from competitors in an increasingly fierce global marketplace. Consumer activists are increasingly demanding that people's medical records be encrypted so that no one who is not explicitly authorized to do so (would you want a potential employer or insurance company to know about that AIDS test you decided to take a few years ago?) can poke about in people's health histories. If you have bought anything over the Internet, chances are the vendor you dealt with used crypto at some point in the transaction.

In general, as more and more things in all parts of life and work become digitized (think of how newer forms of cellular phone service are now digital and not analog) or contain microprocessors / smartchips — and talk to each other — the natural inclination of people in general, and of those who respect the US Constitution in particular, is to ensure their privacy. The natural companion to this inclination is the ever-growing desire to use crypto.

Yet the first-ever Apple Macintosh crypto conference was the sort of event that those outside the computer industry might imagine having all the allure of, say, a refresher course on differential calculus for groundwater hydrologists. Aside from those researchers whose job it is to think about just that arcane branch of applied mathematics, who could possibly care? But times have changed. Cryptography had become one of the central organizing forces in the political philosophy of high tech, and people's attitudes toward it serve as a kind of cultural oath of fealty.

Listening to presentations in one of the absolutely featureless auditoriums on Apple's pretty-well-indistinguishable-from-any-other-industrial-park corporate campus, I felt not so different from when I used to hang around the social fringes of the Weatherpeople in the late '60s. Then and there, everyone played a kind of verbal chicken in proving How Political Am I, questioned each other's credentials for the Revolution (meaning, those you'd need Afterward), and felt very Out Front, clever, and strong, like the daring young men on the flying trapeze.

Thirty years after the time when I used to listen in on the discussions of what used to be called the student protest movement,

I was observing the same kind of righteous rage, familiar to any watcher of technolibertarians, at the stupid and evil government. As before, I was among a fair number of guys with long hair and beards wearing T-shirts. Prevalent was a similar esprit de corps, of "we few, we happy few, we band of brothers," as was the same sense of being a brave member of the Maquis (the underground French Resistance in World War II) — of being on the side of truth and justice.

Similar to what I had noticed in my hanging-about with those talking about the Movement (and in some cases, Armed Revolution) in the '60s, at the Mac Crypto conference I observed yet again arms being covertly linked against the enemy and an affinity group being formed. Back in the '60s, though, this show of solidarity was accompanied by an unstated (or maybe even stated) contempt for the trappings of bourgeois life, for monetary gain or business or profit motives.

But not so here. These outliers and would-be outlaws of 1996 were meeting in a conference room at Apple Computer, one of the best-known mulitnational corporations in the world. The Fellow-resisters were enjoying Big Business largesse (free food, souvenir T-shirts, comfy seats) right alongside their corporate sponsors. In the '60s, a necessary part of the critical political stance was a skepticism toward global monopoly capitalism. But there's a fundamental difference to be found in the absence of such skepticism here, an absence that's not atypical among computerists. In the '90s (often referred to as the '60s turned upside down), politics were creating stranger bedfellows than we ever could have imagined back when we were worried about CIA experimentations with LSD and FBI agents provocateurs at antiwar rallies.

The strategizing, cheering, and booing were as present as they had been absent from the thirty hundred zillion other technical conferences I had attended over the years when, in a previous life, I had been on staff at McGraw-Hill's technical trade magazine for computer-networking professionals, *Data Communications*. Never before had I attended a gathering of geeks, particularly under commercial auspices, that felt so much like the protest-march planning events of my adolescence. This time, the guerrillas were third-party Macintosh developers,[11] in league with Apple staffers.

And to prove how shook up this mixed-up world of politics and technology and Corporate America had become, the Apple technologist who organized the conference was nothing like you'd imagine a Dilbertian cubicle-dwelling Silicon Valley dweeb to be. He was instead the sort of macho-gentle gentleman-warrior you would have wanted beside you on the battlefield in any era: buffed, with previous experience as a military advisor in a country and a war we were never involved in, his hobbies included mastering the combat shotgun. Yet to add to the cultural contradictions he presented, the crypto conference organizer had a picture of his pet rabbit on his Web site. As a joke, in his email correspondence, whenever he would quote your own words back at you for clear reference, he would preface the quotation by saying "Men in black helicopters forced you to say..." As much as he was a freedom fighter, he was able to make good postmodernist ironic fun of the technopolitical cause he was so passionately devoted to: crypto. You can have a sincere love of bunnies and still be a crypto activist.

It struck me that these crypto enthusiasts, most of whom, like many in high tech, had not been remotely political a few years ago, had undergone a singular radicalizing experience, one that had rocked and politicized their worlds. Perhaps these folks had previously acted out with whomp 'em / nuke 'em computer games, or read sword 'n' sorcerer fantasy / sci-fi warrior stuff, or spent weekends involved with paintball. But in the 1990s, with more and more folks attracted to the cause, and with ever-increasing joyous

11 Third-party Macintosh developers are those who develop software for the Macintosh but are not employed by Apple.

ferocity, they got to carry on with the vigor and fun of real issues and a real war: the crypto war. And as for me, those two days in September provided the opportunity to play war correspondent, with all the thrills that implied.

ROOTS AND WINGS

In the '60s, the radicalizing event for the affected group, for those who would be revolutionaries, was the draft. If you could be sent abroad to fight in a civil war for a cause you did not necessarily believe in, you might pause to reflect on the power structures — both economic and geopolitical — that were disrupting your life; hence political consciousness, however naive, is born. For many folks in high tech, their radicalizing experience has come from the US government's mostly awful handling of free speech and privacy as these relate to technology.

One of the catalysts was a congressional bill with the pet name of the Digital Telephony Act (less euphoniously renamed the Communications-Assisted Law Enforcement Act), which passed in 1995. CALEA required all US telephone switching equipment to have a back door (a guaranteed breach of security), so that law enforcement could listen in, if it so chose, on whatever was passing through the switch's circuits. This meant that folks such as MCI, Pacific Bell, and whoever manufactured the PBX in your office would be required to ensure that their equipment made it possible for law enforcement to listen in on all voice or data communications. What has mercifully prevented this act from being implemented are hang-ups with congressional appropriations.

Also in the 1993–1995 era, another similar bad-news measure proposed that all secure telephony (that is, telephones and the equipment they are attached to, such as office switches) purchased by the federal government contain the Clipper chip, which would have embedded within its software a crypto algorithm named Skipjack, which would be crackable by the Feds. Privacy activists were fearful that the purchasing power of the federal government would result, de facto, in all telephony in the United States being manufactured to conform to Clipper specifications. This would mean that in day-to-day ways there would be more privacy, since all your phone calls would be scrambled, but that in an absolute sense, domestic privacy would cease to exist, because the Feds or anyone else with access to the keys to Skipjack *could* listen in. Clipper was shot down, but it left as bad a taste in the mouths of digital privacy folks as Cold War contingency plans to round up lefties into concentration camps in the case of a national emergency left in the mouths of civil libertarians.

But the main catalyzing event, roughly equivalent in raising ire to the tariff placed on tea by the government of King George III, has been the Guvment's bass-ackward / defying-all-sense-reason-and-constitutionality position in the crypto wars. The crypto wars might officially have begun in 1977, when the uber-secret National Security Agency (NSA) issued an executive order warning that participation in an upcoming cryptography symposium on public-key encryption (a kind of very powerful crypto previously in use by the military) might violate the ITAR (International Trafficking in Arms Regulation)[12] decrees that control US munitions. This decree is why so many folks in high tech possess, if not wear, the famous T-shirt that states, "This shirt is a munition," — because a strong crypto key (decoder for a kind of powerful crypto forbidden for export by the US government) is printed on its back.

The roots of the war, as with all wars, go back much further — in this case to the Cold War with its paranoid culture, to the importance of code-cracking in World War II, and really, to as far back as war itself. The Powers That Be (TPTB — Net culture

12 ITAR was replaced by EAR (Export Administration Regulations), when the function moved from the Department of State to the Bureau of Export Administration in the Department of Commerce.

even has an abbreviation for it, since it's a concept so frequently in parlance there) have always known that knowledge is power and that controlling knowledge is just as great a power.

In 1979, former admiral Bobby Inman, then director of the NSA, expressed the federal government's fears:

> There is real and critical danger that unrestrained public discussion of cryptology matters will seriously damage the ability of the government to conduct signals intelligence and the ability of government to carry out its mission of protecting national security from hostile exploitation... While some people outside the NSA express concern that the government has too much power to control non-government cryptologic activities, in candor, my concern is that government has too little. I believe there are serious dangers to our broad national interests associated with uncontrolled dissemination of cryptologic information within the United States.
>
> (*The Electronic Privacy Papers,* edited by Bruce Schnier and David Banisar [New York: John Wiley, 1997])

Although some federal judges and some other government functionaries have come down on the side of all that makes civil libertarians happy, the crypto wars have pitted most parts of the federal government against privacy advocates. The Feds — at various times, the executive branch, the intelligence community, or law enforcement — have wanted crypto algorithms to be crackable, arguing that it is the equivalent of being able to order a lawful wiretap.

Some segments of the intelligence community may be changing their position; these days they probably worry less about whatever the successor is to nasty (but traditional spy-versus-spy) Soviet derring-do, and worry more about what's known as infowar — political blackmail by terrorists hacking into Wall Street's computers or into the US national check-clearinghouses or air-traffic control systems. But this change of focus in demonology has been far less true of the law enforcement apparatus, such as the FBI under the regime of Louis Freeh. Although there are changing battle lines in the crypto wars, and strategic fallbacks by the government, the wars continue to rage.

Government intelligence agencies, ignoring the fact that strong encryption is perhaps the first necessary (though not necessarily sufficient) means for citizens to maintain privacy electronically, cite the usual highly suspect sorts of reasons: national security (a bad reminder of the McCarthy Era and the scariest part of the Bad Government stuff that went on during the '60s), and combating crime (or "if you only knew what I/ we knew"). Or as cypherpunks, computer-privacy desperadoes, sum up the government excuses so well and so sardonically, the Four Horseman of the Infocalypse: money laundering, terrorism, drug dealing, and child pornography. These are the excuses for the government to do away with privacy and the necessity for search warrants in the age of intelligent machines.

The possibility of exporting strong crypto for the purpose of laundering and hiding money offshore is, thus far, only a delicious nightmare enjoyed by both extremists in law enforcement (we won't be able to follow the money!) and their polar-opposite doppelgangers, extreme technolibertarians (they won't be able to follow the money!). What good are dreams if not shared? But whether one law enforcement agent's bad dream constitutes one privacy activist's sweet dream, practically everyone else says stuff and nonsense, for a variety of emotional, legal, and technological reasons. Seeking to gut strong crypto and digital privacy is wrong.

Crypto presents complexity on every dimension imaginable (technical, economic, juridical, psychological, political). But the crux of the crypto dilemma is what's called strong cryptography. Strong crypto is anything that has a key — decoder algorithm — longer than what a computer can break easily. The longer the key, the harder to crack.

Historically, the hottest hot point has been the issue of whether strong crypto should be exportable. But the thing is, strong crypto has been commercially available since 1977 — and available for free all over the Net (and hence the world as we know it) since 1991.

Today you could carry strong-crypto software on hard disk as you take your laptop with you in business class from JFK to Heathrow or the other way around, and who would know? Or suppose you acquired some on that same trip to London and brought it back with you into the United States? In the era of instant global communications, prohibitions against the export of strong crypto have not been practical. While a personal exemption allowed individuals to make this hypothetical strong-crypto run between Dulles and Heathrow, United States businesses were not supposed to be using strong crypto commercially for international transactions. These were mostly unenforceable regulations that US software companies have said have a tremendous negative effect on their ability to compete globally. Software from other countries has not been so hobbled, nor have their manufacturers been required to maintain both domestic and for-export versions of the same programs. Prohibiting strong crypto has slowed down the spread of crypto into everyday mass-market applications consumers could use; for example, strong crypto would enable you to *securely* check email from an airport kiosk anywhere in the world with a smart card not so different from a prepaid phone card.

Weak crypto simply won't do the job anymore. By 1997, students at UC-Berkeley were perfectly able to crack weak crypto keys of the longtime approved-for-export government standard of 40 bits. Other show-offs have since followed their example.

But in a Canute-commanding-the-obdurate-tides act that can be likened to trying to close the barn door after the barn has burned down, the government has made and continues to make intermittent attempts to gut the use of this kind of encryption altogether. Its wrong-headedness has taken the form of banning strong crypto; banning it for export; proclaiming, in 1996, that strong crypto is no longer a munition but a dual-use (military and civilian) technology but still not legal for export; allowing a mathematics textbook outlining strong-crypto algorithms to be exported, but not its accompanying CD-ROM (books and freedom of the press still hold a more sanctified position in our society); allowing the use of strong crypto as long as someone somewhere somehow has a storehouse of decoder keys that the Feds can access if they need to (what's called key escrow); and offering, in September 1999, to loosen the restrictions on the export of strong crypto after a one-time review, a process that might make affordable sense to a large, well-financed corporation, but not to an individual or an academic; mostly freeing strong crypto for export in January 2000, but still demanding that commercial products go through a one-time review, that the government be sent the URL of your company's Web page that contains your crypto source code (and the government reserves the right to change its mind). Think of Czechoslovakia just after the Russian tanks have gone. The immediate threat is gone, but it could come back at any time. Aside from this, no one exactly knows what the one-time review consists of, and the January 2000 deal also has some technical drawbacks and some very nasty antiprivacy stipulations.

STRATEGY, TACTICS, LOGISTICS

Of course, this ludicrous attempted ban on strong crypto has enraged those who care about civil liberties and due process. Of course, this has been a case of government acting as thuggish as those it maintains it is guarding against. The *thought* of government being able to forbid the use of a piece of software is not appreciably different from banning a piece of writing, nor is it less repugnant, nor impossible. That government could even attempt to impede the evolution of electronic commerce, the global growth of the Net, defies sense, reason, progress, and the supposedly cherished American values of freedom of speech and free markets. Algorithms, the mathematical formulae used to encrypt and decrypt data, are as much an artifact of the mind as works of literature, heavy-metal tunes, or the processes used to manufacture Pop Tarts®. So, to imagine the government placing ideas on a Banned Index, much as the Catholic Church did with books, is horrifying, particularly to those who play with code (logical/mathematical ideas of a kind), and in general to anyone who is a communications junkie (which maybe by this point includes anyone who relies on email).

Thus, for a segment of the population (that is, many geeks) that hasn't really thought much about governance, or history (through intention or accident of inclination or training), this *stupid*, rights-trampling government posture, in defiance of the ways technology really has changed the way the world really works, has told many geeks in general, cypherpunks (computer privacy crusaders) and their overt sympathizers (civil libertarians, privacy watchdogs, digital-cash entrepreneurs) in particular, everything they have shuddered to discover about how *illogical* and *criminal* government (any government) is.

Yet maintaining an unfortunate position on cryptography is hardly the sum of what government does, can do, or even has done for the technology community. There are plenty of grisly and neglectful acts the government can be convicted of — but few of them have been perpetrated on the high tech community. For the most part, government has made Silicon Valley a fine and dandy, safe, and regularized place to make scads of money. A gargantuan infrastructure of suppliers and educational institutions, directly and indirectly subsidized by the government, nurtured the defense-electronics industry, which formed the substrate for today's high tech industry. The fact that the food and pharmaceutical supply is basically wholesome (programmers gotta eat, programmers gotta not get lockjaw from stepping on a jagged bit of loose cabling), that we more or less live by rule of law, so graft and protection money aren't usual line items in most high tech companies' budgets — these are results of the invisible hand of *government* when it's acting mundane and low-profile. But these governmental by-products aren't things people in high tech spend much time thinking about.

Less obvious, but even more curious, is the question of *why* these high tech guys have been up in arms about an issue that, as a card-carrying Sand Hill Road venture capitalist remarked to me, doesn't for the most part affect their daily lives, professionally or personally? Yes, it's always wise to be worried about how the government might be encroaching on human rights and personal freedom, and if strong crypto takes over the planet in every guise, maybe governments might have a harder time collecting taxes and might get testy about that. But still, at the moment, the crypto wars have not in the main affected *much* of what goes on in high tech or in most people's everyday lives, granting that this is becoming less and less true as commerce (whether high tech or not) takes on global, electronic dimensions.

The Bad Government! Down! Down! hysteria isn't altogether fantastical, though. A former computer programmer named Phil Zimmermann was threatened with prosecution (and racked up tens of thousands of dollars in legal fees, mostly covered by the civil libertarian community) for infringing on ITAR regulations. Zimmermann's crime, the geek equivalent to signing Charter 77 (a Czech human-rights document of the 1970s — it was brave thing to sign your name to then, considering the country was still under Soviet domination) consisted of his having posted in 1991 on electronic bulletin-board systems a free, home-brewed version of strong crypto for use on microcomputers called PGP (Pretty Good Privacy). A guy with a long record of civil-liberties activism, Zimmermann is considered heroic, for he knew when he set PGP loose upon the world for, say, use by freedom fighters against the despotic regime in the country formerly known as Burma that he would likely face prosecution.[13] The government finally backed down, and Zimmermann ended up being awarded one of the Electronic Frontier Foundation's Pioneer Awards, given for innovation in the pursuit of maintaining the communications freedom of cyberspace — true code heroics.

L'affaire Zimmermann is geek legend come to life: Perhaps nobody else's life during the crypto wars contains so many of the plot points in the crypto-wars narrative. If you do something that benefits all humankind (Point), the government will come down on you (Point) like white on rice. Yet in doing this same something, you also will be heroized (Point) — and best of all, make scads of money (Point)! For freedom from economic hardship is as much a part of the crypto-warrior way as freedom of code: Money and politics and resistance have become all gummed up through the auspices of the crypto wars. In the long strange trip, dharma-becoming-karma, that can characterize cyberculture, Zimmermann was asked by high tech investors to become the highly visible figurehead for PGP Inc., a commercial crypto company, bought out in 1997 by Network Associates, a network-software giant. Trala, trala. Great good fortune for Phil. Virtue should always thus be rewarded.

STYLES OF RADICAL WILL

As in most wars, the crypto wars inspired a Fifth Column. For starting late in the 1980s, lo, a revolutionary vanguard appeared: enter the cypherpunks. Originally a small gathering of geeks, many of whom had met each other at various engineering jobs

13 Zimmermann says this really happened. Burmese resistance fighters in their jungle training camps used PGP on their laptops so that if they were captured, documents would be unreadable — and thus could less likely lead to the arrest, torture, and execution of their families. A similar story was told by Senator Patrick Leahy (D.-Vt.), on his Web site, about human rights in Bosnia.

in the Valley, cypherpunks shared a passionate (and not altogether misplaced, in this instance) mistrust of the government — any government. Their style and tone have since been much imitated. Although the original cypherpunks operated in a fairly low-key fashion, they did create a noisy, quarrelsome, fascinating Net mailing list, alt.cypherpunks, rife with factionalizing, rivalries, legends, scoundrels, wackos, and lunatic geniuses. Over time, the news-group has devolved into a fractious, internecine-bordering-on-fratricidal, narcissism-of-minor-difference free-enterprise zone that attracts far fewer actual cryptographers than it does libertarians of all kinds, including folks such as tax resisters in their thirties still living with their parents. In fact, for Byzantine reasons of personality and policy, there are at least three versions of the mailing list, the original unvarnished, and two that are filtered, or moderated, as is it called in netspeak, by two different netizens, out of the goodness of their hearts and community-mindedness (lots of people want the verbal static on the list tuned out).

One of the codes of honor of the Net is YOYOW — You Own Your Own Words. It's a rule of Net etiquette (netiquette) that even though the cypherpunks' list is public, it's not good manners to go around quoting from what people post online, particularly for use in commercial publication. This rule is sort of a mixture of honoring both privacy (something like not republishing/broadcasting party conversation) and copyright (creators of texts have the right to decide what happens to those texts). Because cypherpunks as a group are particularly fussy about privacy — and often post untraceably anonymously as well, so they can't be tracked down to get authorization to use their posts — I won't excerpt from the newsgroup listings here.

But without violating YOYOW, I can say that what people post on alt.cypherpunks are remarks about privacy issues, news of the day, ways to enact or violate electronic anonymity, proof of how the United States (or any other government) is becoming a police state, privacy issues, the sorry state of the First Amendment, ways to enact or violate electronic anonymity, discussions about pornography (pro and pro), proof of how the United States (or any other government) is becoming a police state, outrageous conduct by the FBI or the White House, privacy issues, firearms, ways to enact or violate electronic anonymity, lawyers guns and money, privacy issues, instances where the Feds really messed up, puritanical or hypocritical offenses by TPTB, proof of how the United States (or any other government) is becoming a police state, ideas for forming an ideal cypherpunk state, ways to enact or violate electronic anonymity, deregulating the telephone industry, privacy issues, Internet spam (junk mail), proof of how the United States (or any other government) is becoming a police state, weaponry in general, ways to enact or violate electronic anonymity, conspiracy theories, proof of how the United States (or any other government) is becoming a police state, and privacy issues.

What's harder to capture is the tone of alt.cypherpunks, which, a decade into its existence, reeks of the furious discontent of hardened bush fighters, rebels with or without a cause, guys who you can feel are choking on their impotent rage. Although many important potential and actual violations of constitutionality and What's Right are bruited about on alt.cypherpunks with sense and smarts, the tone is mostly a mixture of paranoid rantings, reminiscent of what showed up occasionally in '60s underground newspapers, plus something new, more desperate and more scary. The gestalt is of testosterone-poisoned guys with chips on their shoulders and too much time on their hands.

It's perhaps for this reason — the hair-trigger tempers, the conspiratorial rantings, the volume of mean-spirited and sophomoric noise — that the cypherpunks list has spun off two other lists where mentioning anything even *close* to politics will get you banned for life: coderpunks is for computerists wrassling with hard-core crypto programming and mathematical problems; and cryptography is for Big Picture, theoretical discussions of a more abstract nature than what's talked about in coderpunks.

It's useful to once again clear up the confusion between "cypherpunk," the term for one of our code warriors, and "cyberpunk," the term coined by master sci-fi writer William Gibson to describe a genre of near-future dystopian science fiction — grimy, noirish, technology-disenhanced, full of criminality large (as performed by multinational corporations) and small (as performed by rebels and thieves). Think *Bladerunner* or Gibson's own *Neuromancer*. However, creating confusion between the two terms, I've been told, was a deliberate speech-act by the original stylin' cypherpunks — and a source of some delight. There is, perhaps more in thought than in deed, commonality between the two groups.

MEET THE CYPHERPUNKS

The cypherpunk allure of the undomesticated made it no coincidence that the pre-Condé Nast *Wired* magazine, which early on was ever the fashion leader for whoever they thought was part of the digital elite, not only put the founding three cypherpunk forefathers (Eric Hughes, Tim May, John Gilmore) on the cover of their second issue back in the spring of 1993 but also covered the crypto wars as part of its regular beat, in news and features, in practically every issue during its first five years. *Wired* was all about going for the glam and making things digital larger than life. As the '60s proved, revolution — or reports of it as a lifestyle choice — can be *fun*. In keeping with the cypherpunk status as cultural vanguard, the *Wired* issue depicting The Cypherpunk Three, complete with face masks — termed by the magazine the "crypto rebels" cover — blown up way larger than they ever stood in life, was on prominent display in the reception area at the magazine South of Market (SOMA) headquarters until the magazine moved as part of its purchase by Condé Nast.

Eric Hughes, youngest of the three founding cypherpunk fathers, has a degree in mathematics from UC-Berkeley, and wrote the original Cypherpunk Manifesto. He is an executive with a San Francisco Internet/crypto/electronic commerce startup that does Lord knows what (what's a cypherpunk without a startup?) and worked previously with David Chaum, a rather rabbinical former expat to Holland (now returned to the United States) and pioneer of digital cash. Hughes is also the coverboy on *Cyberpunk Handbook: The Real Cyberpunk Fakebook,* a kind of "preppie handbook" equivalent/de facto vanity-publishing effort (though published by Random House in 1995). Self-advertisement is a glorious thing in the media-saturated '90s.

Hughes says he wrote the Cypherpunk Manifesto as a fun piece of agit-prop that codified his ideas about crypto and cypherpunkery. He distributed the manifesto at the 1993 Computers, Freedom, and Privacy (CFP) conference, an annual event that brings together people who care about the interplay between computers, communications, privacy, civil liberties, and society. In part, the Cypherpunk Manifesto professes the following:

> Cypherpunks write code. We know that someone has to write software to defend privacy, and since we can't get privacy unless we all do, we're going to write it. We publish our code so that our fellow Cypherpunks may practice and play with it. Our code is free for all to use, worldwide. We don't much care if you don't approve of the software we write. We know that software can't be destroyed and that a widely dispersed system can't be shut down.

Tim May is a former solid-state physicist who did pioneering engineering work for Intel and then retired off his investments more than ten years ago when he was still in his thirties. He now spends much of his time provoking arguments on the Net with people who have half his IQ points, quantifiable in whatever units you like, and creating his *Cyphernomicon,* a compendium of his musings on crypto and society, easily downloaded from the Web. He remains a very active poster to cypherpunks and was quite vocal as one of the Y2K disaster guys, meaning he advocated that people retire to rural communities with their own power generators and food supplies for six months and learn how to use their AK-47s. This dire situation was abbreviated on the Internet as TEOTWAWKI (The End Of The World As We Know It).

May wrote another cypherpunk source document, "A Crypto Anarchist Manifesto." As he explained in the anthology *High Noon on the Electronic Frontier* (edited by Peter Ludlow, MIT Press, 1996), the manifesto dates back to mid-1988, but May read it at the founding Cypherpunks meeting in September 1992. An excerpt:

> A specter is haunting the modern world, the specter of crypto anarchy... The State will of course try to slow or halt the spread of this technology... An anonymous computerized market will even make possible abhorrent markets for assassinations and extortion... But this will not halt the spread of crypto anarchy.

The third of the holy triumvirate, John Gilmore, was an early computer scientist at Sun Microsystems (the premiere manufacturer of high-end workstations and servers) and now, obviously, is very wealthy. He has contributed much to cyberspace's equivalent of the ACLU, the Electronic Frontier Foundation, both by giving them money and by taking actions such as filing Freedom of Information Act (FOIA) lawsuits petitioning for the release of early cryptographic manuscripts from government quarantine. He has also donated to the libertarian Cato Institute — and achieved a kind of unhappy visibility when romantic intrigues involving his then-girlfriend were brayed about in *New York Times* reporter John Markoff's book *Takedown* (Hyperion, 1996), the tale of the intersection between probably-more-pathetic-than-malicious computer hacker Kevin Mitnick and the photogenic computer-security expert Tsutomo Shimomura.

No cult of personality has grown up around Hughes, May, or Gilmore, but they have been role models, presenting a new way for geeks to represent themselves to themselves: not as nerds and not whiny do-gooders but as warriors in a Just War. It's rather the way gay men worked out in the course of the gay liberation movement that they could be butch and not nellie, or as a cat might say, "I'm not fat, I'm fluffy!" It's for their intriguing butch cultural effects, rather than their day-to-day effect on high tech, that cypherpunks matter.

The cypherpunk/criminal elements of high tech — hackers, crackers, and street users of technology — are but more madcap manifestations of other, better-known, individualistic and asocial qualities that are already present in technoculture: not giving a damn about conventional notions of dress or grooming; keeping vampire hours; amping out for workaholic or recreational overextended stretches of time at the computer; breaking into computer networks and systems in an impish, playful, Kilroy-was-here, and definitely not malicious way; tweaking federal government Web sites to demonstrate that they are not secure, but doing nothing to mess anything up. These last two activities are computer hacking in its time-honored, benign form.

Hacking in its destructive or malicious form is rightfully decried by many people within high tech; they see it as the antisocial mucking-up of the online-world sandbox, and they are at least annoyed by notorious-beyond-the-malicious-mischief-of-his-deeds hacker Kevin Mitnick.

But these many people in high tech are conveniently forgetting that Mitnick and others like him just made the same moves, only to a more extreme degree, as many of them did a few years ago. What's even more important is that hackers act out, although as a caricatured grotesque, the role, so prized within high tech, of the rampant lone rogue tremendously clever at tweaking computers and people and institutions. Hacking can be perceived as technolibertarianism gone feral — which is, come to think of it, pretty much how cypherpunkery could be characterized. But feral cats are kind of adorable in their wildness, no? Because you can still see so clearly how they were formerly tame.

THE CYPHERPUNK STRUT

While terrific at being the choleric punky watchdogs against government that they are (one of my cypherpunk pals defined cypherpunks as "radical pro-privacy activists." So be it), cypherpunks, particularly in their acid-nightmares of government ninjas dressed in black bursting through their doors at 3am, personify what the Jungians call the Shadow-meaning, the dark side of stuff that you don't want to deal with, the repressed, stunted and unexpressed aspects of personal and community life.

One of the shadow sides of high tech that cypherpunks illuminate are computerization's imprisoning, limiting, and dehumanizing capabilities. We should be grateful that cypherpunks are gloriously obsessed with privacy and the intrusions of government at a time when high tech itself is developing and selling ever more tools to monitor and identify every sphere of human life, from which Web sites your kids can access to what kinds of software programs you use in your job. This is a dark/shadow side of high tech that the rush to cash in on e-commerce or boost one's 401k plan too often simply ignores.

But on another level, maybe, just maybe, cypherpunks personify a high tech Shadow archetype: that of the Puer, the Peter Pan character who has never grown up. Assigning cypherpunks such a portentous role is not such an outlandish stretch when you root them within the context of a more general, post-Vietnam American romance with paramilitarism, from Rambo and its endless follow-ons of action movies even unto Tarantino and his spawn, to *Soldier of Fortune* magazine, men's fiction (action-porn written by such authors as Tom Clancy and Richard Marcinko), and even the rise of actual militias. To place the cypherpunks in this larger societal context, I must refer to a remarkable book titled *Warrior Dreams: Violence and Manhood in Post-Vietnam America*, written by James William Gibson (Hill and Wang, 1994).[14]

The relevance of James Gibson's discussion of what he calls the New Warrior subculture to cypherpunkery is that, without knowing anything about them, he describes much of what characterizes the emotional undergirding of the cult of cypherpunks. As he puts it, the ideal of this New Warrior is

> the man who can only live outside society, on the frontier, exempt from the confining laws and moral code that regulate social life. Many men feel symbolically threatened in some way by the world. Just as the New Warrior never grows up, so does he prefer the imaginary battle that lets rage run wild to the moment when the battle ends and a new sacred order is founded.

Sounds like cypherpunkish wrath to me, in its boysclub's unceasing battle cry against the unrelievedly bad government and its general torment of intellectual dyspepsia. "I am embattled, embittered, me standing all alone, and why do TPTB persist in interfering with me? O, woe is I!"

Inadvertently, Gibson gets at it: "If paramilitary culture is to be abolished, then other areas of…life will have to be re-enchanted. Without enchantment, without access to a magical kingdom of some kind, the responsibilities of adulthood are simply too much; people will break down and flee in one direction or another."

Beneath cypherpunk rants about the latest government incursions into privacy, illegal search and seizure, freedom of speech and the press, there lurks the need, so little remarked on, To Act As Hero in My Own Drama. Cypherpunks, and the cypherpunk personae, act like Luke Skywalker taking on the Evil Empire.

14 No relation as far as I know, except in insight, to William Gibson, the science-fiction writer.

Colonel Francis Marion, the Swamp Fox; the Minutemen of the Revolutionary War; the lone gunman (whether protecting the family, lighting out for the Territories, bringing justice to Dodge City, or discovering the headwaters of a gold-bearing river) — they are all guerrilla archetypes ground into the American psyche. I remember a cypherpunk earnestly telling me he had to move out of Palo Alto, leafy bookstore-ridden haut bourgeois Stanford University burb that it is, because the Palo Alto police didn't like his freedom-loving, freedom-fighter-defending activities. Not to comment on the specifics of his situation, but the Palo Alto police department is not known to rival the LAPD or those in pre-Civil-Rights-Act-of-1964 Mississippi for their brutality.

Again, Gibson: "For all the power that the New Warrior seems to have, he is left stunted and diminished inside his hardened boundaries. And for all his supposed autonomy, he remains vulnerable to manipulation." The cypherpunk strut is part Scarlet Pimpernel (though obviously with different politics), part Dungeons and Dragons superhero wish fulfillment.

Cypherpunkery at its most extreme sees government as a monoculture, peopled only by the unprincipled, the dull-witted, the corrupt, and the power-tripping. It is an angry adolescent's view of all authority as the Pig Parent, uniformly cretinous and bad and oppressive and seeking domination — rather than as a complex institution with a variety of good and bad actors with different proclivities, drives, and intelligences. Cypherpunkery in a way pays weird homage to a Freudian view of the world — all base emotion and power drives and secret motivations — where higher brain functions such as altruism or empathy or trying to do what's right or mixed emotions are left out of the mix. For cypherpunkness in its most extreme form, these squishy or possibly nonexistent mythical qualities more properly belong to the province of what William James called the tender-minded — not the tough-minded cypherpunk-hardened boundaries.

Even the possibility of a complex mesh of motivations distracts from the warrior brain. A cypherpunk with geopolitical conspiracy on his mind, to whom the possibility of human kindness or connection is dim, might, for example, have idiosyncratic interpretations of *all* culture. A villainous KKK sympathizer in a John Grisham novel who unexpectedly extends a kindness toward a civil rights worker could only be doing so because the KKKer was actually a government double agent wanting to sabotage the Klan after having infiltrated it. It couldn't be that the Klansman had a change of heart, had mixed feelings about belonging to the Klan, felt some common humanity with the civil rights worker, was capable of a small private act of charity. By limiting the vision of the world through a rather nasty set of cognitive blinders, cypherpunk paranoia reduces the world to a panoptical version of "TIE Fighter," the Star Wars computer game about the Dark Side. This is precisely the susceptibility to manipulation Gibson speaks of.

When we were introduced at a party, a sophisticated, suave, and moderate cypherpunk did not take violent issue with many of the misgivings I expressed to him about cypherpunk anti-society short-sightedness, but he then went on to suggest that his current business, making offshore anonymous banking as available to folks of modest means as it was to the very rich, was a good communitarian response to my concerns. How could I explain to him that for folks of modest means such a deal was bound to be a far lower priority than worries about job security, making ends meet, affordable healthcare, adequate schooling, decent public services, safe streets, and all the rest of the laundry list of anxieties of the vanishing middle and less-than-middle class? That a more fundamental worry would be the struggle of making and saving enough money so that they could conceivably have a surplus that *could* be dumped in an offshore banking paradise? I appreciated the gesture that his startup was trying to make — his equivalent of selling fresh and fairly priced food in an underserved-by-the-big-grocery-chains inner-city neighborhood — but I didn't have the heart to tell him that it reminded me of a cynical joke I heard in the '60s, about the time that the television show *The Mod Squad* was being aired.

As this was during the height of the civil-rights era, the earliest most optimistic days of the Peace Corps, and the beginning of '60s Women's Liberation, the police show *The Mod Squad* featured a white guy, a blonde girl, and a brother with a 'fro administering to the needs of those who had not had responsive advocates before. *The Mod Squad* was marketed in terms of crusading for the poor and down-trodden, and could be seen as a template for other such shows: Mod lawyers. Mod doctors. Or, as the joke I heard went, Mod accountants, who offered to do the bookkeeping for the disenfranchised who had never had this opportunity. Great! Oh, wait a minute, poor people don't usually have unmet bookkeeping needs, they need to make some money first...

As strange as it truly may be to the black obsidian heart of cypherpunkery, sheltering money and preserving anonymity are not, for most people, the most basic of their Maslowian needs and drives,[15] nor the object of their greatest longing. Sure, lots of folks can get a little creative with their tax returns or hide at least some of their assets at certain times in their lives (trying to get college scholarships for their kids; going through a nasty divorce) — but offshore anonymous banking for the masses is like Mod accounting — it's a community-minded business service that stems from a worldview in which paranoia is paramount. It's certainly a novel approach to the world, and, true, Intel chair Andy Grove is famous for his saying, "Only the paranoid survive." But he was, I believe, referring more to business strategy than all of life; and could probably differentiate between healthy and nutso-crazo paranoia.

---

15 Maslow was psychologist who became famous in the 1960s with his positing of the pyramid of human drives. At bottom was baseline survival needs such as food and shelter; after several ascending layers, tip top of the pyramid, was spirituality.

Paranoia does have its strange beauties. Cypherpunks adore the late cult sci-fi writer Philip K. Dick. Although Dick did somewhat accurately predict sex over the Net (jokes about teledildonics aside, we do have X-rated Web sites and hotchat, even if we don't quite yet have electrodes directly jacked into our pleasure centers), it's the lyrical global paranoia of his books that make them fave raves. One of his novels, *Flow My Tears, the Policeman Said* (Daw, 1975), predicted for the 1990s a world where your electroencephalogram, voiceprint, birthplace, and every single move you'd made throughout your life were trackable in government central data banks and encoded on the identity card you had to carry with you because you could be searched at any time by Dick's version of TPTB.

It's much more thrilling to make believe in our millennial times that you are indeed living in a Hobbesian battlefront like the ones that reoccur in Dick's novels than to face whatever internal demons may actually be eating at you. Being on maneuvers on the frontlines of the battles raging in the crypto theater is far better than facing the real hard problems of our era, such as corporate violating of privacy, overpopulation, environmental degradation, and the rise of warlords all over the world. These battles are far more depressing, far less fun, and far more likely to render you feeling impotent than cypherpunk-plenipotent.

Cypherpunkery offers a kind of logotherapy, a method of injecting value into individual lives. It can be viewed as a technique for combating the lack of meaning in postindustrial society, the malaise that results when challenges and rewards can be damnably abstract. Paul Goodman, who wrote *Growing Up Absurd* (Random House, 1960), the germinal '60s book about this dilemma, would have understood cypherpunks. Similarly, cypherpunkery can be understood as a cure for the urban dislocation and anomie first catalogued by Emile Durkheim.

Further, cypherpunkery provides a mechanism for conversion-reaction, neutralizing the internalized slights of being a geek in a society that seems to value less cerebral kinds of prowess. Why did the football players get all the girls in high school? But wait, Henry Kissinger used to date all those movie stars, and power is the ultimate aphrodisiac, so let's claim our very own special personal power. Cypherpunkery's vision of personal power is very, very bewitching. It gets rid of the wimp within.

Given all this, it's surprising that Robert Bly, with his Iron John forays into retrieving atavistic masculinity, hasn't glommed onto cypherpunks. Or as Gibson put it, "One of the most serious problems advocates of a peaceful world have always faced is that while peace means an end to the horrors of war, it also means an end to the travels, challenging situations, and male initiation that war has traditionally provided."

Taking leave of being a crypto-warrior also means an end to giving your noodling with code a High Seriousness and Prankishness combined; an end to feeling like you are a frontiersman striking out for new ground on how civil liberties and commerce will work in the twenty-first century; an end to feeling Important and Dangerous, Righteous and Naughty *flash* all at once. In his oft-quoted call to arms, George Patton said, "We are lucky war is hell, lest we love it so." Cypherpunks have to imagine the hell that inspires their rebel yells, because they love the yelling so.

As the SDS (Students for a Democratic Society) of the technology community — more outrageous than most, articulating the funnest, extremest, most tear-down-the-walls / two-four-six-eight, organize-to-smash-the-state notions of how the world should work, *will* work, once their anti-good-boy vision comes to pass — cypherpunks express and inform the ethos of the rest of the technolibertarian community. And the original cypherpunk manifestos and newsgroup postings, much like the SDS Port Huron statement, coalesced a political way of being, a coherent adversarial pose for being a hardheaded geek.

SCHADENFREUDE

"Anarcho-capitalist," which is how many cypherpunks describe themselves, is as hardheaded as it gets. This dimly veiled social Darwinist / property-is-next-to-godliness / everything-is-contractual political and economic philosophy (with Nietzsche crawling around somewhere inside there, too) was first articulated by economics professor Ludwig von Mises in the 1920s and 1930s, echoed later by economist, Mises student, and Ayn Rand–follower Murray Rothbard[16] — and portrayed in sci-fi writer Robert A. Heinlein's *The Moon Is a Harsh Mistress*, which posited a utopian society based on libertarian, Nietzschean ideals.

This cruelly meritocratic world-to-come described in cypherpunk postings is reminiscent of 1950s science fiction. In these yesterday's tomorrows, the males with superior intellect, as measured in rocket-scientist terms, ruled. (In current terms, benefiting hugely from cash sucked from high tech entrepreneurial activities, generating untraceable untaxable financial reserves and tweaking the global monetary supply through anonymous transactions.) And incidentally, in these Good Societies of the future, the ruling males also scored with the initially reluctant biology-officer bodacious babes. Aldous Huxley, writing years before, commented obliquely on a society of the future based on Nietzschean ideals in *Brave New World* (the genetically determined top-drawer alpha males were explicitly assigned foxy females) — but Huxley wrote his book as a cautionary *satire*. In the same way that the more you run away from something, the closer it gets to you, Huxley's teaching story about a land of ultimate government control doesn't look so different from the cypherpunk social-Darwinist promised land of total libertarian freedom.

A little spookier is that the antigovernment, threats-of-insurrection, the electrical-engineers-will-rule quintessential cypher-

16 Who knows if it was a conscious choice. Any artist knows the unconscious is a wonderful thing.

punk narratives are a bit coo evocative of *The Turner Diaries* (Barricade Books, 1978), the runaway underground bestseller of the white-supremacist world that Oklahoma City bomber Timothy McVeigh had lying around. The eponymous Turner has as his mission to be a "roving military engineer," and the book is filled with references to the monolithic System (reminiscent of the '60s use of the same term to mean the shadow permanent military/industrial/government/power elite) and is replete with lots of nerd-happy details ("11 of us who had come up from Washington...established a...perimeter...enclosing 2,000 houses...with a total of 12,000 occupants"). If you wanted to learn in excruciating detail how to build a secret compartment for hiding handguns in your apartment, you could find instructions in *The Turner Diaries*. Eerily prefiguring cypherpunkery, the book reiterated (1) numeracy as authority, and (2) the System demonstrating that it is not nearly as smart and competent as the Organization (of rebel warriors for a new world order). Yet we are already in transition to a chilly new world order, though not exactly one kamikaze-pilot Turner would have prescribed.

It has been convenient but inaccurate to recall the '60s as solely the era of free love and peace and flower children happily relying on the kindness of others, for it was also the era of Andy Warhol. The icon of pop was *not* cuddly but chilly, and his slick, cynical, daring commodification of pop culture presaged much of what art and advertising and cultural sensibility would come to be about through the end of the millennium. The scene Warhol created around him, including the ascendancy of an out-there gay culture and an antiromantic sexual sensibility, has had cultural reverberations as strong, in its own way, as the antiwar movement and what was then called the Women's Movement.

So it is with cypherpunkery. These techno-rebellious figures and ideas stand in for some of the centrifugal forces that really are pulling society apart: the ways computerization is tainting all aspects of life, and the fact that globalization of capital means there's no governmental body that anyone really has to answer to. And Warholian chill further exhibits itself in commonplace cypherpunk sexual mores.

From a purely socioeconomic viewpoint, it's anomalous that many many cypherpunks are not married, have never been married, and have no kids. Although marriage and offspring are not necessarily markers of emotional health or goodness, it's often the case that straight men older than thirty who have attained prominence in their profession and wealth through their careers usually do acquire these attachments — if only because money and power usually increase the pool of women who are drawn to them. Conventionally speaking, dynasty-making is another expression of power. Or at the very least, a trophy wife can represent another fine purchase. So it has some symbolic meaning that many of these guys are sociological oddities, so different from their counterparts in finance, law, advertising, or just about any other industry. It gives every appearance that they are seeking to opt out from attachment.

Another tilt to the psychosexuality of cypherpunks is what some participate in what they might call their adventurous polyamorous sexuality. In this sexual subculture where many (although not all) cypherpunks dwell, monogamy is viewed as emotional terrorism. Primary partnerships and pair-bonds exist, but it's not kewl to be bugged by the existence of other entanglements. Consider that for those far more interested in masking the Self (How can I keep transactions private?) than in self-disclosure, and who don't want to rely much on trust (whether of other people or a social environment), a sexual ethic of "What I do with other people cannot matter to you" suits.

Hey, Cosmo Girls, the way to snag that cypherpunk Man of Your Dreams is to tell him, "Sweetie, if we get married, I'm only asking for a period of *transitional* monogamy. We can renegotiate the contract after the honeymoon!"

NERVERTS

Polyamory has cultural overlap with other kinds of geekish sexual adventurism. Role-playing and group sex and scenes (whether of the consensual S-M, fetish, or other variants) can work very well with a technocosmology: They all call for explicit and simple rules. Map out and apply the algorithm. Don't rely on those vague, subtle, possibly apocryphal cues that nongeeks *say* they rely on (what do you mean, some people should probably stick to long pants because they don't look too swell in shorts? What do you mean, sometimes when a woman gives you her business card after you've met at an industry function, it's her tactic for getting you to end the conversation so you'll go away and not a sign that's she interested in you?). Don't buy into that antiquated entrapment of the traditional social and emotional mesh of those who aren't Happy Mutants.[17]

Katharine Mieszkowski, in the August 20, 1997, "Culture Shocked" column, which ran in the *San Francisco Bay Guardian* (the city's long-standing free alternative weekly), called the people who manifest this convergence of computer nerd and weird sex "nerverts." When I read her column, I knew exactly what she meant, for I have run into nerverts many many times.

Mieszkowski got a nervert practitioner to explain this connection between wacked-out sex and nerditude:

> Nerds are well aware that they'll strike out every time in the Ken-and-Barbie land of Marina-style bar-scenes. The sexual mainstream has already rejected them. So nerverts seek out situations in which the rules about what is and what isn't de-

---

17 I use the term loosely. Published in 1995 by Riverhead Books, The Happy Mutant Handbook: Mischievous Fun for Higher Primates was put together by and featured people in circulation around San Francisco's South of Market Wired scene and is a scrap / picture book of certified digital-cool pastimes, amusements, players, pranks, listings of who and what is In and Out. Happy Mutants "laugh at authority, use computer tech for fun and empowerment, and like Sea Monkeys. Normals fear authority, have gas from eating at Sizzler, and like Janet Jackson."

> sirable are simply different. One positive consequence of being a life-long social outcast: it makes you more open to interesting alternatives.

This is not to say that all nerds lack social or courting skills, or go in for what are called in the personals columns "alternative lifestyles," or these days, can't be into rollerblading. But a strong intersection exists between nerds and fringe sex, just as a strong intersection exists between nerds and neopagans.[18]

What's going on here has some distinct differences from the subculture of sexual revolution/free love of the '60s, swinging in the '70s, and really, alternative orgiastic sexuality of any era. Its high degree of explicit codification, coupled with a line of work, is unique. Representative is the alt.polyamory purity test available on the Web[19] (purity tests themselves are artifacts of geek institutions such as Cal Tech; they've been around forever at such institutions as ways to self-test sophistication with sex and drugs. It's good to have some metrics!). Polyamory is the preferred term of art: it's gender-neutral, where polygamy and polyandry are not, and allows for all persuasions of partner choice (gay/straight/bi/it depends). The purity test ("Check all boxes for which your answer is yes") is riddled with geek talk:

> ...31. Met all your present sweeties (if n is greater than r) on alt. polyamory?...
>
> 68. Taken part in an alt.polyamory discussion about Heinlein [trying to get people to stop talking about him counts]?...
>
> 71. Made a gratuitous reference to Babylon 5 on alt.polyamory?...

---

18 Neopagans are adherents to non-Christian, syncretic, earth-based spirituality, often but not always with a Celtic influence. Hey, I can really live out a Tolkien lifestyle! Have glamour, power, beauty, and mystery as I don't have much of in my regular life! and have echoes in my universe of something older than a technology or house built before 1979.

19 As the name implies, alt.polyamory is an Internet newsgroup devoted to polyamory.

My absolute favorite:

> ...59. Use the term "NRE" in a post to alt.polyamory?

NRE stands for "non-recoverable engineering" and is an acronym from the world of semiconductor manufacturing, referring to the sunk costs involved in creating a chip. If your NRE is high and you end up making relatively few chips, then it's likely your profits will be low because you will not be able to offset the cost of the NRE. What's your NRE in terms of how much effort you have to put into someone before s/he puts out? What's your NRE in terms of how much energy you put into a relationship in terms of what you get out? As is often said in the Valley, you do the math.

This overlay between geeks and programmatic weird sex does not necessarily exist, but it occurs often enough to comment on, just as it exists between people who were abused as children and those who choose to participate in consensual S-M.

Mieszkowski's essay continued:

> Yet the unwritten rules of human contact remain hopelessly obscure to the real nerd, who fails to grasp the kind of implicit social cues that real people take for granted. This is endlessly frustrating to the supremely logical nerd mind, which thrives in a RTFM ("read the fucking manual") environment where there's a knowable system that can be examined and mastered. Human beings — they don't come with $*%@ manuals!

Which is a bit like the stories I've heard (from geek friends, as well as from teachers of English as a second language) of the difficulties many computer people have mastering non-native *natural* languages (you know, the languages we are born to or come to speak and write in), as opposed to artificial (computer) languages people program in. Their insistence on looking for the rule, as opposed to shrugging off the pattern recognition that needs to be learned onto the irregularities of idiom and exception, is the difficulty. For these are the very things that make natural languages so hard to master after a certain chronological age — but so rich in the ambiguity and generative power that make them suitable for literature. The maddening complexity of natural languages is similar to the very kinds of subtle markers, receptors, and suggestive depths that are the sources of charisma, chemistry, attractiveness — or their opposite, social lunkheadedness and dating cluelessness.

Mieszkowski went on to say:

> But consider this predicament as a lucky "freedom from social skills" and you'll see that it makes nerverts uniquely suited for highly structured sex games and all kinds of role-playing fantasies... They can escape the impossible task of just "acting normal" around others and deliberately, systematically create their own worlds.

Which illuminates again the nerd underbelly that is an inclination toward the human-transcending and the synthetic-universe-preferring. Nerds *like* robotics and cyborgs and may dream of uploading the output of their cerebral cortexes into computers and not being dependent on the imperfections of wetware (that is, flesh). It's an attitude that, more obliquely, is self-loathing. The body as a prosthetic for precisely what? Mieszkowski further stated that

> while nerds don't do well with emotional nuances, they do respond well to the open communications and well-defined rules inherent in S-M and safer-sex practices. All this pragmatic processing is like a Rosetta Stone for the subtle cues nerverts can't read on their own. What a relief.

Thus it can't be surprising that a fellow named Rob Jellinghaus (computer science degree from Yale and vita that marks him as a Silicon Valley cool guy: college intern at Microsoft, stints at Autodesk [premiere CAD/CAM company], Xanadu [whacked-out pioneering noble experiment that failed], Electric Communities [high-visibility virtual-world startup]) wrote the three-part alt.sex.bondage FAQ[20] that explains the terms, comforts the anxious, and generally expounds the philosophy of S-M, b+d, top+bottom. Nor is it surprising that an entire segment of *Beyond Computers*, a one-hour weekly radio show produced in San Francisco and distributed over Public Radio International, was devoted to what its host, John Rieger, called "geek whacking." It's a fun S-M world where geeks create a high demand for custom corsetry and play-for-pay dominatrixes and dungeons.

Robin Roberts, a dominant who's been involved with computers since he first worked with a Univac (the stegosaurus of mainframes) back in 1957, founded the Backdrop Club in the late 1960s as an arena/playpen to act out S-M scenes. A "multipurpose clubhouse" that boasts 3,000 members, Backdrop is enough of a long-standing nervert cultural edifice that it's appeared on HBO and the Playboy Channel. Roberts says there's always been an overlap between geeks and weird sex, and he agrees that the explicitness of rules is integral to geek perversion.[21] As he says, "The elaborate negotiations of S-M courtship are like network protocols [codes for transmitting computerized information] and handshaking [a system for two different pieces of hardware to establish communications connections]." Roberts *teaches* classes in how to read body language ("If I hold her this way, will she resist?"), and agrees that many nerds have difficulty in this area, and with emotions (which are fuzzy and not binary). Using their brains to construct and act out a fantasy, reducing that most maddening and paradoxical and mysterious of human activities, sex and attraction, to codes — it's a magnificent case of making lemonade out of overcerebrated lemons.

---

20 Frequently Asked Questions. FAQ is a common Net acronym derived from early Internet technical documents delineating where the most basic and necessary information on a given topic is contained.

21 "Pervert" is a word rescued from opprobrium by practitioners of weird sex, much as "'queer" was retaken by gay activists.

Nerds are hardly the first folks to make a philosophy out of a personality defect, and technolibertarians are no more guilty of this, say, than some of the Lefties I've known who were so clearly working out some sort of anger or guilt toward their parents. No one escapes from anxiety of influence; everyone is always trying to construct and make use of the best neurotic structures available to them. Neurotic style, though, tells you a lot about the fears and desires being mediated.

CFP

So while cypherpunks often do engage in these libertine raver activities, they also sassily assert, "Nah, we're out for ourselves, the government is clueless at best and dangerous at worst. The center cannot hold. Gotta problem with that?" Their ideology causes a frisson of fear and excitement coupled with a hint of proleptic historical inevitability.

And as with any shiny, dangerous cultural trend, its fashion-forwardness gets adopted by those who recognize freshness of thought. The charge in something new and disturbing cannot be discounted. It can't be that surprising, given the sinister gleam (like the black metallic skin of a nuclear submarine, half visible at surface level, steaming out to sea under the Golden Gate Bridge) of cypherpunkery, that Walter Wriston, the former Citibank CEO, appeared on the cover of the October 1996 issue of *Wired*, with the cover line "He was the most powerful banker in the world. So why is he talking like a cypherpunk?" This ineluctably led to cypherpunk Sameer Parekh, cofounder of the Oakland-based crypto startup C2Net, appearing on the September 8, 1997, cover of *Forbes*, with the leadline "This man wants to overthrow the government." Even the January 1998 issue of *California Lawyer*, the free magazine you get whether you want it or not if you are a member of the California bar, listed on its "new products" page a selection of secure, encrypted email servers for lawyers.

Herbert Marcuse had it right about capitalism being such a marvelous mechanism that all fringes get co-opted and turned into marketing opportunities. So it is with the cypherpunks, and the style and ideas and dark star, black matter they radiate. But it's also true that ideas from the outskirts — whether benign or malign — do have influence, however subtle or indirect, on the town center.

For instance, the changing quality of the annual Computers, Freedom, and Privacy (CFP) conference is in part attributable to the spread of cypherpunk ideology. CFP was first held in a hotel just south of San Francisco in 1991 in the wake of a bunch of patently unconstitutional government crackdowns, such as Operation Sun Devil, where the computers of supposed computer criminals — teenage hackers — were confiscated illegally, among other instances of bad form, bad manners, and bad law enforcement. The conference was a fine attempt to bring together computer scientists, members of the law enforcement community, lawyers, hackers, cypherpunks, civil libertarians, and academics to lessen the demonization on all sides and demonstrate that intelligence and even good intention were distributed all around.

CFP conferences have traditionally included workshops and panels on everything from the Constitution in the Information Age; ethics, morality, and criminality; medical records, privacy, and healthcare reform; to systematic critiques of the use of computers; libraries and access; censorship; mock-court sessions on the constitutionality of the Communications Decency Act;[22] and institutional-database security problems (as with student records and departments of motor vehicles).

Many of the Favorite Sons (and sometimes Daughters) of high tech speak at CFP: from cyberpunk writer Bruce Sterling

---

22 An asinine attempt to censor pornography on the Net, since struck down at the federal district court level. Its bastard child, the Online Child Protection Act, signed into law by President Clinton in the fall of 1998, has been nicknamed CDA II by the Net community and is being met with the same scorn and constitutional challenges as the original CDA.

(who wrote the seminal *Hacker Crackdown,* which documents stoopid rights-violating law enforcement activities), to MacArthur Fellow and copyright goddess UC-Berkeley professor lawyer Pamela Samuelson, to the chairs of the Stanford and MIT computer science departments. A data commissioner from Berlin might attend, as well as too-stereotypical-to-be-real-but-he-is cypherpunk Dan Farmer, a long-haired, androgynous, bisexual security expert (and S-M top/dominant/sadist), who wrote a notorious program called SATAN to sniff out weak parts of Internet security.

Like any conference, the real action at CFP goes on in the hallways and the hotel bars, at ad hoc informal meetings called BOFs,[23] and a good time is usually had by all. Cypherpunks are in full attendance, often using pseudonyms. Ever in pursuit of privacy and in defiance of whoever is purported to be in authority, cypherpunks might wear these pseudonyms on their name tags or, still more mocking of authority and preserving of privacy, hand them as noms de guerre to the volunteers handling registration. Sometimes more than one person at a CFP would register as Kevin Mitnick, perhaps the best-known, but hardly the most dangerous, hacker in the world.

A come-let-us-reason-together ecumenical spirit has been one of the finest aspects of CFP; yet the libertarian cast to the occasion has been there strongly from the beginning. Jim Warren, outspokenly libertarian, was one of the cofounders of the event. Warren, a Silicon Valley entrepreneur who made his early microcomputer-industry fortune from trade shows and computer magazines, very generously underwrote the first CFP so that if the event lost money, he'd take up the slack; if it made money, the surplus would go to Computer Professionals for Social Responsibility (CPSR), the longstanding progressive organization

---

23 Derived from Birds of a Feather. Get-togethers of like-minded souls interested in a particular issue who haven't yet formed themselves into a formal ongoing special interest group

of computer-industry professionals. CPSR was the official institutional affiliation for the first CFP and has been associated with the conference ever since. Warren remains a libertarian and has been active in Libertarian Party politics for a very long time. It's telling, however, that although Warren has had little to do directly with CFP for years, and in spite of CPSR's continuing involvement, CFP remains ever the libertarian stronghold.

By the fifth annual CFP, in 1997, Marcuse's co-optation phenom manifested itself in the remarkable number of hackers and cypherpunks who were now working for corporations or starting ones of their own. Anarcho-capitalists (think of the *Forbes* motto, "capitalist tool"), all in all. Once again street culture and outlaw style had been quickly picked up and profited from by the mainstream. Only here it wasn't African American adolescents but cypherpunks who became legit. Anarcho-capitalism made real. By the sixth CFP, in 1998, the conference had become even more mainstream, so that its program was co-opted by its sponsors that year, the continuing education folks at the University of Texas at Austin law school (Continuing Legal Education, as it's called): refresh-your-credentials courses for lawyers. And in 1999, it took place in Washington, DC, replete with inside-the-Establishment speakers.

But at that 1997 conference, I was struck that the skills of a Kremlinologist had become necessary to make sense of the goings-on. Recall that Kremlinologists were those highly trained Sovietologist subspecialists who became expert at drawing political conclusions from the minute changes in dogma being printed in Pravda or from changes in seating position on a dais where officials were reviewing a May Day military parade. At CFP, the same outrage was pouring out from the same people as it had been for years; for all the praise of evolution in the technolibertarian world, there wasn't too much of it in what many people had to say. You would have to have the acuity of a Kremlinologist to figure out why this CFP was different from any other CFP, who was up, who was out, and what the affairs of the day really were.

Soviet-style reification had set in. Everyone was locked into the predictable positions of a Punch and Judy show — or Kafka's closet. In one of Kafka's novels, the protagonist is wandering around some nightmare structure and happens to open a closet door where one person is in the midst of beating on another. The antihero / observer closes the door, goes off on many adventures, and days later happens on the same closet door. When he opens it, he finds the same actors in the same positions — the vision of embattled stasis at its worst. So it was at CFP: cypherpunks being cypherpunks; civil libertarians being civil libertarians, although some cops and government types have showed definite signs of modulation / mellowing. For the most part, it was the Montel Williams effect: people with polarized positions screaming past each other, or pandering to the audience, or preaching to the choir. Not, of course, that freedom and privacy *aren't* primary human, American, and technological values. But Generalissimo Francisco Franco was still dead.

What's harder to evoke, though, is the increasing psychic freeze I felt throughout the week I was at CFP. It's not that I haven't been outnumbered 307 to 1 by nerds before (I've been attending technical conferences for fifteen years), nor surrounded by those with a voraciousness to Make A Deal (I've been to events whose sole raison d'etre was to put VCs and startups and would-be startups up close and personal). I don't have much of the contemporary bias against lawyers or academics, nor am I so politically fragile that I find comfort only around people who tend to agree with me.

Instead, I was overwhelmed by what I can only call a kind of intergalactic coldness. As Mephistopheles, the devil's own account manager in Marlowe's *Doctor Faustus* said, "Why, this is hell, nor am I out of it," which in his case meant that hell was everywhere God wasn't. At CFP, whose social / emotional tone is so infused with cypherpunk, I felt the hellish lack of humanity. It was cumulative, my getting more creeped out by the hour by a view of human nature that reduces everything to the contractual, to economic rational decisionmaking, which ignores the larger social mesh that makes living as primates in groups at least somewhat bearable, when the weight of days becomes intolerable.

Roger Clarke, a visiting fellow at the Department of Computer Science of the Australian National University, who (along with cypherpunk cofounding father Tim May) spoke on the panel on "Governmental and Social Implications of Digital Money," put it very well:

> The implications of the Cypherpunk/Crypto-Anarchist lines of argument are enormous, and the benefits of their vision (juicily) exaggerated. It would be very helpful...if Eric Hughes, Tim May, and their considerable band of fellow-travelers could distinguish their systemic arguments (of the form: "technological feature X gives rise to social change Y") from their moral arguments (of the form: "the fact that social institution Z will be harmed by this change is a good thing"). Outsiders can see a great deal wrong with American society; but we're not sure that a complete revolution is the only, or the best, way to solve problems.

In other words, the cypherpunk way takes glee in its *Mad Max*/post-neutron-bomb (social structures falling apart with the advent of digital cash) wish fulfillment. It's a delight in destruction rather like that of the lost son of an architect in the Graham Greene short story "The Destructors." The kid protagonist, in the midst of the London Blitz, when all about him is being bombed away, upon finding a still somewhat-intact gem of a Christopher Wren house, gleefully smashes it to bits in a fine fit of Oedipal rage. Pleasure in destruction, or at least in the thought of it. Little to counterbalance it was present at CFP.

> And when the last law was down, and the Devil turned round on you — where would you hide, the laws all being flat? This country's planted thick with laws from coast to coast — man's laws, not God's — and if you cut them down — d'you really think you could stand upright in the winds that would blow then? Yes, I'd give the Devil benefit of the law, for my own safety's sake.
>
> (Robert Bolt, *Man for All Seasons* [New York: Vintage, 1990])

In spite of this love of destruction of laws and convention, the cypherpunk way pays an unconscious homage to one of the most entrenched conventions of the Establishment: the idea of technology über alles. This Establishment thinking was behind the failed strategies of the Vietnam War (the technocrats' war): given our edge in technology and efficiency, we *ought* to win/have won. As James Gibson explained, New Warriors have a continuing love affair with technowar and with what he has called "the hard variables of production as opposed to the soft variables of history, culture, and motivations." These soft variables, as we all know, defeated the French and the United States in Vietnam and, in spite of how technology goes on careening in its madcap way, will continue to matter as much as they ever have.

Witness the Gulf War: Yes, technology kicked off all those gorgeous Mech Warrior–worthy (*Mech Warrior* is a much-loved computer game squaring off monster-robot-machine against monster-robot-machine) computer graphics. But it turned out after the fact that those Patriot missiles weren't really that effective, that the Iraqi soldiers were defeated more than anything else because they were starving and fighting more from fear than for love of cause or country, and that lots of Allied vets are now suffering from the malady known as Gulf War Syndrome (what you might call a disease caused by technology). Nothing really changed except that Kuwait's own corrupt TPTB are back in power. The world in general, and the Middle East in particular, has continued to be as precarious a place as ever. As of early 2000, Hussein remains in power. The technology looked sexy, all right; but it did not matter as much as geeks, whether of sunny techno-optimist or chilly cypherpunk disposition, would like to think.

In spite of what I imagine would be cypherpunk horror at thinking in the same ways as the "Amerikan" [misspelling intentional] government, cypherpunks believe anarcho-capitalism will *also* take over the planet — by technical necessity.

So as I listened, both to formal panel discussions and informal hallway conversations, I kept on thinking, whence this obsession with freedom from intervention? What have TPTB *ever* done to any of you to make you want to do this to them — or at least to insure that you are beyond their hateful (to you) reach? What if you had to rely on all the complex institutional supports, directly and indirectly subsidized and regulated and more or less safeguarded (meds and hospice and SSI and caseworkers and counseling), available for coping with a loved one with AIDS? Have you had a spousal equivalent, friend, or daughter need to rely on the complexly regulated, directly and indirectly subsidized structures of the medical, legal, and forensic professions involved in dealing with a rape? Suppose the startup you dream of fails, and you *need* the legally enforced consumer protection from creditors that bankruptcy laws allow? Even a friend of mine, the finest sort of geek (a conscientious objector who had worked for military contractors, turned alum of the minicomputer industry/Route 128/Digital Equipment Corporation, turned an ex-entrepreneur of his own virtual-world gaming startup, turned ex-staffer at Apple Computer, ex Chief Technology Officer for the crypto division of a multi-billion-dollar network-software company, now to a security startup, where he practices what he calls "software diplomacy"), attending the conference with his wife (also the finest sort of computer scientist), began muttering how stale and tiring all the libertarians were being and how no other points of view were being presented and how psychically exhausting the libertarians and their rhetoric were.

Missing from the debate was a sense of what value there might be in giving something up — an illusion of perfect personal freedom; no chains, no claims, no demands, no strictures — in return for gaining something larger, such as connection, commitment, a sense of being able to rely on the artifice of human society, intimacy and emotional interdependency, and the benefits of a generalized, free-floating social contract. All of which sounds like my fussing over sentimental trash, feminized wringing of hands, vague worries about nothing — except that a week spent where the cypherpunk style sets the tone gets you wondering: *Why* are these guys so morbidly obsessed with privacy above all other civic goods? *Why* are concerns about government meddling in their affairs so paramount — unlike a welfare mother, say, whose life, lifestyle, character, and financial resources really are subject, day-to-day, to all kinds of government-sponsored examination, intrusion, humiliation?

Yes, 1960s conservatives did have it right: The price of freedom is eternal vigilance. But why is this group, so privileged, so poised for flight in any direction if things get rough — to get a well-compensated job, to hire top-drawer lawyers, to live in horse country or exurbia away from urban unrest, to shelter assets, to flee — so flipped about the possibility of being messed with? Of having limits of any kind placed on them?

The point is not to pick apart a particular conference. The dry-ice fumes wafting off CFP '97 were not the fault of the keynoter (the Clinton administration's own Ira Magaziner) or of any of the featured speakers (one of high tech's most overexposed futurists, Paul Saffo, from the Institute for the Future, or consultant John Hagel, from McKinsey & Company, author of e-commerce bible *Net Worth,* expounding on the really old-hat notion that for electronic commerce to succeed, you have to create a trusted community with your customers. This is not new information).

The point instead is that the crypto wars, and their cypherpunk New (Holy) Warriors, eroded much of the humane promise originally held out by the ever-increasing growth of the Net and of computer technology. The guys who developed the Internet and the World Wide Web had an abiding preoccupation with making communication as easy and sturdy as possible, bringing about all the goodies global chatter and information sharing can bring — that is, facilitating what's best about the intersection between people and technology.

And the cypherpunk preoccupation with privacy seems ever more valid, only it's private enterprise, as much as the government, that is cause for alarm. Every kind of bank, insurance company, e-commerce site, Web community, telephone company, and grocery store imaginable is cavalierly selling and swapping personal information they've collected. Privacy? What's that? Get over it. There isn't any.

The crypto wars, alas, brought out the worst: retro bureaucratic alarmist defiance of technological reality and the Bill of Rights going right up against all in geek culture that's antisocial, reductive, paranoid, and celebratory of the virtues of selfishness. As in most civil wars, there has been some merit to the war cries of both sides: Government does have an interest in trying to figure out how to maintain revenue streams and go after criminals in an increasingly digital society. Those being governed, conversely, at least with some precedent in the United States, do have a right to privacy and should not be prevented from following the obvious arc of technology.

As with all wars, it's all been such a waste. But the crypto wars folie à deux is one that really shouldn't have existed.

CHAPTER THREE

WIRED: GUIDING THE PERPLEXED

IN THE WINTER OF 1995, the *Wired* feminist cabal met for the first and last time over lunch in the only place close to the magazine's office we could think of where we weren't likely to be spotted by any other *Wired* employees. Three of the cabal members were smart, engaging, multitalented, multiplicatively experienced female employees of *Wired* magazine; present as rapporteur, I made up the fourth, a contributor who had been on the masthead almost from the magazine's beginning. We were ducking out of the midwinter California rains into a cheesy *sports bar*, of all gawdawful unlikely places in San Francisco's South Park/SOMA multimedia neighborhood. In this déclassé joint with the tacky indoor-outdoor carpeting, we could speak of grievances without fear of word getting out.

I was working that winter on a feminist critique of the magazine for a small-press anthology on women and cyberspace (*Wired Women: Gender and New Realities in Cyberspace* [Seal Press, 1996]. Not associated whatsoever with *Wired* magazine). At the time, there wasn't anyone else Elizabeth Weise, coeditor of *Wired Women*, could have asked to take on the assignment, because so few women had written for *Wired*; the female staffers then had lower-level editorial jobs. I had been both happy and sick at heart to satisfy Beth's request, because I had begun to feel about *Wired*, the *Froissart's Chronicles* of the digital age, like Nora in *A Doll's House*. Since I had been given the opportunity, I was going to have to speak up and out, even if it meant leaving home.

Getting so bent out of shape and also feeling that writing my rant was such a matter of high moral seriousness were typical of the classic battered-wife relationship I had for the couple of years my professional life was intertwined with Wired Ventures: The honeymoon was so sweet, why you now treat me so mean? Nostril-flaring passion, high-dudgeon, fierce loyalty; these were the emotions that the magazine invoked and demanded.

For no matter how much you try to avoid it, are bored with the subject, think it's all been said before, all discussions of the rise and rise of digital culture must eventually devolve to both praising and burying *Wired* magazine. Much like Pynchon's V2 rocket screaming across the sky in *Gravity's Rainbow, Wired* was a thing of beauty and terror when it burst onto the media scene back in 1993, although much of what made it striking has since been copied to the point of desensitization. People have somewhat forgotten what made the magazine so influential out of proportion to the size of its readership; and some of that very distinctiveness has gone away under its new editorial leadership, starting in 1997. But gorgeous, annoying, glossy, enraging, stylish, corrupt, brilliant, reductive, literate, jejune, crusading, sloppy, conscientious, outrageous (in good and bad senses), idiosyncratic, sold-out, literary, journalistically compromised, high art as it was, *Wired* combined new form with new content and defined a journalistic focus of business, culture, and high tech, which has been much decried and just as much imitated.

Wired had published my fiction (probably the first mainstream *literary* treatment of email adultery) in their fourth issue, back in 1993, when publishers in New York were telling me such email exchanges were highly unlikely and that furthermore, readers couldn't possibly care about these computer geeks anyway. The magazine had taken me on and given me room to run in the profiles I wrote about various high tech grand high pooh-bahs (technology-sybil Esther Dyson and Microsoft cofounder Paul Allen, among others), on Internet technical culture (the Internet

Engineering Task Force), and in a humor piece that was sort of a spoof of a *Melrose Place/Max Headroom* proposal for a TV series on technology workers ("Beverly_hills.com"). Louis Rossetto, the *Wired* editor-in-chief / founder / publisher, gave me what Jann Wenner had given rock critic Greil Marcus and other writers in the early days of *Rolling Stone* — permission to write without checking at the door all the rest of my experience, reading, and thinking. Louis handed out to his stable of contributors copies of the classic 1973 anthology *The New Journalism* as a promise — which he delivered on — that *Wired* would go for the original, the personal, the unexpected, the gonzo, and the over-the-top. It was thrilling, and you had to have been there.

Given the joy of working under such an editorial mandate and the deep pleasures of, for the first time ever, writing for a publication that understood to its spine that *technology is culture*, it probably took about a year or more after me 'n' Wired Ventures had first met to realize that we had some Serious Issues and Lack of Agreement in our love affair. Our squabbles became very public and were written about by others in articles on the Web (*Salon* among others) and in alternative weeklies in Los Angeles (*L.A. Weekly*) and San Francisco (*San Francisco Bay Guardian*).

For one, this book itself was originally to be published by *Wired's* now-dead book division, Hard Wired, but I was impertinent one time too many in an interview on the Web site "www.rewired.com" (no relationship to the magazine, "rewired" was written in Berlin by Texan ex-pat David Hudson and Web-published in San Francisco) in the summer of 1996, and so the deal got killed.

Retelling the convoluted detailed histories of those squabbles seems akin to dredging up the details of an ugly divorce with contested property and custody settlements: It's all very upsetting, you have to be content knowing you never have all the facts, but what matters most is that there is a final severing of ties. Suffice it to say that irreconcilable differences sprang from finding out Who The Other Person Really Was, which is often the death of many relationships. Who *Wired* was, in the first five years of its life, before it got sold to Condé Nast / Advance Publications in April 1998, was mostly libertarian, largely in denial that there could be anything wrong with high tech, and dismal with women. It took me awhile to figure this out, dazzled as I had been; and it took the publication awhile to figure out that I couldn't, simply couldn't, entirely get with the program — nor keep my mouth shut about it.

But what was the deal with the other three female *Wired* staffers that drove them to meet me for lunch that drippy miserable day? Why did a magazine cause us all to despair, to care enough to be disappointed and enraged? The opposite of love is indifference; and indifferent we were not.

Only *Wired* could have roused such angst. A magazine funded in part with money from successful high tech entrepreneurs and from Nicholas Negroponte of the world famous MIT Media Lab, *Wired* could only have come into being in San Francisco in the early 1990s: close to Silicon Valley, far away from received notions of what a magazine should be, part of a San Francisco outsider culture that goes back to the Gold Rush days. Its scruffy first offices were in an unfinished loft in a former industrial space in a then barely gentrifying neighborhood south of Market Street. Back then, in 1993, it was a neighborhood where parking was easy; now, you wouldn't want to know how many hundreds of thousands of dollars the purchase price would be for the loft in what's now called South Park / SOMA — a change in real estate valuation caused in part by the existence of *Wired*. The publishing world — and high tech — had never seen anything like it.

WIRED STYLE

Wired, although it had more zine-ish precursors (*Mondo 2000*, *Boing-Boing*, and *Raygun*), which some say have never properly given enough credit for summoning into being the *Wired* way of being, was the first mainstream magazine to demonstrate that "culture" and "computing" were not mutually exclusive. The magazine created mindshare that none of the new copycat competitor consumer magazines (*Computer Life*) or existing technical trade magazines (*Network World*) or newly created sections in existing publications ("Close to the Machine" in the *L.A. Weekly*) has ever been able to attain. The original *Wired* might publish the diary of a game developer, giving readers an inside look at the pressures and pleasures of getting a hot title out the door. The magazine ran features on digital art, computer scientists, populist uses of the Net, use of microprocessors in automobile racing, and new-product reviews of the latest in digital music-making devices, and commented on myriad intersections of technology with culture — all with authority and all sans homogenization.

At the apogee of its media arc, in about 1995–1996, the Wired brand had gone wild, with a short-lived television program, book division, and foreign editions; talk of spin-off business and design magazines; and online empires after successive online empires of a massive multifocal Web site. The magazine had won National Magazine awards and was the darling of trendmeister readers (well, purchasers, if not readers) who wanted the latest thing for their coffee tables.

Wired materialized the idea that the technology economy and digital culture were juicy and vital and necessary to The Way We Live Today. In a sense, the entire magazine can be seen as the equivalent of the section that used to appear in *Vogue* called "People are talking about," which meant, really, what *Vogue* editors were talking about. Which was what everyone in the beau monde, or who wistfully wanted to observe the beau monde, should be concerned with. *Wired* created the mold out of which have been stamped so many copies of the story, now a perennial favorite of the media, of the cool guy who has succeeded with his cool new technology. *Wired's* pioneering effort has led to the mainstreaming of its fashion-forward sensibility, such that the *New York Times* now has a computer lifestyle section, "Circuits," and one of *USA Today*'s lifestyle reporters covers the Internet. And since it contributed to the heroization of the technology entrepreneur, guys cashing in on the getrichkwik.com/dogfood.com Internet investment plays of the late 1990s/2000 still see themselves as Net heroes, even though what they are really are speculators.

The permanent change that *Wired* wrought on mainstream media is reminiscent of how the countercultural gazette of Berkeley in the '60s, the *Berkeley Barb*, along with other underground newspapers of the time, raised the consciousness of more traditional media outlets. By the early 1970s, Establishment publications such as the *New Yorker* began absorbing the counterculture into their perspective, running regular columns by rock critics alongside its traditional tony writing on traditional tony culture. The same absorption of an outsider sensibility was repeated two decades later at the *New Yorker*, where John Seabrook and John Heilemann (who went from the *Economist* to *Wired* and then to the *New Yorker*) now periodically write on high tech.

Wired also led to the creation of more literal flatterers-through-imitation: *Forbes ASAP*, a quarterly special issue about the grooviest in high tech; *Fast Company*, spawn of *Harvard Business Review*, financial cheesecake/beefcake for those who want to be involved with Way-New Business — you know, the kind where you make money off the flows of the new global information economy and think outside the box and use your wireless Internet connection while skiing at Telluride; *Industry Standard* (whose publisher, John Battelle, was the former managing editor of *Wired*), a weekly described by this same publisher as "*Variety* meets the *Economist*"; *Business 2.0* — the name says it all: that is, all business should borrow from the traditions of software releases (casual dress and no rest for the weary); and the latest from the Bay area, Time Inc.'s *eCompany*. But in spite of these publications, which are so clearly spirit-children of *Wired*, there has been no *Wired*-killer, no publication that has gone on to steal away *Wired* readership directly. And strangely and sadly, *Wired* under its new owners is now imitating these business-porn magazines who are its imitators.

By the summer of 1993, roughly half a year after *Wired* began publication, guys wearing ponytails getting into limos at LAX could be spotted wearing WiReD baseball hats. *Wired* was name-dropped in television ads for IBM and appeared as a prop in the James Bond movie *Golden Eye*. Art directors everywhere drew inspiration from the *Wired* look and feel, which quickly became so admired, and so emulated that the companies who scampered to place their ads in the magazine modeled their layouts to look like the editorial copy their product-plugs ran next to. By 1998, *Wired's* visual style had so passed into the mainstream that it showed up in places as unlikely as the annual report for the California utility company Edison International. The same year, the newly revamped and higher-profile San Francisco Museum of Modern Art put on an exhibit, with material culled from its permanent collection of architecture and design, of a selection of opening spreads from *Wired* magazine.

The libertarian politics of *Wired* during its pacesetting first five years under the direction of its founders was as integral to its presentation as its whack use of color and its insistence that what was geek was chic. Whatever *Wired* turns into under its new ownership by Advance Publications, it will be remembered for what it was in this earlier epoch — good and bad but never ugly.

Most readers don't pay much conscious attention to the politics of a magazine, unless they are reading it explicitly for its politics, as with the *Nation* or the *Washington Times*. But think of how "The Playboy Philosophy" was both implicit and explicit:

Though never fully fleshed out all in one place, it was enumerated all the time and all over the place in *Playboy*. The tone and content of the magazine made its political philosophy apparent. The message of (1) enjoy the sybaritic cosmopolitan cultivated good life, particularly as expressed in suave things to buy; (2) be sex-positive and pro-civil liberties; and (3) be daring but not mean or intolerant, rippled through the magazine both directly (in the advice of the Playboy Advisor) and indirectly (in the choice of articles printed, people profiled, writers published). Because *Playboy* was such a saucy good read, while still being fun to look at, and was slightly more culturally avant garde than its readers, but not so much as to be inaccessible, its readers went along for the ride with its philosophy, whether consciously or not. So it was with *Wired*, with its downtown/global aesthetic, its I'm-so-cool-I-can't-stand-myself appeal, perfuming the air and seducing its readers with its philosophy of libertarianism.

Wired's packaging of its libertarian mix (so compelling, so maddening) consisted of fine old-school I. F. Stone–ish government muckraking, classic ACLU-type outrage, reports of infringements abroad on what would be Bill of Rights issues if those countries had such a thing, and more insidious, general-purpose free-market/privatize-it-all rantings. As an old hippie with artistic pretensions, I too was seduced by the magazine (yes, the government is capable of supremely bad things; yes, wonderfully artful and original combos of text and image are only to be wallowed in). It took me awhile to realize how tunneled was the *Wired* vision of digital culture *Wired* was selling.

EXAMINING THE TEXT

Looking at *Wired* in its first year of publication (1993), you find, among the stories on computerists and high tech CEOs and futurists and digital artists of all kinds, numerous examples of the magazine's consistently antigovernment editorial stance. It's worth examining a year's worth of issues in some detail in order to comprehend how unremittingly libertarian its beat was from the very beginning.

Premiere issue (undated – first came my way right after it came out, in February 1993)

- Feature titled "Public education obstructs the future. Would you send your kid to a Soviet collective?"
- Feature on Inslaw, a notorious scandal in which the Department of Justice, with much bad intriguing and seeming criminality, stole case-management software.

May/June 1993

- The famous crypto rebels cover, featuring radical pro-privacy and terribly libertarian computer activists.
- News stories on the death of the US postal service (its incompetence and the coming all-digital/all-the-time economy that will do it in); on an IRS ruling that might have negative consequences for self-employed geeks with home offices; and on the damages Steve Jackson Games won from the Secret Service when it unconstitutionally and mistakenly busted the Austin computer-game maker and confiscated all its computers.
- Feature on dishwallahs, satellite dishes used to get around India's prudish censorship of media.
- Feature titled "EuroTechnoPork/Memo to Bill Clinton: Europeans have a lot of experience with government tinkering with technology. Bad experience. From London, John Browning reports on why Europeans feel that technology policy is an idea whose time is past."

September/October 1993

- News stories on the Nader group's attempt to make House and Senate internal online systems public; and on a ruling by the California Supreme Court mandating the carrying of state-issued ID, going on appeal to the US Supreme Court.

- Interview with George Gilder, Ur-supply-sider *Forbes* columnist, high tech's Promise Keeper, and author of techno-idolatrous books such as *Microcosm* and *Telecosm*, in which he says "The Internet is...an exciting metaphor for spontaneous order. It shows that in order to have a very rich fabric of services, you don't need a regimented system of control... If you are a winner, you don't go to the government. You've got too many customers. It's the people with no customers who are besieging Washington... The dog technologies run to Washington, decked out like poodles. The politician is always the dog's best friend."

November 1993

- News stories on the crusade of a former spook, who upon discovering that 75 percent of the information in classified data bases is wrong, has been on a mission to demonstrate that better (and cheaper) information is available on the open market; and on a recent post of a Department of Justice bulletin board system stating that hackers were lining the doorposts of their homes with copper wire so that if they were busted, all their data would be deleted as the info-narcs walked the hackers' confiscated computer equipment through the portals.
- My own profile of Esther Dyson, who talked about when she "used to be a liberal."

December 1993

- News stories on pro-privacy/bullied-by-the-US-government activist Phil Zimmermann; and on attorney general Janet Reno making Freedom of Information Act (FOIA) suits easier. This was, of course, considered a good thing.
- Feature titled "Uncovering the secret history of the cold war," about how FOIA requests for POTUS (President of the United States) email will be honored.
- Feature titled "Big Brother wants to look into your bank

account (any time it pleases)," on the federal financial crime enforcement network.

January 1994

- News stories on conflicts between government information being made freely available online (it's our right to be able to read it) and commercial database providers who want to charge for the same information — specifically on the SEC's data; and on the stupidity of US representatives requiring constituents to send snailmail letters requesting their congresscritter's email addresses so that they can then contact them electronically.
- Feature titled "Direct Democracy. Are you ready for the democracy channel?" on electronic town meetings: "Ask the average person on the street whether he or she can do a better job than the average politician and the answer will usually be: Hell yes!"
- Feature titled "The White House Phone System Boondoggle. The Clinton administration may have broken the law": "...appears new contracts in clear violation of the federal Competition in Contracting Act."
- My profile of John Dvorak, computer columnist-curmudgeon-wisenheimer weasel and libertarian.

February 1994

- News stories on Kuwait possibly jamming satellite channels to ensure censorship; and on Bionomics.
- Op-ed titled "Get on track: There will be no info highway": "Regulation was the last of the worries of highway builders. Their problems lay largely in stimulating investment."
- Feature titled "Stealthwatchers. Armed with Radio Shack PCs, a small group of private citizens are unmasking the US Defense Department's black budget aircraft."
- Feature titled "Nobody fucks with the OMV. Simson L. Garfinkel investigates how the government is using your driver's license to play Big Brother."

March 1994

- News stories on Bruce Sterling placing his exposé Hacker Crackdown on the Net for free: "I didn't write this book in order to squeeze every last nickel and dime out of the mitts of impoverished 16-year-old cyberpunk high school students... Well-meaning public-spirited civil libertarians don't have much money, either. And it seems almost criminal to snatch cash out of the hands of America's direfully underpaid electronic law enforcement community. The information inside this book longs for freedom with peculiar intensity. I genuinely believe that the natural habitat of this book is inside an electronic network"; on an easy-to-use version of PGP; on Extropian cypherpunk Romana Machado and Stego, her software for encrypting information through digital visual camouflage; and approval for a Washington Post op-ed opposing the appointment of former arch-spook Bobby Inman as US secretary of defense.
- My interview with Cal Tech professor and rank libertarian Carver Mead, who is one of George Gilder's demiurges.
- Feature titled "Heard Not Obscene: How the Supreme Court might debate the constitutional implications of a case when V[irtual] R[eality] meets kiddie porn."
- Feature titled "Can the BBC be saved? Britain's most powerful broadcaster with the world's most respected broadcasting brand name is fighting to keep the television tax that pays for its operations. But winning this battle will have little effect on the larger forces besetting the venerable Beeb: Competition and new technology from without, rot and intransigence from within." Government is so tediously big and bad, you know?
- Feature by Barlow titled "The economy of ideas: A framework for rethinking patents and copyrights in the digital age (everything you know about intellectual property is wrong)." Another *throw out your tired old laws, nature and the market will provide* song lyric with a world beat.

And during its second year of publication, simply skimming *Wired's* covers, you'd find listed:

April 1994: "Jackboots on the Infobahn."

June 1994: "The super-secret NSA answers Clipper critics. A *Wired* exclusive." "The EFF is fighting for your rights in cyberspace. Just who are these guys?"

July 1994: "Bruce Sterling on the NSA." Cover of John Malone, CEO of cable giant TCI, photoshopped into looking like the Road Warrior. In his interview, Malone says, "You know, shoot [Reid] Hundt [then chairman of the FCC]! Don't let him do any more damage, know what I'm saying?"

September 1994: "Universal service, an idea whose time is past." Universal service is the notion that everyone should be guaranteed at the same affordable rate what's called POTS (plain old telephone service), even if living in rural or inner-city areas where phone companies might not make money providing service. Never mind that many would argue that universal service historically made the US phone system the best and cheapest and most domestically omnipresent in the world.

October 1994: "Meet the Extropians." Jumping-over-the-moon raver anarcho-libertarians.

November 1994: "Prophet of Privacy: Steven Levy on Whitfield Diffie." Diffie is rightfully considered one of the gods of strong crypto.

The pattern was pretty clear, and it wouldn't change for years.

As high tech entered its biggest boom of all time and *Wired* grew ever more sleekly fat with ads, its editorial slant only became more reified and stubbornly, religiously set in its rabidly free-market libertarian ways (interviews with Newt Gingrich by Esther Dyson; lots of stuff on the New Economy) — until a decision by Wired Ventures investors installed new editorial management — a team with credentials more journalistic than evangelistic — early in the winter of 1998. But my favorite *Wired* cover line of all time appeared on its September 1995 issue, with the dazzling phrase (take one *Wired* style word from column A, one from column B, and one from column C): "anarcho-emergentist-Republicans."

The magazine almost never ran anything that was other than laudatory of technology or other than libertarian in outlook. There was as tight a filter on what ran and what didn't as in any Soviet publication before the fall of the Iron Curtain. Lower-level staffers, not so in agreement with the party line of the executives at the top, were always trying to see what they could sneak through; I heard these tales all the time from people I knew who worked there. Readers of a political stripe other than libertarian, but who had no other publication to turn to that was about technology *culture*, would scan it every month to see if there was any sign of things changing. This hoping for the best but so often finding only the worst in *our* magazine was an ever-recurring topic of conversation at the San Francisco dinner parties I was attending at the time.

When *Wired* ran as a cover story (March 1996) Po Bronson's slyly subversive profile of George Gilder (it's not enough that there was a Q+A with the bloke back in the magazine's first year of publication; never can have too much of a good thing), I immediately sent the author a congratulatory email: How had he snuck such a clever critique of Gilder, one of the *Wired* elect, into the magazine?

In reading Bronson's piece I was having an experience akin to what I had heard members of the Russian intelligentsia felt when *One Day in the Life of Ivan Denisovich* was published during the Khrushchev regime. Solzhenitsyn's novella was the first above-ground treatment of the gulags in a state-sanctioned magazine, and everyone wondered how he got away with it — and if anyone would be able to get away with such a thing ever again. The answer was: not really. Not for a long time. Bronson's sardonic article was so at odds with the run-of-the-mill oogie-googie praise of all things libertarian that had characterized the magazine from its humble beginnings — and would continue to do so until new management took over. You weren't "so *Wired*" if you held to a view of things that wasn't libertarian and techno-utopian. In other words, it wasn't *Wired* to question whether technology was going to do anything other than bring good things to life and make us all healthy, wealthy, and wise. And if you thought otherwise, you certainly weren't wise and probably couldn't be wealthy.

HOT MEDIA, COLD WAR

Wired and its political seductions (during the Korean War, this was called brainwashing) bring to mind a one-page short story I read as a kid in one of the Seven Sisters women's magazines (*Ladies Home Journal*? *McCall's*?) during the fallout-shelter-happy early '60s. In the story, after the thinly disguised Commies came to town and with deceptive kindness took children away from their families to live in fun camps/dorms/stalags, one of the Commie pseudo-Mom den mothers suggested to the little girl protagonist that it might be fun to cut up the American flag that had been flying in front of her elementary school. The colors would look so pretty, like confetti sprinkled all over the school-yard! — which chilling act was the climax of the story. The point, of course, was that by making the reprehensible and politically offensive fun and colorful and novel, no one could object. As a preternaturally skeptical child, I understood how I was being propagandized and that the moral of the story was that it was a Bad Thing to do craft projects with the Stars and Stripes. Still, if it really looked that great, what was the harm? Though I would not have had the language to articulate the thought, a part of me then sneakily considered the proposition that maybe the political agenda wasn't as important as the aesthetic one. Homo ludens.

Wired created its equivalent of red-white-and-blue confetti. The magazine, so singular and so charismatic, was especially effective as a propaganda vehicle because as definite as its agenda was, as narrowcast as that of *National Review* or *On Our Backs* (the first lesbian-bi-sex-positive zine), its biases didn't come packaged as politics but as lifestyle/decoration. It could work its encompassing magic far better than any communique from a revolutionary cadre. What can't really be answered is how much it expressed in smashingly original fashion the technolibertarian gestalt that was already out there, as opposed to how much it manufactured the technolibertarian consent that suited its founders' and their sympathizers' points of view. It's a perception/reality, nominalist/realist epistemological quandary: How many of the technolibertarian leitmotifs and eidolons (entrepreneur as hero; freedom fighter by virtue of digital tool-using; netizen/digital citizen; government, at best, as semi-dangerous semi-intelligent being, and at worst, the enemy of the people) that have been equated with *Wired* were *fostered* by editorial dictat, and how many were there waiting to have their manifest glories brought into proper public view? How much did the editorial founding fathers deify a vocal *minority* culture as culturally dominant — and how much did they merely amplify what was already there?

Louis Rossetto, *Wired*'s former Fearless Leader (barred from the magazine by investors in January 1998) personified the magazine's counterculture-libertarian schtick. A man whose personal style exuded the dress-down Indie, vaguely boho charm of an artsy American who had knocked around Europe for years (all true, in his case), Louis nonetheless had been a young Republican who flirted with the Libertarian Party while a Columbia University undergraduate — a contrarian place to stand for someone coming of age in the late '60s, particularly at *that* particular multiversity. He became friends with John Perry Barlow: cowboy/Robert Waller stud-about-town/free-range technolibertarian.

Barlow is perhaps the most high-profile member of the digerati on the planet. He wrote for, and was written about in, *Wired* perhaps more than any other tech celeb. Quick! There's

Barlow quoted in the *New York Times* once again! Or is it the *Wall Street Journal*? Over there! There's Barlow giving a speech at Cannes! Psst! Have you heard the rumor about Barlow fixing Darryl Hannah's fence in Aspen? With a persona that employs the hortatory moves of a circuit rider, he gives out digital-culture gospel-shouts that carry more than a scent of roguishness. Barlow *was* the Playboy Philosopher for the *Wired* generation.

Vintage Barlow, from the November 1995 issue of *Spin* ("Our body politics, our selves: John Perry Barlow proclaims the new Net Order"), guest edited by dreadlocked Virtual Reality duke Jaron Lanier:

> Many federal governments are already both fibrillating with data-shock and increasingly incapable of convincing taxpayers who support them that they are getting anything like their money's worth. I think it unlikely that there will be a federal government left on the planet in 50 years...
>
> It is difficult to enforce a credible order upon people whose activities can take place in any terrestrial jurisdiction...
>
> We can be reasonably sure that it will not be easy to impose order on anything as slippery as a virtual body politic...
>
> Because one thing is clear to me. We are at the end of the world as we know it. Our grandchildren will obtain their order by methods we cannot imagine; our legacy to them should be a virtual landscape open to all the possibilities they might try. Let's be ancestors for them as great as Jefferson and Madison were to us. Let's leave them freedom. They can decide how much of it they're brave enough to keep.

Another important *Wired* editor-philosopher bond formed between Kevin Kelly and George Gilder. Kelly, number two at *Wired*, had been the editor in chief of *Whole Earth Review*. There, he had displayed how smitten he was with self-organization, chaos, complexity theory, and the rest of the let-it-be hive-mind-think of how bees don't need environmental impact reports to figure out where the best flowers to sup from are. It's Creation Theology (the Lord in all Munificence provides enough, and enough order, without our pesky meddling) masquerading as borrowing from Nature. KK formed a special-affinity group with Gilder and did the interview with Gilder in the magazine's fourth issue. Classic Gilder, from the September/October 1997 *Cato Policy Report*, "Regulating the Telecosm":

> Today technology is crying out in pain. The danger is that the government will try to find a solution to that pain... The essential conflict is between the inescapable laws that govern technology and government regulation, what could be called Morons' law. Morons' law is inexorably hostile to the flood of creativity we have witnessed.[24]

Both Gilder and Barlow are high up on the totem pole erected in front of the technolibertarian village and thus are not your average Joe-Six-Mbyte technolibertarians. People whose value may be more symbolic than actual deserve to be examined closely as the potent symbols that they are.

Between Gilder and Barlow you have the two cultural moieties of technolibertarian culture: Barlow, the raver Wild West neo-hippie; Gilder, the sui generis cultural conservative. Both were all over the magazine, from its first issue up until the first issue of its sixth year, the notorious "Change Is Good" edition, which summed up the self-congratulatory technolibertarian ethos in pieces by the all-male Usual Suspects, plus the Token Girl, Virginia Postrel, editor in chief of the libertarian flag/mother-ship publication *Reason*. If

24 Moron's law is Gilder's haha homage to Moore's law. Moore, one of the founders of Intel, posited decades ago that microprocessors would double in capacity every ten to eighteen months — more technically, that the number of transistors that can be placed on a given area of silicon doubles every ten to eighteen months. This has more or less been the case for years, but increasingly less so due to the limits on the physics of miniaturization.

Wired was the foremost retailer of technolibertarian style, Gilder and Barlow were its most prominent salesmen. It was a natural linking of arms, between grandiloquent spouters-off and a magazine looking for libertarian grandiloquence. The magazine co-evolved along with whatever Gilder and Barlow were thinking about.

Very much in keeping with the general tone of *Wired*, both men proposed that computer and communications technologies constituted heroic enterprises. Gilder worshiped entrepreneurs and inventors and appeared to have found God in a microchip. Barlow intimated that the great work of being on the Net was going to lead to the omega point of creation, the high point of evolution we've been heading toward for centuries, ou quelque chose comme ça in the key of Teilhard de Chardin. As exponents of the *Wired* philosophy of digital revolution, both men played to the need that geeks and others had to feel that they were engaged in paradigm-breaking, paradigm-creating work.

Everyone wants to be the star of his/her own movie. Everyone wants to believe that the life they are living is unparalleled in excitement, import, and drama. But what was unique about the *Wired* philosophy, with Gilder and Barlow two of its most emphatic champions, was that for the first time the natural progress in microelectronics was touted as *epic*. In epics, the protagonists are, by definition, more important to the gods and to men than random mortals could be, which is exactly how people participating in high tech culture of the 1990s came to see themselves. They had become More Important. The capacity for improved self-regard now available to geeks of all kinds through the *Wired* philosophy, in combination with the capacity for arrogance and obtuseness many geeks unfortunately are already prey to, made for improvements in self-esteem and egocentricity that were stunning. Party to this improved self-concept (when had geeks *ever* received such attention?) was the money these guys were making as never before: Money is the most measurable way for society to say "attaboy!" So obviously, the free market works.

WOULD MARGARET MEAD BE PLEASED?

Some evidence on the side that *Wired* was merely documenting much of what was there to be seen inadvertently comes from findings made by J. A. English-Lueck, who is part of the anthropology faculty at San Jose State University (SJSU), which is devoting itself to the ethnographic study of Silicon Valley. She coauthored with C. Darrah a fascinating paper, which I've read in draft: "The Ethnography of Silicon Valley: Visions, Values, and Virtuality in a High Technology Community." The anthro team interviewed folks associated with various high tech high-profile institutions: the so-often quoted think tank Institute for the Future; the Tech Museum of Innovation, a San Jose interactive museum that creates ahistorical shrines to high tech in the Valley; and an only-in-Silicon-Valley non-profit (publicity and streamlining regulation are main features), Joint Venture Silicon Valley, which had its Smart Valley project. Smart Valley was charged with "creating electronic community" by developing electronic infrastructure and recruiting users for that technology, with initiatives such as its Telecommuting Project, Smart Valley Schools Internet project, Public Access Network (Net kiosks in libraries, etc.), the Bay Area Digital GeoResource, and so on.

The SJSU data collectors strived to sample widely, interviewing the Tech Museum volunteers, corporate partners, and staff; and at Smart Valley, they spoke with insiders such as past and present executives, staff members, advisory board members, and volunteers. To reach out to folks who really were dealing with the more quotidian aspects of the Silicon Valley labor market, and trying to prepare others for it, they spoke to counselors and administrators in the region's community colleges and vocational programs, as well as to teachers throughout the Valley.

The SJSU team interviewed these native informants using a structured technique called Ethnographic Futures Research (EFR), in which people were asked about their best, worst, and most likely scenarios for the near future, as a way at getting at their embedded belief systems. The aggregated self-inventory of Silicon Valley that comes from their interviewees maps beautifully onto the worldview *Wired* was selling. As English-Lueck put it:

> [Silicon Valley] is stridently conscious of itself as an important place in some larger firmament, be that national or international. It is seldom sufficient just to solve local problems, but... spokespersons in Silicon Valley believe its solutions must serve as paradigms for other communities. The region also promotes itself as one which is constantly "reinventing" itself in order to avoid falling from the "cutting edge," an apparently unthinkable fate.

Wired had it right. Its audience's demand for self-importance and novelty was as great as any of those in the high courts of the Hellenistic Mediterranean or of France in the pre-Revolution eighteenth century.

If you were part of geek culture — or simply wanted to immerse yourself in a worldview that seemed the Newest Thing around — you cleaved unto *Wired*. And if you hadn't thought much about political economy, and all you knew of government were its wrongheaded attempts at sabotaging the Bill of Rights in the digital '90s, then the libertarianism the magazine shoved at you, so emphatically and so constantly, directly and indirectly, made perfect sense. It was perfectly in synch with the self-glorifying rhetoric you heard all around you all the time anyway, from the "excitement" marketing assistants spoke of when describing the latest tweak to a software upgrade your company was selling to the elephantiasis of expectation Wall Street analysts had for IPOs and quarterly growth in earnings from high tech companies.

And you almost never read other points of view in *Wired*'s pages, and mainstream media really hadn't caught up or on and was either dismissive or inaccurate in its write-ups of high tech. Or, just as bad, other print offerings were doltish-looking or obscure: Who other than a CS grad generally wants to read journals for historians of technology or serious computer scientists, such as *Communications of the ACM*?[25] There wasn't really any other editorial product to be consumed. Readers of *Wired*, the first genre-creating/busting mass-circulation commercial magazine on the US cultural scene in a decade, were probably not much different from the little girl in the short story with her American flag confetti. It looks so great and is so much fun, what could be wrong?

History belongs to the victors — and the *Wired* version of digital technology's impact on society has been the victorious one, if only because it got there first. Perhaps only when libertarianism has slipped into being just one of thirteen ways of looking at digital culture will it be possible to see what was really going on as Silicon Valley came into zeitgeist dominance and tire companies acquired URLs. For now, the tropes *Wired* crusaded for are still the Truth that is Out There — no countervailing metaphors to live by have prevailed. Nothing really has come along to replace *Rolling Stone*, although no one necessarily believes anymore that sex, drugs, and rock 'n' roll are alternatives to anything or that *Rolling Stone* is much of an alternative to mainstream publishing. Still, *Rolling Stone* defined the genre of gonzo reporting and of lifestyle/buying patterns as political acts.

Some high tech commentators profess to have progressed from *Wired*-style technolibertarianism to a middle-of-the-road position of gravitas and sobriety (not all regulation is bad and government can do some good things and an untrammeled marketplace isn't necessarily the best thing going). A manifesto

25 Association for Computing Machinery, the fine old scholarly organization of the computer world, where many of the sociocultural implications of technology are discussed.

manqué promoting this point of view, called the Technorealism Document, existed for a media moment of very short duration. The rather innocuous eight-point statement("5. Wiring the schools will not save them") was formally signed onto by a bunch of technology journalists (I was one) and launched with a companion Web site with great foofaraw in March 1998 at an event sponsored by the Berkman Center for the Internet and Society at Harvard Law School. Technorealism, when reduced to its essence, said neither a techno-utopian nor dystopian be, follow the sane middle path, cyberspace is grounded in the real world, and governments will continue to matter. Some of the criticism and negative press coverage we TRs received said, "No one buys into that excessive foolish *Wired* flavor of libertarianism anymore anyway." Perhaps, but this "we've evolved past all that" critique came more, I think, from the 5,000 or so Net-culture insiders who have spent much time debating these issues online for years and who bothered to let their hurt feelings be known because they hadn't been consulted on what Technorealism should and should not have been (don't they have day jobs?) than, say, from rank-and-file Silicon Valley sales managers.

I gotta say, I do not run into many of these modulated, evolved, next-generation technologists when I attend group dinners with nerds, or into geeks at parties, or read most of the computer press. My experiences are more likely to take the form of the pleasant encounter I had on a flight back from New York to San Francisco in June 1998. I was sitting next to a man with at least twenty years' tenure in Silicon Valley, who had just come from attending the 100,00-plus-participant microcomputer conference PC Expo. He had never heard the term "libertarian," but he marveled at how I seemed to know and understand so exactly how he thought about the world. He was a very nice guy, and no one wants to be reduced to type, but he was technolibertarian to his bones. Government bad, market good; someone said it, I believe it, that settles it!

Other members of the high tech rank and file say now they never really bought into *Wired*'s vision anyway. Again it's worth looking to the 1960s. For though the portents were that the Hippie Dream was over by the end of 1969 (the Haight was a mess, rock stars were dying, stagflation was beginning to make the economy a place not forgiving of alternative lifestyles), guys continued to grow their hair as sign of rebellion, experiments with sexuality and mind-altering substances only increased, and identity politics (women and gays and ethnic groups) took on ever greater force well into the '70s. The cultural trends that started with the Free Speech Movement did not end with Altamont — or even with the move of *Rolling Stone* to New York (sold out!). And nothing came along in the '70s to articulate as hipster an image as *Rolling Stone* — even if the magazine's editorial direction, and the consensus of some its readers, was changing.

So even if the new *Wired* has backed off from the outré libertarianism of its progenitors — in fact, away from politics altogether — the ideas it promulgated are djinns that cannot go back in their bottle. The magazine is still associated with that stance, even if it no longer corresponds with reality; and the whole situation is rather like what happens when giardia contaminates a watershed.

Once the parasite gets into those streams, it is there forever. You can never drink from mountain springs again, no matter how far into the backcountry you hike. Technolibertarianism continues unabashed and unabated — in small part because no publication has come up with a compelling replacement narrative.

Wired also offered cross-generational appeal: to kids who had grown up, or were growing up, with computers; and to the grown-ups in chronological age, who were making lots of serious new money as computing and digital communications became ever more a part of Other People's Lives. More cynically, its attitude-up-the-snout (most extremely expressed in its "Viacom doesn't suck" cover. Sumner Redstone as Beavis. Or is it Butthead?) appealed to guys in their twenties, or those older ones who want to think of themselves as still being in their twenties and having an Inner Bike Messenger. The expensive toys and tales of other successful hunter-predators on the digital Great Basin appealed to guys thirty and older, who really were hauling down the bucks to buy those toys or hoped real soon now to be the subject of their own suck-uppy *Wired* profiles. Brilliantly, and conversely, *Wired* also offered a pillowbook full of dreams for the young'uns to aspire to. Discussion of the kinds of guys *Wired* profiled and who those profiles were pitched to leads right into the boys-club critique of *Wired*. As done to death as that feminist deconstruction has been (at least in my petit cercle, of women who make their living through technology, particularly in the Bay Area), it also cannot be ignored.

THE WOMAN QUESTION

Just as technolibertarian culture is *morbidly* hypermale, so *Wired* magazine reflected this probably semiconscious bias. And by semiconscious, I mean that Louis and Kevin and John probably had differing degrees of consciousness about trying to make *Wired* such a male rag from the beginning; but it seemed to them to be a good choice to stick by, as the magazine became such a big shiny golden carp in its very scenic koi pond. Never mind that some of their female staffers — and readers — protested this male bias from the very beginning. I've brooded on this a lot, because *Wired's* libertarianism, as well as its silly sexism, took me so naively by surprise.

On deeper consideration, though, steering *Wired* into the male market segment of magazine readership was an inspired choice. To guys in their thirties and older, such a female-ignoring appeal probably lay in a bit of a "backlash" phenomenon (how can I have fun if there are damned females *everywhere* I go these days? grumble grumble...reminders of constraint, of Mom or Significant Other or Sunday School teacher); to guys who were younger, having come of age and gone to college in the era of politically correcting freshman comp instructors, a brash male culture that unabashedly does not mince words, that abjures the caricature of screechy leftiness so common on college campuses and so tokenized in the media, is a relief from a prissiness they had endured for too long.

This orientation meant that in *Wired's* first five years, the number of articles *written* by women, the number of articles written about women, the number of women who appeared on the cover (is there any reason a cover story on kids and computing couldn't have a girl instead of a boy illustrating the piece?) were appallingly few. The treatment of women editorial staffers was disgraceful (often ignored, mostly segregated into editorial pooper-scooper jobs), with competent women passed over for less-qualified men.

When I mentioned some female-specific issues about Esther Dyson in the article I wrote about her (nothing programmatic. I was simply wondering how she felt about making her way through a male-dominated industry, coupled with some of my own puzzlement about how some sources I interviewed about her made personal comments [not liking the way she dressed] or asked personal questions [who was she dating?] that guy subjects of profiles don't seem to be subject to), my editor, Kevin Kelly, found it very odd. He said didn't think about whether Esther was female or male, so why was I bothering? At worst, I thought it might be valuable for other women to see how a successful woman dealt with the weirditudes and tensions of high tech. Oh (what a novel idea). Click (the term *Ms* magazine coined to signify one of those Feminist Moments). Duh (not so hard a concept to wrap yourself around, if women as actors and agents are in an everyday sense part of your worldview).

Rossetto, in an interview with Paul Keegan in the February 1, 1997, issue of *Upside*, said:

> Women are biologically different from men. They have different hormones, they have different neurotransmitters, they have different body chemistry, they are created for different biological functions that lead them to be more inclined to do certain things. Men are content to sit in front of a screen for hours on end and do things with it, interact with inanimate objects, and men have been doing that, from computers back to cars, back to factory equipment, back to farm implement, back to whatever. Women are more social; they prefer to spend their time interacting with others than in solitary quests.

Louis, I suppose, never read another neo-caveman philosophe, Lionel Tiger, whose *Men in Groups* posited that women can't amount to much precisely because they don't bond in groups. Hey, whatever it takes to create false dichotomies. Presumably Louis also never heard of Rosie the Riveter, or the women who operated anti-aircraft artillery in England during World War II, or the women who have spent their working lives chained to sewing machines. Hell, when computers first got going, and programming was considered a boring repetitive task, it was largely women's work. And yes, there exist women at this very moment doing interesting things in high tech. But Louis is not here for me to argue with, and he is gone from the magazine anyway. What's more to the point is that his retrograde foolishness signifies the curious cultural conservatism, so counter to *Wired*'s rhetoric of revolution, that underlies much technolibertarian thinking. It's not for nothing that Camille Paglia, the counter-feminist of the moment, was the *only* woman featured in the first issue of the magazine.

Which brings up George Gilder, the Tory leader of the *Wired* technolibertarian revolution. Not talking about his sexual politics would be like not talking about the former KKK membership of David Duke when he was running for governor of Louisiana.

GILDERVISION

Gilder, the pet of *Wired*'s then executive editor, was a former Republican Party speechwriter and is a family-values Cotton Mather. His *Sexual Suicide* (Quadrangle/New York Times Books, 1973), updated and expanded into *Men and Marriage* (Pelican, 1986), is famous in some circles, infamous in others. He now flits about high tech (at one point, he wrote some of the semiconductor coverage for Esther Dyson's newsletter) as a figure of technolibertarian High Intellect — and like any proper member of the high tech chattering class, he has a newsletter and conference biz to show for it. Cover boy for *Wired* 4.03,[26] he is also singled out for special vivisection by Susan Faludi in *Backlash*. In his 1981 *Playboy* interview, Gilder comes up with zingers like "Upper-class feminists all believe that any man who makes it just by working harder than a college-educated feminist must be an evil oppressor"; "Women will never pursue careers with the same determination and drive men do"; "The Pill mainly liberated men, allowing them to find more opportunities for their short-term, compulsive sexuality"; "Anti-feminist women tend to be more intelligent and interesting than feminist women, because they are not conformists." There is, of course, more, but Gilder's fearlessly backward-looking high-mindedness about women matters, because Gilder is a much-quoted Big Thinker.

As much as he puts women in their place, Gilder also puts men in their own very special place. Of Cal Tech professor Carver Mead (*Microcosm*, Simon and Schuster, 1989), Gilder writes:

> A gnome of quiet voice, pointed beard, and kindly smile, he would bring his vision — tenaciously, trenchantly — to prestigious men who disdained it, to old friends who bitterly opposed it, to allies who betrayed it... His word became law... In

26 That is, issue 3 of Wired's fourth year of publication. Wired style dictated that issues be numbered like software releases.

> the end, the microelectronics industry would transform itself… to conform to his message.

Or in the section called "The Economy of Heroes" in *Recapturing the Spirit of Enterprise*, (ICS Press, 1992), the updated version of his *The Spirit of Enterprise* (Simon and Schuster, 1984), J. R. Simplot, the Idaho potato king (dried potatoes for the military in World War II, frozen french fries for McDonald's) and early investor in Idaho semiconductor-maker Micron, is described as the son of

> a…farmer of Scotch and Huguenot ancestors, with a wiry frame, keen eyes… Seeking more space and freedom, he had left behind in Iowa a fertile spread and a young wife, heavy with child… It was in [a] one-room cabin that Jack, as he came to be known, first exercised his echoing voice and sturdy limbs… In photographs, he appeared as a happy, freckled youth… But already Jack had learned that life consisted of stern duties… Without the duties of [farmwork], though, he simply invented new work. Somewhere in his thick Scots Presbyterian bones, the eight-year-old Jack Simplot was an irrepressible entrepreneur… Leaving a mother he loved and a father he feared and a farm that needed his labor, he suffered all the guilts and anxieties that entrepreneurs everywhere report when telling of their crucial moves.

A chapter in *Recapturing the Spirit of Enterprise* is also devoted to Milos Krofta, a paper-manufacturing and water-purification expert/entrepreneur who is described as

> a blond, erect, fastidious young man…a Slovenian engineer with…proud bearing… [He] married Maria Hybler, also bright and blond and Catholic… At seventy-one years of age still an erect and handsome man of courtly European bearing…he erected a white marble monument in memory of the family that had raised him… The elegant stone…also symbolizes…

> triumph through a...son, who had...found purity and peace, and expiation for the past, in an entrepreneurial revolution halfway around the world.

Gilder's bordering-on-homophilic hero worship of high tech coffee achievers (whether entrepreneurs or technologists) embodies to the point of self-parody the caricature-male quality of technolibertarianism. He always appears to be seeking the latest John Galt/Howard Roark who best represents this year's Spirit of Enterprise, with a male reverence that can even override his avowed libertarianism. It's a phallus worship he has in common with Ayn Rand — only in her case it takes the form of reverence for rapaciousness and rough sex as characteristics of the male heroes (well actually, there aren't other kinds of heroes) in her fiction.

Gilder recast the proposed preposterously monopolistic merger of MCI with Worldcom (now running circa 60 percent of Net traffic. Regulators in Europe and the US put the kaibosh on the deal, until MCI promised to divest itself of its Internet dealings) by getting all googly-eyed and fluttery when he described Bernie Ebbers, Worldcom's CEO. He is quoted in the October 9, 1997, issue of *Salon* webzine: "Welcome to the reign of King Bernie, who will be the salvation of the Internet. Like John D. Rockefeller and Michael Milken before him, Mr. Ebbers has shown the magic of entrepreneurial guts and vision." Indeed. What a droll set of heroes for one who is said to value soundly competitive markets — or who pretends to understand technology, high tech culture, or data communications.

The strength of the Net has always been its decentralization, it being a network of networks that no one in particular controls or owns; most people who truly understand and love the Net would be grossed out/enraged at the prospect of it needing a Savior, or there being *anyone* in charge — and it's a definition from classical economics that majorly controlling the means of distribution means you majorly control/dominate/price-fix a market (wasn't that what the breakup of the Bell System was all about? Or how about Frank Norris's *The Octopus*?). In fact, for all his libertarianism of convenience, there's something in his slobbering over great men and happily-dwelling-in-his-fancy-of-the-past social agenda that's a little reminiscent of the early celebrants of Eurofascism from the 1930s — when the notion of Germany or Italy having a strong Man to lead us all out of chaos got *such* a bad rap.

As with the cypherpunk shadow, what you are most intent on denying is precisely what may be driving you the most. Psychological common sense dictates that the way Gilder depicts his male-warrior/hommes des affaires somehow resembles the forward-striding, eyes-ever-fearlessly-on-the-horizon, Soviet New Men so beloved of socialist realist art. Only here, instead of bulging necks and tractor quotas, his Guys have had something to do with technology, Guys deemed worthy of an IPO. In this regard, he's like Ayn Rand before him, who never really shook off her experience of postrevolutionary Russia (her fiction demonstrates all the humorlessness, lack of irony, 2-D heroes, and political exhortation of the collectivist world she despised).

Although cloaked in the language of libertarianism, there is inherent in the Gildervision (ever since now-commonly-buffooned John Scully got into that vision thing during his '80s tenure as CEO of Apple, everyone at VP level and above in high tech has grand things to say about everything) a worship of (male) power — so often an enemy of the liberty libertarians are *said* to value above all. Gilder's infatuation with male prowess erases women from the picture, suggesting they would be better to be homeschooling their kids and that their only reason to log onto the Net would be to have some safe exposure to certified non-scary entertainment (maybe fashion/grooming/health/fitness/childrearing tips) and to be able to stay away from the nasty cities where those anarchic secular-humanist values seem to rule and there tends to be *true* diversity of point of view — and where the vast majority of folks who actually are Net entrepreneurs dwell. And where many women actually live work thrive love and yes even are technologists and entrepreneurs.

And although I may think Gilder's wallpaper-paste-thin sociobiology is so over, nonetheless in less audible and cartoony form, some version of it informed *Wired* editorial direction from the start — and remains a miasma that creeps about on little cat feet throughout high tech. And it reminds us, that in spite of its dressing-up and body-modification through the Northern California of self-realization and experimentation with lifestyle, engineers as a group have always been more conservative than not.

The Gilder/*Wired* focus on individual accomplishment and those who break the rules (though that's a stretch, when you're lionizing the heads of cable companies) had a lot of DC Comics Action Hero appeal to those so understandably weary of the collectivist bummer of identity politics. What a concept: cyberspace and hightechlandia merchandised as a place where the buffalo roam and dogs run free.

Never mind that many people working in high tech are most likely grunt programmers doing stuff like maintaining inventory-tracking modules for construction-management accounting software or working at ghastly huge man-in-the-gray-easy-care-twills places such as Ross Perot's own data processing feudal kingdom, Perot Systems, or at former defense-aerospace contractors such as Lockheed-Martin. Manning their computers like Kiowa braves on vision quests, most high tech droids ain't. But how much more rewarding, if Walter Mitty–like, to imagine such consonance between who they are day to day and what *Wired* told them they were in their pilgrim souls! And who could make a snazzy literary splash out of the fact that, actually, according to an article in the January 1994 issue of *American Demographics*, more women than men use computers (think of the pink-collar ghetto of secretaries, data-entry personnel, and phone customer-service reps)? Given how secretaries are asked to perform ever more *computer* work (producing desktop-publishing reports; creating PowerPoint displays; maintaining databases), it's possible that these numbers have gotten even more skewed in the direction of women as actual users since 1994. Who, after all, maintains the computers in small offices?

Bue these women are using computers in decidedly unadventurous, untransgressive, un-world-changing, poorly-compensated ways. In fact, computers are often used in dehumanizing, dispiriting, downgrading-the-quality-of-work-and-life-and-privacy ways. But we live in a noosphere of ideas, so don't complicate things with facts.

Facts such as that a magazine like *Wired*, which passed itself off as being on the cultural vanguard (which in some regards it was, for it was very queer-friendly, if not female-friendly), was very oldschool old-boy in its sexual politics, stranger still, during a time when the World Wide Web (whose rise coincided with the hockey stick of *Wired*'s own growth curve) was increasingly serving as a port of entry for women getting involved with computer technology. The Web, with its multimedia capacities (literary writing and images whose appeal was aesthetic, with sound and animation and film possible) attracted a more gender-balanced crew to computerized projects of all kinds. But you would never know much about this increasingly female audience from reading *Wired* — though its Web site (originally called "HotWired," now "Wired Digital"), perhaps because it had greater operating distance from the editorial founders, was far more female-friendly and female-honoring (in management and content) than the magazine. Perhaps it's because the Web site hemorrhaged money for years and so, in a way, was less valued.

In spite of any hurt tender feelings I or other women may have had about the original *Wired*, I have come to think that its boysclubness and libertarianness and its lift-off splash-down success were all tied up together. Sad to say, generally that which is female-identified is generally *not* seen as daring and culturally innovative. Ask the Gorilla Girls, women in the arts community who don gorilla masks (to preserve anonymity) as they speak and write about the sexism in the art world (e.g., the number of women in group shows, the number of women with solo shows, the number of women with senior curatorial positions). In fact, the opposite is well documented: The extent to which a profession or activity is female-friendly is the extent to which it loses status — or has subtly already *lost* status, so that the barriers to entry aren't what they once were (consider the loss of status in these once entirely male but now largely female professions: Secretary. Pharmacist. Psychiatrist. Branch-bank manager). Although there's much evidence, given who the founders were and what they have said, that the magazine was never intended to be other than an obviously guy-mag, perhaps a digital-culture bombshell could not have taken a different, more gender-equitable shape.

"But where else can I go?" No one else got digital culture so well, could publish work with such panache. This love-hate, we-are-hurt-and-angered-by-what-it's-tuming-out-to-be-but-there's-no-greater-publication-on-the-planet-right-now reaction is what steered the *Wired* feminist cabal to have lunch with me that day. We were feeling something like the woman who enters into a passionate relationship with a charismatic man, only to discover with horror that our concerns were not his concerns and that who we were and what we had to say weren't valued. And in a way, the many public and private squabbles I had with *Wired* were about this codependency.

The complex *Wired* woman-problem backstory explains why no one thought it was a coincidence (though it might well have been) that when a new editorial team was brought in during the winter of 1998, both the editor in chief and the managing editor were female. This was as strong a signal as could be sent that Things Were Gonna Be Different. Think of when an organization is seen to have gone bad: When the United Way and the NAACP were besmirched by executives behaving badly, *women* were brought in at the top to clean up the joint and elevate the moral tone. The implication was that with the old libertarian team gone, women would not face as high a bar to entry. Having women at the top at *Wired* (even if the choice of these two women had an element of right time/right place: both had been esteemed, if lower-level editors, at the magazine before the putsch) was a way of saying, "No more bad boys around here."

NATTY BUMPO, LEVI STRAUSS, AND YOU!

Coterminous but not precisely synonymous with the male-supremacist mind-set reflected in *Wired* was the cult of the entrepreneur, the rebel hero genius god who walks among us. *Wired* genuflected to this cult repeatedly. To examine this creed in one of its purer expressions, let us again turn to Gilder, who wrote an entire book/love letter in this vein about guy entrepreneurs in *The Spirit of Enterprise*:

> Bullheaded, defiant, tenacious, creative, entrepreneurs continued to solve the problems of the world even faster than the world could create them. The achievements of enterprise remained the highest testimony to the mysterious strength of the human spirit. Confronting the perennial perils of human life, the scientific odds against human triumph, the rationalistic counsels of despair, the entrepreneur finds a higher source of hope than reason, a deeper well of faith than science, a farther reach of charity than welfare. His success is the triumph of the spirit of enterprise — a thrust beyond the powers and principalities of the established world to the transcendent sources of creation and truth .

> ...Entrepreneurs everywhere ignored the suave voice of expertise; the economists who deny their role as the driving force of all economic growth; the psychologists who identify their work and sacrifice as an expression of greed; the sociologists who see their dreams as nostalgia for a lost frontier; the politicians who call their profits unearned, their riches pure luck .
>
> ...The spirit of enterprise wells up from the wisdom of the ages and the history of the West and infuses the most modern of technological adventures. It joins the old and new frontiers. It asserts a firm hierarchy of values and demands a hard discipline. It requires a life of labor and listening, aspiration and courage. But it is the source of all we are and can become, the saving grace of democratic politics and free men, the hope of the poor and the obligation of the fortunate, the redemption of an oppressed and desperate world.

Yet as much as making like an entrepreneur is a fine thing, and has worked to great advantage in Silicon Valley, reality again is sadly more complicated. AnnaLee Saxenian, a city-planning professor at UC-Berkeley, wrote an influential book that provides some explanations of why Massachusetts's former high tech corridor, Route 128, which had historic and other advantages on its side, had faded until the late 1990s, and why Silicon Valley, the relatively underprivileged hick from the provinces, has bloomed. *Regional Advantage: Culture and Competition in Silicon Valley and Route 128* (Harvard University Press, 1994) describes the network of social and professional relations, private- and public-sector partnerships, and community-building that were integral to Silicon Valley's rise and rise — factors missing from Route 128 technoculture, and which Silicon Valley's community memory forgot for a while as it stumbled through a recession in the late 1980s:

> Lacking a language to describe this unusual mix of cooperation and competition, they saw themselves through the lens

> of American individualism. They attributed their spectacular growth to individual technical prowess and entrepreneurial risk-taking. Just as the vocabulary of rugged individualism, entrepreneurship, and free markets blinded Silicon Valley's engineers to the institutional and social underpinnings of their industrial success, it also left them unable to ensure their own survival. Assuming that the dynamism of free markets would be self-perpetuating and self-governing, they saw no need to attend to the institutional foundations of their vitality. This lack of self-understanding would lead them to make choices that would threaten the long-term dynamism of the industrial region they had created.

Saxenian has all kinds of smart things to say about the origins of Silicon Valley's wealth and glory, but the relevant part here is her suggestion that the myth of the solo entrepreneur is embedded deep in the Silicon Valley psyche, a myth only partially grounded in reality. And like many myths, this one ignores the larger culture it springs from. The male, alone on his search to earn his manhood, isn't exactly how it really works.

ANGELS AND INSECTS

But Gilder wants us to make that leap of faith, in language that's only explicitly more religious than what's articulated by other denizens of high tech:

> Yet more than any other class of men, they [entrepreneurs] embody and fulfill the sweet and mysterious consolations of the Sermon on the Mount and the most farfetched affirmations of the democratic dream. They come, like Andrew Grove [Intel Grand Master]...and a million others — as outcasts and refugees...
>
> "Do unto others as you would have done unto you" and "Give and you will be given unto" are the central rules of the life of

> enterprise. They require institutions of property (you cannot give what you do not own) and personal freedom (a planned economy cannot allow the surprising gifts of entrepreneurs). But it is a life that most deeply springs from religious faith and culture. The act of thrift, suppressing your own desires in order to serve the desires of others — the act of committing your work and wealth, over a period of years, to bring into the world a new good which the world may well reject — the act of putting your own fate into the hands of unknown others, freely deciding your future in a market of free choice — these are the essential acts of a religious person. It is a commitment made in the darkness of time to a process of dangerous creation unfolding in an unknown future; and it partakes of that "mystical and godlike" impulse of personal giving, that continual play and energy of new acts of fellowship, which makes possible the progress of men and nations.

Or this, from *The Soul of Silicon*, a talk delivered to the Vatican in May 1991, reprinted in the June 1, 1998, issue of *Forbes ASAP*. (The speech is also anti-Darwinian, anti-environmentalist, and decrying of secular humanism. But that's not within our purview.):

> The true spirit capital of the current capitalist economy is not material. It is moral, intellectual, and spiritual... Capitalism begins not with taking but with giving... Profit is an index of the altruism of a product — a measure of the extent to which an investment reflects an accurate understanding of the needs of others.

Note the not-very-hidden religious tone that slips into much of the language of this technolibertarian zealot — and which is not at all unique to Gilder. In featuring Gilder and others inclined to charismatic high-intensity sermonizing, *Wired* fastened onto the need to be a True Believer. Soul hunger crops up in strange ways — and if you don't know how to identify this hole in your soul, you may end up unconsciously filling it with very miscellaneous stuff. In spite of what many of us were taught about the Renaissance and the Enlightenment and the Age of Reason and how science is so divorced from religion — actually, it isn't. Physicists have so often been inquiring into the cosmos for Higher Reasons that they are in effect more metaphysicians than not. Higher-ups in NASA (including Wernher von Braun) were famously professing Christians. The Great Divide between science / technology and religion may not be so profound as it is reported to be. And the religiosity may take the form of adamancy of technolibertarian belief, or fervency of response to various technolibertarian preachers, such as Gilder.[27]

What could be better for a religion of the tech 1990s and Naughts (2000s) than one that is cyborgish (we wanna be as much like machine-hybrids as we can), money-centric (obvious), and nature-worshipping / chaos-theory-endorsing (we are all living in the shadow of the '60s ecology movement, starting with the success of Clairol's Herbal Essence shampoo — and maybe we all have a vague sense that Nature is Going Away? Recall the much-documented, decades-long communion between neopagans and nerds.)?

If, in your craving for faith, you are put off by the Calvinism of Gilder, and you seek something less upright and less endowed with the whiff of the lamp, you can choose the other likely technolibertarian credo close at hand. You can sign on with Barlow.

Barlow, Barlow, Barlow. Or maybe it should be, as in the opening lines of Nabokov's *Lolita*, John. Per. Ry. Bar. Low. His rhetoric is call-and-response for the Dionysian technolibertarian cult, as opposed to the Apollonic. His me-so-horny ("A Ladies' Man and Shameless") confession for "*Nerve*," a "literate smut" erotica Web site, says he likes 'em young and gets bored with

27 These themes are well explored by David Noble in his *Religion of Technology* (Knopf, 1997), by Margaret Wertheim in her *Pythagoras' Trousers* (Norton, 1997), and by Erik Davis in *TechGnosis* (Harmony, 1998)

that which becomes too familiar and he's a ramblin' kinda guy. He's a prime specimen of a Gilder Male, untrammeled male sexuality! The essay bespeaks a sexual politics that's just as shopworn, and just as eye-rolling, as Gilder's, though of course, for entirely opposite reasons (again, opposite ends of the same spectrum tend to look and feel awfully similar). Contrast with Gilder, a last Puritan. Barlow made being oppositional *fun*, sexy, racy, and daring.

Curiously, his language is also crypto-religious, perhaps from opposite causes than that of Gilder: Hanging around Timothy Leary can give you religious visions. Be that as it may, Barlow, like Gilder, insists on the liberation from matter than cyberspace offers.

Witness his Declaration of Independence of Cyberspace, which was signed into existence on February 9, 1996, at the Illuminati-type World Economic Summit in Davos, Switzerland. It came on the heels of Congress signing the Telecom Reform Act of 1996.[28] Some choice bits from Barlow's document:

> Well, fuck them. Or, more to the point, let us now take our leave of them. They have declared war on Cyberspace. Let us show them how cunning, baffling, and powerful we can be in our own defense...
>
> Governments of the Industrial World, you weary giants of flesh and steel, I come from Cyberspace, the new home of Mind. On behalf of the future, I ask you of the past to leave us alone. You are not welcome among us. You have no sovereignty where we gather.
>
> We have no elected government, nor are we likely to have one, so I address you with no greater authority than that with which liberty itself always speaks. I declare the global social space we are building to be naturally independent of the tyrannies

28 The act, among other provisions that were supposed to further the deregulation of the US communications industry, gutted some essential Bill of Rights protections for cyberspace.

> you seek to impose on us. You have no moral right to rule us nor do you possess any methods of enforcement we have true reason to fear.

LIVING IN THE MATERIAL WORLD

I have wondered if this celebration of the divorce from matter is so entrenched in the technolibertarian ethos because it is in matter where the Dark Side of high tech, and libertarianism, exists. Gilder loves prattling on about quantum mechanics and the idea-and-spirit-driven qualities of high tech entrepreneurialism, so divorced from that nasty materialism of Marxist states and of base popular culture. Barlow likes to talk about the republic of ideas cyberspace creates and about how in the realm of intellectual property, if you give it all away, magically the Universe will provide. This luftmenschery was generously sprinkled throughout *Wired* and in the writings of these two guys elsewhere.

But it's precisely in the realm of the material that technolibertarianism can stumble. For instance, although the Grateful Dead (Barlow's rock-'n'-roll connection; so he can, for the rest of his natural life, swagger that sobriquet, "I'm with the band") made a point of being good sports about the amateur taping of their shows and the swapping of these tapes among their fans, as far as I know the band still charged (and received) good money for their commercially made recordings, for the concerts Deadheads attended, and for the sales of Grateful Dead chotchkes. This is hardly a case of making a living by living in a culture of mind.

Yet it was the *Wired* ethos — oddly Marxian and materialist in this one regard, when so much of the rest of its pitch was so blatantly Idealist — that the tools you use define who you are. Netizens are those citizens of the world whose unifying trait is that they are frequent users of computers with access to a global communications network, although why this should determine political identity or serve as a marker for enlightenment is unclear. In a way, it's as odd as saying that driving a car or drinking municipally treated water defines who you are politically. How people use and create their material culture does somewhat define them, as historians of technology and cultural anthropologists have explored. But Political Animal as defined by tool-use evokes the language of a debunked political movement that also defined and glorified people by the tools that they used and their mode of employment: all hail soldiers, peasants, and workers!

But, but, but aren't I trying to make that very case that the Peculiar Institution of a very certain kind of politics (that is, libertarianism) is soldered firmly onto the motherboard of a particular kind of tool (that is, high tech)? Only in that certain kinds of thinking have sprung up in a particular time and place — that a certain political-economic culture has sprung up on the Net and in high tech in the 1990s. But I would not presume that it had entirely to be this way or that computer or Net use logically demand a certain worldview. Although their use may amplify certain personal and political inclinations, I don't think they necessarily imply it.

The *Wired* way had it both ways: It was Materialist in its obsession with high-tech toys and the highest-end computational devices for work, but Idealist in philosophically separating itself from the nagging messy world of matter — where we all actually live, and which the high tech world relies on for its existence. Actual people and businesses do have to *buy* the products of the geek mind, or where would the new wealth of nations come from? The e-commerce *frenzy* to detach shopping from place, with the damage to local businesses and tax bases (all libertarians get gleeful at getting away from taxes) implicit, is yet another iteration of this thinking. The revolt against *matter,* against the intrusion of the real world in all its imperfection and intractability, is well documented in the suggestive Netizen findings of the San Jose State EFR research. It's a very special kind of wishful thinking that Idealist high tech is prone to engage in:

> Although globalization is taken for granted, it is a relatively thin or flat world that is described. Significant cultural differences are non-existent or deemed deviant, and everyone who matters speaks English and shares the same values and assumptions about the world. This homogeneity results from the global replication of Silicon Valley clones, which are populated by people with beliefs similar to those found in Silicon Valley. Thus, globalization does not really connect the diverse people of the world, but specific transnational colonies of like-minded souls... Indeed, the emerging networked products and services are more valuable if they are accompanied by social models for their use. Thus, Silicon Valley becomes the "value added" to their consumers... [The] Silicon Valley worldview is better characterized as one of global provincialism .
>
> ...Worst case scenarios were blamed on the failure of the public to embrace the new electronic services and products and the enthusiasm needed to make them publicly viable. But our interviewees, those educated and mobile, could leave such a scenario, while the masses who fail to adopt the new technologies are expected to stay and pay the price of their shortsightedness.
>
> [And] service providers — educators, restaurateurs, janitors — are envisioned to serve the needs of the techno-elite that really "matter" in the Valley.

TECHNOLUMPEN

Yep, it's those buzzing annoying gnats of the non-elite that we best ignore, those so uninterestingly dogged by material reality. For it's precisely in the realm of the material that the cult of the entrepreneur can be shown as the dehumanizing folly it really can be. On the Web site that spun out of *Wired*, www.suck.com, (the *National Lampoon / Spy / Private Eye* of webzines), there appeared on June 24, 1996, "Dining with Cannibals," by the necessarily pseudonymous POP. In it, s/he wrote a tale of toil that blows apart the path to glory that entrepreneurial culture is supposed to be about, and it generated an endless stream of email tales of toil to the site, saying, yeah, me too, you don't know how miserable *my* job is.[29]

> The computer industry eats people, consumes them whole... While corpulent, sickly white prepublic CEOs masturbate over their vested stocks, their Dockers-and-button-down-clad minions push and push and push the people who do the actual work until stomachs writhe in the acid and sleep disappears and skin goes bad and teeth ache...
>
> People who work eight hours a day then go home to families and lives are derided as not being "team players." People who throw themselves into criminally unreasonable lumber-mill schedules (part buzzsaw, part logjam) are rewarded with more work. People who point all this out are threatened with the loss of their jobs and labeled attitude problems.

Which reminds me of a friend, with a 4.0 average and joint degree in technology design and English, who had extensive experience running the Macintosh labs at her college. After the startup she went to work for tanked and bounced the payroll checks for its employees' last two weeks, it took her a year to find another full-time job. She quit one of the contracting jobs she was able to find in that scary time period, for being forced to do the work on a per-job and not per-hour basis; with the overtime demanded of her, she ended up earning almost nothing. It's not that she's inexperienced in costing out her time; it's that exploitation of the most nineteenth-century type runs all over

29 "Tales of Toil" was first coined to describe first-person anonymous accounts of jobs that suck in Processed World, the playful, groundbreaking, anarcho-situationist zine that started in San Francisco back in the early eighties, as the first ongoing critique of the culture of data-processing. POP would have likely found a place for his/her rant there, had the magazine still been around.

high tech culture. As Jonathan E., columnist for *Microtimes* — a formerly reputable, long-standing, advertising-rich, free micro-computer tabloid available at fine kiosks all over the Bay Area, bought by an outside media conglomerate and now turned into a purely bits-and-bytes, speeds-and feeds product shopper — said in the March 25, 1998, issue,

> How else to explain the huge number of internships and unpaid jobs at some of the industry's better known names while their executives pull down fat numbers for themselves? How else to explain the near ubiquitous short-term contract positions in blatant defiance of the intent of state labor laws and any fundamental sense of fairness? How else to explain the incredibly high number of responses to any halfway decent job opening?

What Jonathan is talking about sounds like a description of what it's like to labor in the traditional glamour fields of film, music, and publishing businesses, where long years of low pay and reliance on the intercessions of luck are occupational hazards. But high tech is not supposed to be like these old-school, insubstantial, faddish industries. It is supposed to be creating actual value, real wealth, and awesome upside income potential for anyone who signs on. But increasingly, the reward comes from being at the right venture that the right VC firm has smiled on — grace, not works.

But to continue with POP: "Human costs aren't considered, families don't exist, there is no Outside… 'Tell them they have to work weekends,' the boss says to his winged monkey. 'Tell them that they are not working hard enough.'"

Wired documented the glorious prizes that could come your way if you went the workaholic/geekoid way. What you almost never heard talked about anywhere, or read about anywhere, was what price you might pay to get those prizes. Or that in spite of trashing yourself and your life in the approved way, you still might not be able to claim any of these prizes. Richard Howard, in "How I escaped from amazon.com" in the July 17, 1998, issue of the *Seattle Weekly*, wrote about his McJob travails at the largest online bookstore and perhaps the most widely known e-commerce site:

> If you are an idealistic college grad with one of those ubiquitous liberal-arts degrees and a dream of moving up the ladder in a hot, technology-based Seattle startup, the price you pay in this case is an entry-level job worthy of the Electronic Sweatshop Seal of Approval... made marginally palatable by the constantly whispered mantra of "stock options."... Reduced to taking a $10 an hour job in this, one of the "hottest" regional economies in the nation...with no health-insurance benefits or sick leave, [this] was viable only as long as nothing went wrong... You're hard-pressed to pay your share of rent on such a wage, much less even to entertain the requisite fantasy of sport-utility vehicle with cell phone... To find yourself *competing* for [such] a job that demands as much of your loyalty, commitment, and zeal as Amazon.com does, and which then pays you back with a poverty-line wage — *that* signals the real issue:
>
> American workers' lack of leverage in the face of globalizing labor markets, deregulation, merger mania, and a stock-market-driven impulse to maximize short-term corporate profits at all costs... The company's '97 sales figures show...a ninefold increase over the previous year to somewhere in the $150 million neighborhood...
>
> "But what about those stock options?"...A new employee has the option to purchase "up to 100" shares of common stock over a five-year period for the price it held on the day you were made a permanent employee... Amazon.com CEO Jeff Bezos... has become a multibillionaire due to a recent turn-up in the company's stock prices (he holds a modest 19.8 million shares).
>
> A paltry 100 shares certainly *won't* make any of his overworked customer service minions wealthy. Even those fortunate few

> who got in on the ground floor and have seen their holdings, say, quintuple in value since Amazon's IPO are tallying profits in the neighborhood of perhaps $10,000–$12,000 thus far — a welcome payback for all those underpaid hours...but hardly the stuff of Microsoft-millionaire fables .
>
> ...There's a more pervasive issue here — of which Amazon.com is more symptom than cause. I recognized it...when pondering how a company that enjoys the backing of Silicon Valley's premier venture capital firm, Kleiner Perkins Caulfield & Byers, and touts itself as the harbinger of the "next big thing" — serious online profiteering other than pornography — can get away with paying the bulk of its employees essentially unlivable wages in trendsetting Seattle. I mean, aren't the local and national media constantly sounding the drumbeat about the overheated economy...how there's a dearth of qualified workers, how it's a job seeker's market, how businesses (particularly technology-related ones) are forced to engage in bidding wars...for scarce labor resources?

It's precisely these sorts of problems arising in the grubby, uninspired, rooted-in-the-nasty old-hat real world offline that show up the bugs in the system of the New Information Economy. And these bugs are precisely those that would be brushed off as inessential details in the cosmology *Wired* was attempting to both construct and document. Even more irritating, they are bugs that Wired Venture employees and key business partners (yes, even I was offered a bit of this deal) got to know too well, when two failed Wired Ventures IPOs meant that the stock options that people had been offered in lieu of decent compensation became pretty much worthless except as nostalgia items.

WE ARE FAMILY

Probably without intending to, POP's "Dining with Cannibals" inadvertently reveals the subtle antiwoman bias in high tech, which tends to make women technologists leave the field at twice the rate men do. For like it or don't, whether it's nature or nurture, women tend to get stuck with more of the domestic management of a household. Caring for and about children runs right into the demands of a 70-to-80 hour workweek, and tends to feed the suspicion that such weeks are not necessarily worth having. Yet on paper, in theory, it would appear that in the telecommuting, free-agenting roaring digital '90s, women could work well at home, programming at odd hours between tending to toddler upchuck and carpooling daughters to aikido practice. But it doesn't happen this way, at least not very much — or can't, in a runrunrun business culture where you are either too busy or have no work at all.

Especially with family and women's issues, San Jose Seate University's English-Lueck's "Tactical Ambiguity in a Post-Modern Company Town: The Case of Silicon Valley," a paper presented at the American Anthropological Association meetings in Atlanta, Georgia, in December 1994, points up the difference between high tech's self-representation ("the widespread belief that microelectronics is," as historian of technology Langdon Winner wrote in his 1992 "Silicon Valley Mystery House" paper, "an inherently human, democratizing force in contemporary life") and the reality (as English-Lueck says, "even though it is not particularly borne out empirically at any level").

> Companies portray themselves as the champions of family rights, yet the overriding concern of work productivity combined with the lack of job security threatens...the family... Family values discourse and corporate policy foster a very narrow vision of family — father as breadwinner, mother in the informal economy at most, and children happily on their

> computers or at school... Upper echelon men, whose psyches have been reshaped to fit the 'Silicon Syndrome' of work (and with 60-plus percent divorce rates)...find it difficult to cope with...exposure to family life."[30]

The reality is that, as reported in the 1990 US Census, 24 percent of Santa Clara households were single-parent households, and 64 percent of women were in the workforce. Yet women in high tech work almost anywhere other than in R&D or in decisionmaking roles, where, in the flexible (read: downsizable at any moment) New Economy, rehiring is most likely to happen. According to English-Lueck, only one Silicon Valley company, Silicon Graphics, was cited by *Working Mother* magazine as a good company for working mothers (women in upper management, support of childcare, generally family-friendly benefits). You have to wonder how long that will last, given the company's very fading fortunes as of the winter of 2000. But let's hear more about the company town that is Silicon Valley: "Uncertainty [in the sense of the anarchic qualities human lives actually have] that characterizes the contemporary family is viewed as the enemy, not something to be fostered. That style of rhetoric undoes support for the families that exist in life, not rhetoric. Extended or intensive families that may be part of immigrant cultural traditions are not acknowledged."

And from the SJSU EFR: "Families and family life were defined amorphously... How work at home would become part of — or remain distinct from — family life was not addressed. Ironically, in our industry-based informants' worst case scenarios, people would be working somewhat less and would have more time with their families."

Okay, that's the untidy messiness of those goshdurned emotional family ties. But might it all be worth it for the Little

30 "Silicon Syndrome" is taken from the eponymous book by Jean Hollands (Bantam, 1985; subtitled How to Survive a High Tech Relationship), which describes the total-overtime, work-above-all ethic of Silicon Valley.

Woman and Junior and Princess if, through the short-term pain, there is long-term gain? Giving a smack upside the head to the notion that hard Horatio Alger work will get rewarded, and smile handshake slap on the back, it will all have been worth it, POP tells us instead that

> for the people who make it through the entire vesting period, the shares almost never add up to anything significant: yes, yours for just the cost of four years of your life-friends, sex, contentment, peace, and an apartment free of that sickly smell it gets when you haven't been there for a long time — a new car!
>
> ...The equivalent of, what? A 10 percent raise? At the cost of a stomach lining? A decent night's sleep?... A life?
>
> Never before in history have nerds, as a class, become economically viable. It was never worthwhile to exploit astronomers... And they overfocus anyway! Convince them that The Product is somehow important to their lives, more important than their lives... And Bang! Coding machines! Machines being the operative word.

POP's lament is similar in tone to an exchange between a programmer data-beast and venture capitalist (VC) that appeared in installment 10 of "The VC," a comic strip (www.thevc.com), clearly written by insiders. There, the VC inquires, "How were the holidays at my favorite portfolio company?", to which the programming-machine replies, "We coded every night until 3 A.M." The conversation continues in this vein:

"And New Year's Eve in Aspen was a riot!"

"We debugged 'til midnight, then fell asleep watching the ball drop on TV." "Then unwound for a couple days in Palm Springs."

"Really? I was thinking of heading to the desert this weekend."

"Ahem..."

"I mean, if we get all the docs written."

"Now's probably a good time to tell you about the revised product schedule."

POP would understand.

English-Lueck talks about how in the mining company towns of Arizona, "the values of administrators come to be supported by residents, their conformity and compliance determine their 'goodness' as residents and workers... [Similarly, Silicon Valley] company elite manipulated the concept of worker 'loyalty' to reinforce their hold over worker time, family life, even identity formation."

POP connected the dots: "It's sick and it's immoral. A friend of mine was beeped to work — he had to carry a beeper — on a weekend, on his wife's birthday, and he didn't return home until 2 A.M. The video-game he was working on had a bug. The video-game. The manager who called him in probably got a raise."

Even in and of itself, the place of "home" is rather nervous-making in Silicon Valley, for in the composite EFR findings,

> homes were viewed with great ambivalence...[and] were presented as poorly defined, residual places. After people leave work and school, they must be somewhere, and that place is home... Indeed, skepticism about the educational system was only exceeded by suspicion of the capacity of families and communities to produce workers...of tomorrow .
>
> ...Homes were presented as "platforms" for various media... [and] were viewed with great ambivalence, particularly by industry informants... Many interviewers argued that a threshold of non-commercial use was necessary to lower the telecommunications costs to commercial users. Isolated homes were vaguely sinister...[and are those] that [have] failed to purchase the products and services that underlie being part of the electronic community .

> ...The implication for the home is clear. Although it is a refuge, it is one that will increasingly be like the workplace. Indeed, the home was often presented as just another workplace, along with a cubicle provided by an employer and the use of dedicated telecommuting stations .
>
> ...The electronic community of Smart Valley manifests itself as a commercial venture delivering services to individuals and employers (seldom to families)... Community is an external object... It can be engineered to integrate it with electronic technologies, but people are not the focus.

VEAL PENS

So homes, who needs them, except as satellite offices? The demographic sector whose situation POP was describing (those in their twenties and thirties, who aren't necessarily much into nesting anyway) is part of the culture of what in South Park/Multimedia Gulch are sardonically called veal-fattening pens: places where the young are kept immobilized indoors to be sacrificed for greater economic productivity. And ooh, they have such tender white flesh because they don't get out at all! The evil astral twin to the veal pens is the rampant age-discrimination in high tech.

In the material world, as folks age in high tech, if they have gone (or been forced to go) from company to company, they very likely may have no pension plans. One-third of the labor force in high tech is contract/temporary: The culture of free-agentry, so celebrated by *Fast Company* and Scott Adams, the creator of "Dilbert," the nerd's Snoopy Dog, is scary if you have a mortgage or a child with ongoing health problems.

It's another of those raver/gilder epistemological quandaries: If you don't choose to believe or see that something is there, maybe you can act as if it doesn't exist. A little after the Conventional Wisdom had it that there were two unfilled job openings for every available technical worker (fault the education system; open the immigration golden doors; ignore the fact that those same immigrants consider the education they can receive in the United States better than what they can get at home), there began to be disquieting outing of the long-not-talked-about-publicly age-discrimination: Maybe there *were* enough technologically trained folks — only they were age forty and older and nobody wanted them.

The Information Technology Association of America claims that 80 percent of programmers are under age forty-four. The Institute for Electrical and Electronics Engineers (IEEE),[31] hardly a radical labor union, hardly a Luddite antiprogress organization, says that median pay for its members *fell* 2 percent in the past decade. Shankar Lakhavni, who heads the IEEE's workforce committee, said in a February 24, 1998, story in the *San Francisco Chronicle,* "There is no overall programmer shortage, just spot demand in newer technologies." What's even more cuckoo is that when IEEE takes a modest, *wait a minute, let's consider the consequences long-term of raising skilled-worker immigration caps,* its members complain in vigorous antigovernment terms about how bars to immigration are interfering with the growth of industry and progress.

Meanwhile, back at the ranch, our heroic high tech CEOs are lobbying like crazy to increase the cap on H-1B visas, which permit immigrants to enter the country and work for six years. The great thing about this is that H-1B workers typically earn less than native-born engineers. What's more, they are rather like indentured servants: they can't move on to other jobs or complain about working conditions, because their visas are tied to the employers who obtained them for them. H-1Bs are a great

31 The IEEE is something like the geeks' American Medical Association. You have to have a CS or EE degree from an accredited four-year institution to belong this organization of several hundred thousand members.

way for startups to get employees who can be intimidated into working however long or hard as their execs demand. There's also the tacit threat (or advantage, depending on whether you're siding with management or labor) with H-1B hires that they can be sent back when whatever skill they had is no longer in demand. Just as intriguing, if high tech workers come in on shorter-term B-1 visas, they can be brought over to the United States to be trained at their sponsor companies — and then sent back to a country where the sponsoring corporation can open a much cheaper operation (probably one not burdened by health, safety, environmental regulations, or pesky taxes), staffed with their trained-in-the-USA employees. Oops, there goes the neighborhood. Yeah, yeah, this is the trend in global capital anyway, so what's the big deal?

There are other aspects to the demand for H-1B Gastarbeiter: The immigrants who have powered through Bangalore Tech (IIT in reality) or Taipei State (NTU in reality) or Jerusalem U (Technion in reality) and then made it over here (either recruited right away or after putting in some time in a US graduate school) probably had a kind of scoring-top-of-the-class desperation that would make them so *happy* to be here, and so unquestioning of whatever high tech companies are shoveling, that they are ideally docile workers. Their experience of government in their homelands may have been of far more corruption, brutality, and inefficacy than what is commonly experienced in the United States — but that hometown experience would fit quite nicely with the libertarianism encountered in Silicon Valley. They *know* for a fact how yucky government can be.

What's more, immigrant engineers may have cultural and educational traditions that are much more conservative and much less questioning of authority than those of the native born — perhaps the equivalent of the desirability of the supposedly more biddable mail-order Asian brides. "Technocoolies" is the term English-Lueck found in common parlance to describe the hard-working, make-no-waves, Fresh Off the Boat (FOB) Chinese engineers. Mo bettah than the older American guys, who perhaps might be compared to older divorcees/first wives who find themselves with little value on the marriage market.

Cast-off older tech workers, who had they chosen another career path would be in the prime of their earning years and considered seasoned and valued professionals, finally began to be the subject of news stories in the mainstream media in 1997 and 1998 and 1999, though their plight, much like that of the victims of female circumcision, had been known about, if ignored by preference or mild distaste, for years (if we don't look at the problem, it's not a problem). A "Wired News" (Wired Ventures' online news service, which has alliances with more conventional news outlets such as Reuters) story on February 25, 1998, detailed case after case of computer oldsters with fine academic and industry credentials, many of whom had kept their skills perfectly current, who would get one response to 250 resumés sent out, or be grateful to get the opportunity to manage a Radio Shack.

Some of the problem lies in the way high tech recruiting now works: Resumé-scanning programs don't have the intelligence (because, after all, they are simply tools of dumb machines and can't make independent judgments about novel situations) to see that a candidate whose resumé lacks certain key words denoting certain absolutely specific up-to-the-moment skills might be able to do the job just fine, because the breadth and depth of experience would indicate a compatible skillset. It would be as if you were looking for an employee who could build bridges in Italy, and your resumé-scanning program couldn't see that someone who had experience overseeing major construction sites in Switzerland (where Italian is one of the four official languages, and Italy forms one of its borders) might be a plausible, non-absurd candidate. Similarly, high tech recruiters themselves may not understand the technology well enough to be able to make such leaps. All they may know is the set of buzzwords on their requisition lists (C++, Perl, SQL) and may not realize that someone with slightly different kinds of object-oriented or relational database experience might be amply qualified.

The age factor may intervene in other ways, in that people who are older, who have been around high tech awhile, may be less likely to get caught up in this year's technology craze, since they probably saw it come around, though maybe in a slightly different form, five or ten years ago. For example, client-server is a technology that started coming into vogue at the beginning of the 1990s; but really, it was just a newer version of timesharing with smart terminals that I learned on ten years before that. And now it too is passing into history, being replaced in the Information Technology (IT) jargonosphere with "N-tier computing."

So having already seen attempts at solutions to technology's hard problems, older programmers might have a kind of halt/wait/have-you-considered-these-sorts-of-problems-that-might-crop-up world-weariness that doesn't sit well with today's impatient, impetuous high tech world. Much as teenagers feel that they have discovered sex for the first time in the history of the universe and of course are doing it better than anyone else possibly could have before them, so it is with high tech. It may not be that older programmers are less capable of thinking out of the box but that they have better built-in bullshit detectors. Or maybe they have justifiably less enthusiasm for a work life of Brownian motion, bopping frantically but aimlessly from startup to startup.

More from the EFR reports:

> Skills were conceptualized as luggage that could easily be carried from employer to employer, and workers become more like entrepreneurs who have little long-term attachment to employers. In order to compete successfully they must be highly skilled, even though the specific skills required are vague. In general the prized skills are expected to be communicative and

> social in nature. It is not clear, however, whether the increase in required skills refers to greater mastery of specific skills or an expansion in the breadth of skills required. Nor is it clear whether the driving forces are technological change, the characteristics of jobs in changing industries, or loosened ties between employee and employer. The latter suggest that any worker can increase his or her chances of being employed by mastering more skills, although few of those skills might be used (and paid for) on any of the many jobs the person ever holds.

Which made me think of a childhood friend, a guy who all on his own made the transition from clerk at a museum bookstore to word-processing temp to database-programmer/sys admin, acquiring the technical skills he needed on his own time — and who went to school at night to earn his bachelor's degree. Attracted by the vision of the Good Life in the Bay Area, he took his severance package from being downsized from the corporate MIS department where he had worked well and loyally for years on micro-to-mainframe installations and moved out to San Francisco.

But here on the West Coast, his years of experience were for naught: The next wave of technology (local area networking; client-server) had already taken hold. The problem for him was that you *can't* learn about networking on your own: Think about it. A network consists of the links between multiple computers. So you can't install a network in your studio apartment unless you decide you don't need a place to sit down and eat your soup, or unless you go absurdly into debt to buy multiple computers and networking gear (I promise you, you do not want a router in your pied a terre) so they can be linked across the distance of a bridge table. What's more, when you are unemployed, the prospect of what might seem a plausible alternative escape route, that of spending thousands of dollars to take a class where you can get officially network-certified seems iffy, since corporations may hold such certificates in less esteem than actual work experience.

So my friend, the ideal self-starting autodidact skills-improving employee, spent a year trying to find a job. He did get one, eventually. No. Scratch that. He didn't get a job; he got a gig as an independent contractor with no benefits and no job security past the three months of the contract terms, but not before he racked up tens of thousands of dollars of debt by living off his credit cards. He was in his mid-thirties when he made this scary, barely-getting-by job transition, and he had no dependents. He also didn't have major health problems — or none that he couldn't put off tending to until he could afford to buy insurance. What of other mortals less lucky? The EFR testimonials offer this response:

> Mirroring international rights discourse, the rhetoric of prosperity intimately linked with the phrases "flexibility" and a "free market" are portrayed as the avenue to security... Companies need to be flexible (able to downsize) if they are to remain competitive and herald in new eras of prosperity. The problem is that workers have forgotten to be "loyal." By placing the burden of security on the worker — suggesting that good, loyal, and obedient workers, even if laid off, will survive — the powerless are then left with the moral guardianship of a right they cannot realistically affect.

High tech is sure as heck beginning to look like advertising, a comparison most technolibertarians would find odious. Advertising is famous for wanting kids fresh out of school (they know the newest trends) and winnowing people out by their forties. If you haven't made it to the top by then, you're something of a loser — or at least are perceived to be such — and will become increasingly unemployable. As Chris Brenner of Working Partnerships, a non-profit associated with the South Bay Labor Council of San Jose, said in a March 9, 1998, issue of the *San Francisco Chronicle*, "If they [programmers] don't make a fortune in their first 10 or 15 years, where do they go?"

It's telling that a field that is seen to be so much the opposite of high tech (about image and aesthetics, the subjective and elusive. About vagaries in fashion. About the quintessential intermediating no-obvious-value-created middleman) tracks the high tech trajectory. But maybe it isn't so strange, as feature-creep and Moore's Law and companies created not because a programmer had a smart idea that s/he is passionate about but because a Suit or a VC saw a nano-market-niche that might be exploitable are indeed making high tech *seem* like an industry that creates consumer demand rather than serves it. Just like advertising.

Who becomes obsolete more quickly, and hence is more disposable, than the programmer who has precisely today's skills? It's a bit like being a model — who wants you after you are this year's girl? And if you didn't make it to the financial security of supermodel status, which meant you could sock enough away for when you got past your realistic earning lifetime (say, age thirty) — well ain't it awful, Mabel.

So *Wired* really did have it right. A magazine about tech culture should be packaged as a magazine about ephebe culture — or for those who think or want to be like the golden youth of our new Athens. And Condé Nast, already owning titles such as *Vanity Fair* and *Vogue*, which sell youth and beauty and glamour, was right to buy it. Eternal youth culture has always been the best way to move units.

Only the superficial think style doesn't matter. *Wired* created style and, in doing so, set the pace for politics and religion among the geek class. It doesn't get any more important than that. And I'll remain one of the many whose heart was broken by the promise of *Wired*.

CHAPTER FOUR

CYBERGENEROUS

ONE DULCET SPRING AFTERNOON in the late 1980s, I was out for a drive on a first date with a guy much enmeshed in Silicon Valley (house: one of those scarily overpriced-by-the-standards-of-the-rest-of-the-world bungalows in Palo Alto; friends: folks who had really made it big there *then*). As people do when they are trying to display who they are and where they came from to a potential Love Thing, I talked to him about what it was like to have lived in Manhattan before the stock market crash of 1987 and how one day, at rush hour, I saw a young black man, looking clearly country and not at all like a hardened urban dweller, sitting in front of the McGraw-Hill building, with a sign that read, "I need money to go home to North Carolina to get some food." I was telling Mr. Possible about the midtown beggar because he represented to me how hard and how heartless life had been during the years of my captivity in New York. Yet all the sleek accomplished male who was driving us both in a BMW along Skyline Boulevard had to say was "A long way to go for groceries, don't you think?" I was stunned; this from a guy who'd been a scholarship boy himself, who'd traveled all over the world in rough and not cruise-line conditions. His reaction was my first encounter with the strange lack of philos in high tech.

What I couldn't have known then is that nothing much would come along to change my picture of high tech's curious nyah-nyah-nyah-I've-got-mine-so-screw-you orientation to the world. An article written in the early 1990s for an industry publication, *Upside* ("Silicon Valley Scrooges," December 1992), decrying the lack of philanthropy in high tech, suggesting the reasons why, and offering vague intimations that maybe things now might finally be getting better, reads eerily like an article written much later in the decade ("The Wealth and Avarice of the Cyberrich," January 7, 1997) for the mainstream publication *Newsweek*. The *no thank you, not for me, I didn't give at the office* attitude toward charity appears to be deeply embedded in the Californian Ideology[32] present from the beginning (with the exception that proves the rule being Hewlett and Packard and the companies and foundations they built).

It's no surprise that the old-line, East Coast high tech firms IBM and AT&T are notable exceptions to the general lack of fellow feeling, or giving back, that characterizes the rest of (mostly West Coast) high tech. According to the 1997 *Yearbook of Facts and Figures on Private, Corporate, and Community Foundations*, published by the Foundation Center, in 1995 the AT&T Foundation topped the list of the fifty largest corporate foundations, as measured by volume of grants. Of the fifty largest foundations overall, only Hewlett and Packard's and AT&T's showed up to represent the world of digital technology. To indulge in a few more lies, damned lies, and statistics, in terms of per-capita income and housing costs, this wealthiest area in the country had as its community foundation one that did not make it into the top twenty-five in the US until 1998, whether defined by grants or asset size.

Personal wealth in Silicon Valley grew by $100 billion from 1991 to 1998 — but the attendant regional United Way annual goal remains at $25 million. The percentage of corporate philanthropy

---

32 Californian Ideology is a term Richard Barbrook, founding member of the Hypermedia Research Team at the University of Westminster, London, coined to describe the bizarre fusion of the cultural bohemianism of San Francisco with the high tech industries of Silicon Valley. It promiscuously combines the free-wheeling spirit of the hippies and the entrepreneurial zeal of the yuppies."

as measured in profits before taxes *dropped* from 1.14 percent in 1993 to 0.92 percent in 1997 — while the high tech industry has roared on, to quote Louis Rossetto in the first issue of *Wired*, like a Bengali typhoon.

A study released in September 1998 by the Community Foundation of Silicon Valley, as part of its Giving Back Initiative (funded by the David and Lucille Packard Foundation), relied on a survey of high-net-worth households and of the general population in Silicon Valley.[33] Although the average percentage of annual charitable giving in Silicon Valley (2 percent of annual income) is similar to the national one, and the percentages of those giving in each income bracket are somewhat above national averages (83 percent of households versus the national average of 69 percent), one-third of Silicon Valley households earning $100,00 or more give $1,000 or less to charity, and 45 percent of the wealthiest households give $2,000 or less to charity. Only 14 percent of Silicon Valley's wealthiest households say that it is even somewhat important "to be a lead investor, helping attract others" to philanthropic opportunities.

Although there is some evidence for greater professionalization of corporate philanthropy in high tech (increases in corporate volunteer programs, increases in local philanthropy), consider that per-capita income in San Jose is $42,000, about double the US average, the highest in the country. According to the American Electronics Association (a Silicon Valley–based trade organization), in 1998, the average salary at high tech companies was $49,586, contrasted with an average $28,582 in other industries. But local charities do not receive twice the US average in donations. One in nine — approximately 65,000 Santa Clara County residents — were worth more than $1 million, and

33 "'Silicon Valley is defined as Santa Clara County (San Jose north to Palo Alto), north through San Mateo County as far as San Mateo itself, the section of the lower East Bay that's in Alameda County (Fremont, Newark), and over the coastal range to Santa Cruz County.

there were at least thirteen billionaires in the Valley, who had a combined worth of more than $45 billion. By February 2000, it's been said that the Valley was generating sixty-four new millionaires per day.

There may very well be a touch of something geographic that predisposes Northern California high tech to act this way: Peter Dobkin Hall, senior research scholar and director of a program on nonprofit organizations at Yale Divinity School, studies philanthropy and says that nonprofits actually didn't have that large a presence in community life outside of the Northeast until after World War II, and that the farther south and west you travel in the United States, the more dominant *public* institutions become. Still, in this era of instant communications and bicoastal lives, this shouldn't be an excuse.

Geographic factors may come into play, even if at a microeconomic level. Most of the Great Wealth in Northern California high tech has emanated from the suburban peninsula south of San Francisco (with all the insulation and monotony suburbs imply), and its very suburbanness may have something to do with the problem. In cities, social problems and glorious institutions and art-making are all in your face, on the street for all to see. Suburbs are famous for keeping things calm, for cutting people off from one another, for gating communities, for ensuring tranquillity and uniformity. It will be interesting to see if the Net-based businesses of San Francisco, which generated $2.2 billion in 1997, will differ because their wealth is rooted in the city, not in the suburbs. Though by the winter of 2000, the main effect of new wealth arriving in San Francisco has been the evaporation of the middle class.

CIRCUMSTANTIAL EVIDENCE

When I wrote a profile for *Wired* of Paul Allen, the other billionaire cofounder of Microsoft, one of the instances of true censorship I experienced in my writing career at the magazine came when I wrote about Allen's then-pathetic record of philanthropy. At the time, in 1994, his record was so marginal (kept hidden?) that I had to write to the state of Washington's secretary of state to dig up what little Allen's foundations had actually done. Aside from a meaningful chunk to the University of Washington (where his father had worked as a librarian), a gift to the Oregon Shakespeare Festival in Ashland (a donation sizable to you and me, but nanometer-size for someone with Allen's assets), and a guaranteed loan to an iffy Seattle urban-renewal project, the foundations were either inactive or doling out modest amounts (in the $5,000 to $10,000 range) to local charities. When editor/founder/publisher Louis Rossetto came across the section of my article describing these minimal efforts, he slashed it out with the comment, "Who are we to say what he ought to do with his money?" It's the technolibertarian way to celebrate wealth, no matter how randomly or questionably it's acquired (in Allen's case, his wealth comes from having had the winning-the-lottery-of-all-50-states-combined good fortune of being Spin-and-Marty 50s Disney TV early-adolescent best friends with Bill Gates since about the time they both hit puberty), but not to question its use — -except if it's the durned government that's got it.

It's hard to quantify how many people worth $100 million or more are in the Valley. There are enough of them that no one knows any easy way to track them — not to mention those worth only between $10 and $100 million, much less those worth only a few million. But in any case, no one has stepped forward, as Dave Packard did, to take on the role of Resident Great Philanthropist. There is some personal generosity (either anonymous or known only to a small circle of friends) that does exist among the good guys of high tech (and there are many). Still, personal generosity is different from philanthropic giving. Smoothing the path of friends and relatives is a noble act; but philanthropy implies going outside what might be called kinship circles, extending generosity beyond those whom you immediately care about and with whom there exists the potential of reciprocity. It's a noble act of a different order, the difference between the altruism of the selfish gene — that is, the notion in sociobiology that you'll sacrifice for a sibling or an offspring, acting in enlightened genetic self-interest because they carry some of your genes — and altruism for the hell (and pleasure) of it.

Jim Mitchell, longtime business columnist for the *San Jose Mercury News* (Silicon Valley's hometown newspaper), who has rightfully complained publicly for years about the "Philanthropy-NOT" social practices of high tech, says that "anonymous benefactors are not common, according to Silicon Valley charities." Or as Susan Miller, director of the New Langton Arts gallery in San Francisco put it in one of a series of articles in the December 9, 1997, *San Francisco Chronicle* on the state of the arts as the National Endowment for the Arts falls into decline, "We're waiting to see if Silicon Valley will ever come forward, because up to now, they have been pretty stingy." This sentiment is echoed by nonprofits all over the Bay Area.

The Giving Back Initiative survey reveals a very counterintuitive pattern: 21 percent of the households making less than $40,000 annually give 5 percent of their income or more — compared to 8 percent of those who make above $40,000. Those living in Silicon Valley not making money in high tech — or at least not very much — give far, far more, proportionately, than their neighbors who do. This says as much about culture as it does about class.

Yet high tech's putative stinginess doesn't mean that all of its wealth remains out of circulation. Many wealthy guys may give angel money to startups as yet too small or too risky to warrant venture capital attention (as with Broadway shows, angels are private, as opposed to institutional, investors). Angels placing seed money (small amounts of money to get a venture going) are a beneficent part of the high tech landscape. These private investments may very well play out as acts of philanthropy if the ventures they subsidize end up doing nothing other than providing employment for a few guys for a few years until their efforts come to naught. Nonetheless, seed/angel money is intended as an investment, not an act of charity. It's the Silicon Valley way to think foremost about the upside of all transactions.

When I have talked to folks newly enriched by high tech, some of them confess they don't understand how to do philanthropy (hint: the point at a charity auction is not to get the best deal but to give away your money). According to Peter Hero, executive director of the Community Foundation of Silicon Valley, "I don't want to look stupid" is a rationale he hears often for why people don't give. Which is an interesting statement in its own right. Look stupid to whom? In what respects? There's a strange social-shaming at work here. If, as the theory goes, you are smart enough to make money in the New Economy, in which respects do you worry you might be maladroit? In social skills? Empathy? Not being able to think outside the box to bring innovation to philanthropy? Not figuring out how to acquire the expertise of those who could provide counsel? Will the slackers and poseurs and layabouts and crackwhores whom you thought you were helping use your gifts of cash to come mock you at your workplace? Will a philanthropic gift that has only equivocal or only moderately successful results make you look worse than majorly mismanaging a company, announcing products that are never delivered or don't work, or flaming out spectacularly in a startup that runs through all its funding without shipping a thing?

These confessions of intellectual inadequacy are odd for people who seem to be able to do stuff like make their way through Stanford engineering or business school, acquire and/or flip founder's stock, and live the 24/7 professional-merging-with-personal life of the Valley.[34] So you have to hypothesize

34 24/7 is a term borrowed from the desired available uptime of computing resources (24 hours a day, seven days a week) and the demanded availability of

that it's a strain of geek myopia. Meaning, maybe this skillset, of understanding what philanthropy means, was neither handed out at birth nor developed at any time since then. But it's unlikely this deficiency is congenital, since geeks in other times and places haven't had quite these problems. Maybe what these modern geeks are saying indirectly is that there's nothing here to learn that's worth any of the metabolism of their precious complex carbohydrates.

People in high tech claim they don't have the time to sort out the claims being made on their parvenu noblesse oblige — and it is true, the higher up you go on the corporate ladder, the more vulnerable you are to all the centrifugal dynamism of global competition. So what's likely to happen at the corporate level is that the responsibility is fobbed off onto a public affairs drone, indicating that the issue is about as important as planning the annual Christmas party. If the corporation can get a photo-op out of a gesture and placed in the major media, great (hey, lookit our CFO with his arm around that cute kid-of-color next to a computer monitor!) — but what? Ongoing support? For *what*? Giving time and effort to charity is not going to give the impression that you're maintaining your place on the bleeding edge.

Still, there are some efforts afoot to meet this unmet need for high-tech-stinginess remediation: Citibank, for example, is now offering seminars for high-net-worth individuals in the Bay Area in how philanthropy can be part of an overall financial and tax strategy. The Community Foundation of Silicon Valley, following a model pioneered in Seattle, has created SV2 (Silicon Valley Social Venture Fund), where people in the Valley invest their money and attend quarterly meetings to brainstorm and figure out which programs seem to be working best. At least part of the function of SV2 is educational.

---

people who work to support them — and by extension, the workaholic people who work in the globally competitive computer industry.

A SAD STORY

Consider the story of Lightworks Technology Foundation. The charity was founded by a guy named Josef Woodman, one of Silicon Valley's own (well, not technically Silicon Valley, but Marin County, just over the Golden Gate Bridge from San Francisco). Woodman made his money (a teensy mini-fortunette by high tech standards: under $10 million) as the education director of Autodesk, the market leader in CAD.[35] With much to-do, Woodman debuted Lightworks at the 1996 Comdex, the largest annual microcomputer trade show in the world, which routinely pulls more than 200,000 vendors and resellers and press people to Las Vegas. According to its press release, the goal of Lightworks was to provide "an efficient tax-deductible means for corporations and individuals to set up endowments and provide technology-related grants." These were to be technology-based projects that addressed poverty initiatives for people and institutions, cultural programs "addressing cutting-edge technology applications": information access, Internet, and computer provisioning for schools, libraries, colleges, and low-income areas.

In the Lightworks press release, Woodman said, "This young industry, though well-intentioned, makes charitable contributions at less than one-half the business norm of 1 percent pre-tax-earnings. I have to think it's because we're all too busy. Lightworks was formed to do the footwork; participating companies and individuals will enjoy the limelight." Lightworks forecast a perpetual endowment of $200 million by 2003, so that the foundation could give away at least $10 million annually in funding technology grants.

Sorry to say, by May 1997 Woodman realized that no way, Jose, would Lightworks reach its goal of $2.5 million in gifts for the year — so the foundation shifted gears to become a provider

35 Computer-aided design: software that does stuff like help architects render buildings and floorplans or that helps engineers visualize dams or machine parts.

of technical expertise for pilot projects in the nonprofit sector. High tech is so much more inclined toward offering expertise (propagandizing new converts) than coughing up cash.

In the May 2, 1997, issue of *Philanthropy Journal*, Woodman delicately stated the problem: "I was naive about how slow and jaded the giving environment in Silicon Valley is." Not to pick on Woodman or his failed attempt to do good, but you have to wonder what really went on in his attempts to get money out of the business community where he made his bucks. "Slow" is an odd word choice to characterize a culture and economy that thinks in Web weeks (jargon for how business and technology fads change week to week on the World Wide Web — a Web week is a manageable unit of business time) and is seeking ever faster ways to move bits and make money. And "jaded" describes an equally unlikely state of mind for a culture that can hardly be said to have overdosed on acts of community spirit. What's more likely is Woodman ran into the lack of empathic imagination that characterizes much of high tech — but he was too much of a gentleman to say so.

Lightworks couldn't cut it, even with a new, non-entrenched-bureaucracy-type enterprise specifically set up to fund *technology* projects by someone well-acquainted with technology and the technology community — in which corporations and individuals could have all the control, efficiency, and inspection of the books they wanted. Lightworks offered the kind of middle-management-lite, low-friction way to do business that Silicon Valley *says* it admires in any enterprise — and the absence of which Silicon Valley *says* is part of the reason high tech finds traditional charitable organization contemptible. Yet even when Lightworks invoked all the safewords and conditions that should have pushed the pleasure buttons of people in high tech, Silicon Valley just hasn't wanted to put out.

An enterprise such as Lightworks should also have assuaged the fear of getting ripped off that is often expressed as a reason for not giving. The logic of this fear lies in the unconscious tendency toward scroogehood within libertarianism. If you do believe in a world pitting all against all, then fear of rip-off is warranted. If I am only out for myself, then I have to assume everyone else is, too. But you'd think in an economy where so much wealth is being generated, folks wouldn't be worried if there was a little shrinkage, as it is called in the retail environment. What is it these people have so little of *spiritually, psychologically,* that they leap to the assumption that if they give something up or away, they're being stolen from?

It's the same emotional-financial anorexia that lands people in high tech work tens of millions of dollars to do their shopping online only — at venues that charge neither for shipping nor sales tax. Just can't give an inch...

THE BELL CURVE

The most common rationalization you hear throughout Silicon Valley whenever its lack of philanthropic spirit is mentioned is that high tech money is new money. The way this tape gets replayed is that these folks who came from middle-class or even more modest backgrounds are not in the habit of having money to give away (never mind that people all across the socioeconomic spectrum do give, and often; it's the less well-off who give *more,* as measured in terms of percentage of income). It's an argument that creates the false impression of high tech as the refuge of people playing out the Horatio Alger myth of today — as if there were not many people in high tech who came from privileged backgrounds, of the upper-middle class or higher. Increasingly, high tech is a place where you *need* that CS degree from Stanford, that MBA from Wharton.

Contrast with the generation who went through the Great Depression: They shouldn't feel *secure* about the money they have made since, because it hasn't been around all their lives

— yet this group is not notorious for its lack of charity. Being newly wealthy doesn't necessarily make you feel uncomfortable doing anything philanthropic. And the "it's new money, stupid" excuse is not offered up to explain the behavior of other people who have newly made it to the top in other fields.

The "it's new money" stinginess explained more in terms of geek culture is that those who have been so heads-down with coding or consumed by the drive to make money haven't gotten around to thinking about what ought to be done with the money that they have made, aside from making more money. Geeks think more about creating cool stuff, and acquiring wealth as proof that the stuff was indeed cool, than about what they might want to do with the wealth once it's acquired.

A corollary to the "it's new money, stupid" apologia is that things will all change after this generation of technologists starts getting older and thinking about estate planning. This proposition declares that the Tech-Rich will give it all away later in life, when perhaps the competitive hormones have waned and the more meditative ones, concerned with legacies (in the traditional sense of what lives on after death, not in the computer sense of obsolete technology you are stuck using because it's too complicated / dangerous to replace it), have kicked in. Yet according to the Giving Back Initiative survey, only 48 percent of those surveyed plan to donate more to charity when they get older. Of the 74 percent who have engaged in estate planning, only 11 percent have named a charity in their will. Oh well. It's just more evidence that high tech is locked into a perpetual youth culture mind-set, even if that doesn't match the actual chronological age of many who work within it.

But who knows. As with Rockefeller and Ford, it's possible the offspring of those who have made The Big Money will set up major charitable foundations and take on the occupation called philanthropist. Maybe. Wouldn't it be pretty to think so.

The "it's new money, stupid" argument has some other

shortcomings, among them the fact that not all high tech money is *that* new. You can look at industry benchmarks such as Intel Corporation, which has been around for more than twenty-five years and dominates the market globally in its sector (microprocessors) almost as widely as Microsoft dominates in its sector. Intel's profile, and that of its multimillionaire founders, has been pretty subdued as far as philanthropy goes. True, a foundation (which hasn't done much yet) has been started from one of its cofounder's money — that of William Noyce — but the snide comment might be made that, yeah, that's only because he's dead. And although other companies that got their start in the high tech world of the 1970s and 1980s may not have turned out to be as world-straddling as Intel, they nonetheless generated enough wealth that something philanthropically interesting could have come from them.

Contrast with Digital Equipment Corporation (DEC), the Apple Computer of the 1970s and 1980s. A Massachusetts computer manufacturer that gave IBM a run for its money in the 1980s and created a new class of computer, the minicomputer, DEC was the underdog-made-good success story of its day. In 1990, during its tiptop earning years, DEC donated 30 percent of its pre-tax income (about $37 million) through its corporate-giving programs. DEC's money was certainly the New Money of its era — but it was being earned in a time and place that operated under a different set of values. Although DEC has since fallen on hard times and been absorbed into Compaq Computers, no business analyst or former employee would ever suggest that DEC's community-mindedness contributed to its downfall.

The difference between DEC and the exemplary Sun Microsystems (premier manufacturers of high-powered Unix workstations, machines used for power number-crunching and network-serving) couldn't be more pointed. Sun, which has been around for more than ten years, occupies a mindspace similar to that once occupied by DEC (well-respected underdog with special strengths in academic and scientific computing). Sun's CEO, Scott McNealy, said in that December 1992 issue of *Upside*, "It bugs me when a company gives away stockholders' money so the CEO can be seen at the ballet," followed by the equally oxen-hearted statement in that January 7, 1997, issue of *Newsweek*: "If you want to redistribute wealth...why don't you go out and earn it and give it away." Charmed, I'm sure. Still, sad to say, companies in Silicon Valley have a better record than *individuals*.

And even when a company is new, its executives may have money that is not. People who score move from company to company: the way to really score points in the game is to keep scoring with new companies. So the money is always new and always insecure. But economics is not all of life.

A parallel to the "it's new money, stupid" rationalization is that high tech has a large immigrant population, whose community values may be different from those in the United States. The explanation here is that giving may be extended within a specific immigrant community or church, or to the folks back home, and not to traditional American charities or in traditional American ways; that surplus income goes to support aged great-aunts back in Taipei or Bombay. A fine theory with much validity; yet American/new-homeland culture can exert *strong* shaping behavior when consensus-reality demands or entices. Immigrants to Silicon Valley seem to have no trouble enjoying American pop or mall culture, sending their kids to public schools or accompanying them to local theme parks such as Great America in Santa Clara, and generally acting like everyone else along the 280 corridor. If community standards were set such that philanthropy was just one more wacky Yankee custom to be adopted, whether embraced or grumbled about, these country-of-origin straw-man/woman arguments couldn't be evoked.

Peter Hero thinks the immigrant problem extends even to those who are native-born Americans: the people who come from all over the United States to work in the Valley have no connection with the communities or institutions here. If they think about giving at all, it will be to their hometown institutions, or maybe the alma mater that put them in their current happy circumstance. Forty percent of giving within Santa Clara County goes outside Santa Clara County.

ART NOT SCIENCE

There is some philanthropy that does go on in high tech; and sometimes it very much walks the "we'll do it *differently*" line that high tech says it wants to walk.

For example, the Entrepreneur's Foundation (EF) encourages startups to donate stock, which EF then reinvests in selected non-profits. This may be the *only* sort of giving that can work for Net startups: If they donate pre-IPO stock, it effectively costs them nothing. For they may never *make* a profit, and so never have cash to give; and once they go public, they become beholden to their stockholders, and community relations is obviously lower down in the list of priorities than earnings.

And if you are willing to give over your Web browser's default homepage to advertisements narrowcast to your interests based on the demographic information you've revealed, half of what these advertisers pay to for-profit Eyegive will be turned over to a charity you specify. My personal favorite is the Duffield Family Foundation, whose assets stem from the personal wealth of the founders of PeopleSoft, the giant of HR software. This foundation has committed $200 million to build no-kill animal shelters all over the United States, all because of the founders' dear departed miniature schnauzer, Maddie. Score one for imagination and doing things differently.

And even when high tech isn't doing things all that differently, all is not totally terrible as far as its philanthropic actions go. T. J. Rodgers, the infamous libertarian badboy CEO of Cypress Semiconductor, has egged on his company to be the winningest contributors to Second Harvest food bank and to Valley Medical Center (VMC), the local trauma center of last resort for those who can't pay to go to the Stanford emergency room. Choosing the food bank and VMC is all for the good; the decision to support these two charities was based on their efficacy at delivering the services they offer. Business discipline is a good thing. And, indeed, much of the philanthropic thinking in high tech is that it's important to reward the programs that work and not reward the charity bureaucracy — definitely a sensible businessperson's point of view.

But embedded in this fine act of charity lies one of those libertarian contradictions. Rodgers touts the competence of the docs who work at VMC, saying they *could* all be making much more big bucks elsewhere — but choose to, in a sense, donate their surplus wealth by working at VMC. But if the market is the best measure — aren't then the VMC staffers chumps because they choose to work for less at a less Glam institution? Or at least chumps by the terms of the Valley they are working for? True, large-minded technolibertarians believe in choice above all — so that if you choose to minimize your wealth and play Crusader Rabbit, that's your lookout. But in practice very few do make that choice or — more important, in terms of the Valley's libertarian culture, understand value that is not always, cannot always be, market-certified.

And the Valley's libertarian culture, which has little place in its Cartesian world for the intangible, runs smack into one of the Hard Problems of philanthropy: the lack of formal rigor in human services, whether in the problems themselves, the potential solutions to them, or the soft-hearted and frequently touchy-feely-verging-on-politically-correct institutions that have been set up to address them. Daniel Ben-Horin, director of Compumentor, a well-established San Francisco nonprofit that links up computer resources and training to nonprofits, would agree that many folks in the nonprofit world annoyingly don't have the competence and tough-mindedness of those in high tech, so high tech's intolerance with philanthropy becomes somewhat understandable. But many human dilemmas (whether it's creating more equitable healthcare and health-education delivery systems or supporting a local dance company) don't lend themselves to notions of efficacy, either because they can't be solved quickly or obviously, or because the end result isn't very measurable.

This also explains why the small grunt charities that do the un-sexy uninteresting day-to-day support, such as daycare for forty-year-old chronic schizophrenics, get so little attention from high tech. These are nonprofits that may have been supported in the past by government grants, many of which have since been cut; and their mission is to take care of those who do not represent problems to be solved. The only problem they present is the eternal one of human vulnerability, imperfection, and suffering — something high tech would always prefer to pretend doesn't exist.

This discomfort with squishy stuff and the intangible and that which can't be reduced to formulae or program may be a partial explanation of *why* what charity there is in high tech so seldom goes to art and flows instead to X numbers of neonatal isolation units, or Y numbers of turkey legs with stuffing handed out at Thanksgiving. Art is damned hard for everyone, even for experts, to quantify. Art so often has defied, and still continues to defy, the logic of the marketplace: That Mozart died a pauper and that the French Impressionists whose work now commands such ridiculous prices in the global marketplace were not the market leaders of their time is a counterintuitive throughline that exists to this day. Art has always depended on patronage (either personal or communal — the royal court or the high priesthood or the community's generalized support), but its areas of tangency with high tech are few. Art is precisely that human creation that lasts and lasts — a state of affairs totally at odds with technology's joy of obsolescence.

Since our techies honestly may not perceive the difference in aesthetic value between a Lichtenstein and some DIY (Do It Yourself) computer art exercise in primary-colored movie special-effects knockoffs, how could there be art worth subsidizing? How do you explain to folks who may not understand that there is value-added proposition to be derived in experiencing a painting in person (that is, in a museum) as opposed to on the Web?

And for some strange reason, although the math-music/computer-programmer-cum-MIDI-dilettante connection is well established,[36] visual art is famously resistant to penetration by the nerd heart. The ghastly art at raves (think cheesy '90s knockoffs of the art displayed at '60s rock-'n'-roll light shows), the abuse of Kai's Power Tools (think cheesy computer-generated visuals, with overuse of fractals[37] and a repetitive psychedelic palette) are mere examples. You might find a plasticine sculpture of a nubile woman riding a dolphin in a place of proud display in a nerd living room, or paintings that are a dyspeptic mix of the Goth, the computer-generated, and the tribal-global (of a vague ethnicity that's from everywhere and nowhere). One can observe a fashion sense that runs to the fake-medieval for dress-up, or to chunky crafts-fair leatherware (hats, belts) reminiscent of the Carter administration. There's the nervert proclivity for dressing as for scenes, especially as something Dark Shadowy in black leather. And I admit to making horrid value judgments as someone who has hung around museums a lot and has very conventional middle-brow taste (Cindy Sherman yes; Thomas Kinkade no).

Whereas Internet startup Pointcast CEO Dave Dorman has compared Silicon Valley to "Florence during the Renaissance,"

---

36 The mathematically minded understand the algorithms of music instinctively. The computer scientist who is the talented amateur musician. the musician who takes to digital forms of music making is a personality archetype that's been around as long as computing-even longer, if you consider the scientists of any breed who have deep affinities with the pattern-language of music.

37 Computer-generated images suggestive of ferns unfurling or paisleys morphing.

Simon Firth, a British writer and TV producer living in San Francisco, sees the Valley as

> a sprawling mess of unremarkable development that struggles to match the cultural interests and output of any typical affluent American suburb, let alone a major US city or global cultural center... Look in Palo Alto, Cupertino, or San Jose for examples of what has really endured from the Florentine Renaissance — buildings of architectural significance, commissioned public monuments of distinction, galleries of the finest contemporary and classical art... They're nowhere to be found... In the long-running fight between developers and preservationists...the developers aren't bothering to argue the architectural merits of the homes they want to build. (*Salon*, March 30, 1998)

It is an issue of culture, rather than of moral superiority: Unlike other educated professionals, who see good works and support of the arts as symbols of having arrived, or payback to the society that has treated them well, the average set of geeks, through their libertarian views, seems to be espousing a world where the only art would be whatever had withstood the test of the marketplace (Don Kingman museums? Leroy Nieman traveling exhibitions?).

If technolibertarian guru Esther Dyson honestly believes artists should always think in terms of licensing to support themselves, how can you explain to her that Disney creating *Lion King* lunch boxes cannot be compared to, say, demanding that Michael Ignatieff or Katha Pollit ghostwrite doggerel-on-demand to commemorate the bat mitzvah of a client's daughter in order to support their novel- and poetry-writing? Revenue models borrowed from the world of software (where support and custom enhancements can create a fine income stream) don't match up well with the world of fine art. I don't know whether it's more risible, absurd, or simply in bad taste to think it plausible for

Magnum photojournalist Susan Meiselas to license her work for printing on tote bags, or for novelist Denis Johnson to take excerpts from his brilliant, dark *Resuscitation of a Hanged Man* for use on a daily *Chicken Soup for the Soul* inspirational desktop calendar. Branding as a concept can't apply to all acts of creation, nor is software the model that all acts of creation should be patterned after. But a confusion between commercial and fine art is not that surprising in the context of the know-nothing philistinism of high tech. It's a skewed understanding of the way art worlds work.

This is not to say that artists historically have not sought patrons, and might, for example, paint portraits of their patrons, popes and fine ladies. At best this *was* their work and was, at the very worst, for most of them a very acceptable form of day job — just as a novelist today might write screenplays as a day job to subsidize her fiction. Classical composers were glad to have commissions — as would be an architect today. But the eons-long tradition of patrons and day jobs (whatever form those might take in any era) does not vitiate the demand creators make that they be fairly compensated for their original work, or that there be fair compensation for commercial duplication. The rise of digital technology makes reproduction of works of art easier but does not do away with the need for artists to be compensated so that they can keep producing. Giving away a photograph or a novel or a piece of music to promote brand recognition so you can make money from a line of greeting cards does not always make sense where art — and not software or cartoons — is involved. Art endures, and that which does may not have any obvious commercial tie-ins. At least, not initially.

A former senior editor at *Wired* remarked to me that he'd seen a dance performance, and it was boring, a reaction not that uncommon or unlikely. But it was the proud Know-Nothing stance, from a fellow who was otherwise an Urban Sophisticate, that was disturbing — as well as the implication that since it was art that wasn't to his taste, it had no value. He also asked the rhetorical question: Why did the United States need more than one symphony orchestra? Why, as a society, support any of it? This from a young man educated in the best private schools and with a BA in anthropology from UC-Berkeley.

The Problem with Art may have other roots: As one thoughtful ace technolibertarian pal o' mine explained, it was always the arty kids in high school who had no use for the nerds. And now, ten or twenty years later, they are coming back and asking for money? No way! Think of Nozick's explanation of the resentments that exist between the class of wordsmiths and the class of the numerocratic. My friend even admitted, mostly kidding but sorta not, that deep within many nerd hearts dwells the sense that We Are Not Like The Others/We Could Never Figure Out their rules of attraction or strange social customs. Nerds are always looking for algorithms or heuristics to model the world: Think of the nerverts. No, I can't explain why catching typhoid while traveling in Africa is romantic and might be the basis of an interesting novel or movie but coming down with hepatitis in Mexico is not. Which makes geeks understandably ask, where do The Normals get off asking Us to subsidize their bordering-on-inexplicable needs and claims?

As Firth says in his *Salon* piece, "an integral part of the Valley's success myth...has come to be defined almost in opposition to culture. You can only get to the top and stay there...if you banish from your life the artifacts and interests that define culture for the rest of society."

The socially moderate/fiscally conservative congressman from Silicon Valley, former technologist Tom Campbell, has voted against the continuation of funding for the National Endowment for the Arts. It is a budgetary frill, in his mind, at a time when deficits need reducing; but considering the microscopic fragment of the US government budget NEA funding takes up ($200 million), this position says more about the trivialization and discomfort art can inspire within high tech than it does about community-funded art and theater and dance's realistic drag on deficit reduction. Since art doesn't save lives — and may or may not lead to greater productivity, jobs, or export dollars — its value perhaps is seen as questionable; it's just so damnably subjective. Still, money given to the arts is often as big an economic generator as money given as a small-business loan: think of how the Oregon Shakespeare Festival has transformed the economy of Ashland, Oregon.

REBUTTAL TO CYBERSELFISH

High tech alternately ignores, is semi-secretly proud of, and dances around the accusations of being philistine and cyberselfish. Although I tend to believe these accusations are more true than not, I would be delighted to be disabused of these notions. So in December 1997, in spite of the predations of El Niño, I couldn't wait to attend a panel discussion in Santa Clara titled "Cybergenerous: Time to Debunk the Myth That Silicon Valley Companies Are Tightwads."

As I flew past the off-ramps on 101, I couldn't help but be reminded of the article I had just read in the *San Francisco Chronicle* about the wretched-excess, silly-money knocking around Stanford Shopping Center (where merchants earn out per square foot in the realm of Rodeo Drive and Trump Tower). This happy Silicon Valley boomtown news appeared in the paper simultaneously with a discussion of a report by the Center on Budget and Policy Priorities. Its highlights included the fact that the incomes of the richest one-fifth of California families had risen by 30 percent since 1978, but those we normally call middle class (making under $60,000 per year) had lost ground, and the incomes of the poorest fifth had decreased almost 30 percent. The executives in the electronics industry earn more than two hundred times what production workers make; in 1998 the Valley's top ten executives received $442 million (mostly in stock), and the average wage of software engineers exceeded $90,000.

What's more, in Silicon Valley, the hourly wages of 75 percent of workers were actually lower in 1996 than 1989. And in 1999, the fastest-growing job sector in the Valley was entry-level positions paying less than $10 per hour. This in an area where a two-bedroom apartment will cost you more than $1,300 per month. Twenty years ago, a gardener could live in the Valley and support a family; now Palo Alto cannot recruit teachers because they cannot afford to live in that community.

Anyway, "Cybergenerous" was a meeting of the Churchill Club, "Silicon Valley's Public Affairs Forum," founded by Rich Karlgaard and Tony Perkins. These two men started *Upside*, a technology magazine geared toward high tech executives and investors, and each has gone on to better things in the magazine world. Perkins is now editor in chief of an even-more-rahrah technology-industry publication, *Red Herring*, geared toward VC readership; Karlgaard has become publisher of *Forbes*, (cuz there's so much going on in the Far West, he gets to stay Out Here and is not obliged to move Back East to the magazine's traditional headquarters in New York).

On the "Cybergenerous" panel, there were non-cyberselfish CEOs: Eric Benhamou, 3Com (if your computer is on a network, it's likely it uses one of his company's cards; if you use a modem, it's likely it's one of his company's models; if you use a Palm Pilot, you are also familiar with his company, which owned Palm for a while. And if you follow baseball, you may be familiar with how San Francisco's Candlestick Park was renamed 3Com Park); James Carreker, Aspect Telecommunications; Ramon Nuñez, IKOS Systems; and Harry Saal, founder of Network General. The panel was moderated by consultant Dori Ives, a woman with experience helping mostly high tech companies work on philanthropic issues.

While waiting for the panel to get started, I recalled my post-graduate years of the 1970s, when I lived in Berkeley for a living (studying acting, groveling at tables, working for a peace group) and learned many things, among them that I was not born under the protection of St. Jude, the patron saint of lost causes.

In my brief '70s flirtation with the nonprofit do-gooder world, I realized I simply did not have it in me to keep up peppy advocacy in the face of far more defeats than victories. I remember listening to a bright young woman who I think had recently been made head of Amnesty International's Latin American section (or whatever it's called) chirruping about someone her organization *had* gotten sprung — great, of course, but what about the thousands of Disappeared that remained? Not to dis her, but I learned the signs then of those who are relentlessly upbeat in the face of adversity and impossible odds. Much like those who have the temperament to be successful salespeople, they celebrate the one deal closed and not the nineteen rebuffs. I think of them as being the special charges of St. Jude.

It wasn't so much the CEOs at "Cybergenerous" who played the role of special charges of St. Jude (though the argument could be made for them, too) as the local nonprofits and volunteer organizations with handouts and brochures in the back of the room. "It's a matter of constant education!" "It's getting so much better!" they chirped — referring to high tech's notorious Bad Form when it comes to philanthropy, whether at the rank-and-file level of the hypothetical grunt sales engineer now waiting for his options to vest, at the level of executives and investors who have already cashed in on the New Economy very well, thank you, or at the level of corporate giving. (Exceptions *always* made for Hewlett-Packard and for the members of the Hewlett and Packard families, of course.)

Dori Ives had the upbeat quality of the Amnesty International staffer of my youth: Isn't it grand that Microsoft and IBM are getting into a competition over who can be most generous? Never mind that it's about donations of *computer* equipment.[38]

38 Microsoft donating computers to libraries is a special problem in its own

Bue whenever the presence of the special charges of St. Jude is felt, look for the impossible odds. For although CEO speakers Carreker and Nuñez each outlined thoughtfully designed programs for corporate giving (with much employee consensus and fiduciary and financial sense) and Benhamou proposed a more typical Silicon Valley self-interested one (wiring schools in communities where employees live), they all gracefully agreed with their fellow panelist Harry Saal that it's very hard to implement these programs midway through a corporation's life. This was something venture capitalists (VCs) and obsessed engineers and bordering-on-piratical entrepreneurs give little thought to. The rule of thumb given out on the panel was that companies routinely have to grow to $1 billion in sales before they give community involvement a thought.

So for there to be any kind of meaningful corporate philanthropy (because who knows if or when a company will reach $1 billion in sales), the corporate commitment has to, instead of being an afterthought, be there from the beginning. Getting in at the beginning weirdly echoes where the vast majority of high tech philanthropic dollars do go: to education, primarily to K-12.

---

right: Who needs books when you can use Microsoft Encarta, where the earlier non-Microsoft-published editions described Gates's entrepreneurial ruthlessness and post-Microsoft-acquisition editions describe his philanthropy? Not to mention, hooking generations of kids early on the Microsoft way, regardless of the buggyness and derivativeness of Microsoft software or the greater value placed on software and software retrieval than on books. A controversy arose because, typical of not-playing-fair Microsoft, it wrote off its donations at full manufacturer's suggested retail price (which no one on Gaia's green earth has ever paid for anything), whereas IBM took the generally accepted good-accounting practice of writing off the wholesale price of the gear.

But Microsoft is simply being slightly more egregious, as it usually is, in practices that are common throughout the software industry. For example, in a September 9, 1997, *Wall Street Journal* piece on the software-giveaway scam, Novell (a giant of networking software), acknowledged that its 1996 declared gifts of $1 million cost the company only $4,820. Which is not exactly playing fair to mention, I know; it's not as if the nonprofits would have been likely to buy the software on their own, so the gifts can be seen as treasured luxury items the organizations might never have considered. Who are these nongovernmental organizations to question gifts reigning down from above?

To pick out the most cynical motivation in a situation where there is a multi-variate set of forces at play, it might be argued that high techsters intuit that you gotta catch 'em/brainwash them when they're young — or they won't be good workers in their cubicles, won't be good purchasers of your latest rev (that is, version of software), won't have formed the strong brand loyalty you want them to have. Not to mention, how are you gonna keep your workforce, aghast at the ridiculoso housing prices on the west side of the Bay? At least their kids will be attending public schools with Net access. Who needs art, anyway?

This allocation of philanthropic resources to kids' causes may be Silicon Valley's peculiar version of a growing trend in the rest of the United States: leaving the cocoon of your own life only where your kids intersect with the larger world. Peter Dobkin Hall suggests that children are a major organizing factor in communities in a way they were not when safety on the streets meant that kids could grow up in a condition of less-supervised benign neglect. Whereas people often don't know and don't care about their neighbors or what goes on in their neighborhood, they *will* get involved in the parent-teacher organization at their kids' schools. Or, as the cliché goes, soccer moms will talk to each other in order to form a carpool, when they may have lived in the same neighborhood for years and ignored each other.

Just how does this Silicon Valley permutation of bowling alone, except for the league your kids play in, play out? Some St. Jude-ish statistics can be derived from the survey of "Corporate Community Involvement in Silicon Valley, 1994–1997" conducted by the Community Foundation of Silicon Valley and the American Leadership Forum.[39] No surprise, the study was

39 The American Leadership Forum is a national organization that plucks likely senior executives who have demonstrated some tropism toward community engagement and regrooves them with expertise in working cross-institutionally, building cooperation on a regional basis (coalition-building across municipal and county lines), dealing with government issues, and all sorts of right-minded stuff. Eric Benhamou and Jim Carreker and Harry Saal are all graduates of this

funded by the Packard Foundation — of David Packard and Hewlett-Packard fame.

The one hundred largest companies in Silicon Valley were asked to respond to the survey.[40] From what the companies who responded to the survey said, service on nonprofit boards declined by 13 percent from 1994 to 1997. This decrease fits with Ben-Horin's longtime grappling with Bay Area high tech, as one whose organization, Compumentor, was one of the first to attempt to bring technology expertise to the nonprofit sector. Compumentor has found that geeks at the grunt / production-line level are happy to volunteer their time wiring schools or donating equipment or explaining the intricacies of getting a dial-up connection to the Internet, but that senior executives, who form the class of what used to be called business leaders, in general have not exerted leadership in philanthropic directions — not in time, not in money, not in anything.

Some of the self-interested cultural operators that encourage such participation in other business climates don't seem to be present in Silicon Valley. Many don't see that serving on community boards, and making like a big macher, is an effective way to perform business networking — though there's no reason this shouldn't be the case.

This was made very clear when the United Way of Santa Clara County basically went broke in May 1999. What happened then was very interesting. Had this occurred in, say, Minneapolis or Cleveland, the powers that be would probably have heard about the problem and fixed it in their boardrooms

forum.

40 Only about half answered. It is not clear whether this means that the silent half don't care enough about their philanthropic efforts to bother responding or that philanthropy is so absent from their overall activities that there's little to say (or whether this is simply a statistically normal response). However, given the hundreds-of-millions-blending-into-billions dollar size of these companies, it's hard to believe that corporate philanthropy isn't an issue.

("We can't allow these 100 member agencies in our community to lose their funding"). But, initially, *no one* came forward to do much of anything. Then Steve Kirsh of Infoseek finally stepped forward with some money, but when he asked his friends, equally or comparably by mere-mortal-standards wealthy, to do something — no response. What finally bailed out the organization was Bill Gates swooping down with a large donation, which then, in the spirit of competition and Microsoft-loathing, made others cough up the rest of the deficit in a matter of days.

With the exception of a few companies, such as Cypress Semiconductor, the celebrated high tech competitive spirit doesn't manifest itself when it comes to philanthropy. This is compounded by the fact that there is little community stigma in *not* participating in charitable giving — except maybe you'd be thought a fool to not use "philanthropy" as a way to write off excess inventory, that is, overstocks of software and hardware you have sitting around. And to speak of competition in another sphere, the institution of the trophy-wife, whose job in a couple is to perform social-climbing and to atone for Veblenesque conspicuous consumption by practicing dramatic acts of noblesse oblige, is far less visible in Silicon Valley.

MATERIAL CULTURE

Another signature of the crazy world of philanthropy in high tech is that almost half of giving is in kind, not cash, in contrast with the rest of the country, where the rate of in-kind giving is 12 percent. Reasons for this are complex, a mix of the ingenuous and disingenuous — and regardless of motivation, computer products and services cannot serve all philanthropic needs.

This in-kind track record for Silicon Valley is somewhat about stinginess — no, call it business prudence. High tech companies are beholden to their stockholders, even before their customers

— much less their community. Their motivation for donation can be to write off excess inventory, get a great tax deduction, and not waste any bandwidth or employee hours or executive attention on thinking very far about what might be of greater societal value. Both reprehensible and nonreprehensible forces make this practice commonplace. Kirk Hansen, a professor at Stanford's Sloan program for midcareer MBAs, says that leverage is the reason that companies give away software: When companies give away a product that sells for $1, and it only costs them 10 cents, they've given the charity something theoretically worth a dollar at one-tenth the cost. Such a deal appeals to business-like notions of efficiency. What's scandalous about these gifts is that the donors may not supply documentation or copies of the software beyond one master copy. In other words, these are donations that do not involve any actual dipping into corporate, real-world resources, such as the expenses of burning CDs or printing and shipping user manuals.

It's not just the software-giveaway scam that is so at odds with what the spirit of philanthropy is supposed to be about. Another example of adhering to the letter, and not the spirit, of philanthropy is the way Jerry Yang, one of the founders of Web startup success Yahoo, has conspicuously given money to computer science departments — and he is only among the most conspicuous in high tech performing this ode to corporate self-interest. Gordon Moore, a retired Intel founder, recently gave a big chunk of change to his alma mater, UC-Berkeley — but, of course, it was in support of its extremely commercially viable electrical engineering and computer science efforts. After all, computer science departments are where companies get their next-generation research done, and they benefit from tech goodies directly and indirectly subsidized by federal, state, and local governments in various ways.

Jim Clark, the focus of Michael Lewis's bestseller, *The New New Thing,* typifies many of the characteristics of high tech's wealth. For one, even when a company is new, its executives may have money that is not. Clark, who more than ten years ago founded Silicon Graphics,[41] went on to cofound Netscape, the company that made the World Wide Web really popular through the deployment of its browser, Navigator — and which has since been purchased by AOL. Clark is not a twerp in his twenties. According to his Web site, he was "the first Internet billionaire," and he has since moved onto two other startups, Healtheon and My.CFO. His main philanthropic move has been to endow the Stanford University Program in Biomedical, Engineering, and Sciences (Bio-X) with $150 million — whose focus is to create better prosthetics, artificial eyes, and so forth. A fine thing. And imagine the patent possibilities flowing out of such a center.

In fact, the ideal partnership between university and industry now held up as a model for all the world was created by Frederic Terman, former dean of Stanford's engineering school and provost and vice chairman of the university, who encouraged technologists to enter industry. Terman, in the 1950s, created the Stanford Industrial Park: university as über-tradeschool, explicitly tying industry and university to each other. Terman's tenure at Stanford prefigured the '90s trend favoring the market as the measure of all good, even in academia. He gutted what might be considered debit-centers (such as the classics department) and shifted the focus of its biology department away from ecology and toward the more potentially industrially lucrative fields of biochemistry and molecular biology.

Giving in kind and giving to fund research with high potential for profits from intellectual property are radically different from and far more self-interested than Andrew Carnegie's funding of libraries. Imagine if Carnegie had funded only a school of mining (and not even metallurgy) in the Mesabi Iron Range

41 Silicon Graphics is a multi-billion-dollar high-end graphics workstation company. You might be familiar with the results of their work if you saw the computer-rendered dinosaurs in Jurassic Park or the Mars Voyager photos.

of rural northern Minnesota — the locale for the ore that made Pittsburgh steel possible. This kind of giving is different from the giving of another of today's plutocrats, George Soros, who has given away millions of dollars to foster democracy and fair business practices all over the world. True, he is a global financier, and he will benefit from the better business climate that a more stable world will provide. But Soros has not done the equivalent of what the people in high tech do — which would be to endow a chair in currency speculation at Columbia University's business school, famous for its international orientation, and to call it a day, philanthropically speaking.

A question from the audience at the "Cybergenerous" event echoed Terman: Since nine out of ten startups fail, shouldn't we be teaching people about business and not about all kinds of stuff that happened 200 years ago? In other words, shouldn't universities be mostly business incubators? The thing is, it's possible that people exposed to history, economics, literature — yes, even the classics (if you want to understand the basis for most business scams, you can do worse than read what the Romans had to say) — might do no worse in business, where people skills count (it's called management), than those who have only and always been head-down among the quantitative, say a BSEE with a minor in business administration. If you know something about previous cycles of boom and bust (such as the hyperinflation-then-crash trade in tulip-bulb futures in seventeenth-century Holland), you might have some distant early warning system about the dangers of hype and speculation. Calling the shade of George Santayana...

One *tiny* example of how giving back to the world beyond the frames of high tech might ultimately benefit it is a 1998 study by Stanford English professor Shirley Brice Heath. Her results demonstrated that kids who study art after school are four times as likely to win academic awards, four times as likely to participate in math or science fairs, and had higher math and verbal

SAT scores than those who did not study art. As Heath said in a November 13, 1998, issue of the *San Francisco Chronicle,* "young people in...arts programs engage in lots of communications similar to the kind you find in a venture capital company where everyone is sitting around the boardroom talking about the kind of project they want to develop."

TOMCATS IN LOVE

The disinclination to see how the world outside high tech can have positive value to the world inside high tech isn't just about self-glorification. It's also about love: Very much at play is the cat–dead-rat phenomenon. To wit, if a cat really loves you, it will give you what it loves — which is a dead rat on your pillow or doormat. Never mind that you may not *want* a dead rat. And so it is in high tech: In a culture as workaholic and self-validating and insular and technology-besotted as high tech, nothing could be finer to these Valley cats than the gift of dead-rat computer equipment. So they give what they love best, what they think has the greatest value; that is, computers and communications systems. These cats range through territories that are clumped way toward the "have" end of the "have"/"have-not" spectrum, where schools are definitely above average and it's safe to walk the streets at night and the libraries are stocked and you can rely on your late-model car to get you where you are going and you can buy the books you want or need at Kepler's; their basic needs are very much being met. Thus results a true lack of understanding that throwing a copy of *PhotoShop* on a Pentium clone may not solve an East Palo Alto kid's problems. This kid may not have a safe and quiet place to do her homework, enough to eat on a regular basis, or a home where the phone and the gas and electricity aren't in frequent peril of being turned off. The fact that there are neighborhoods where pizza cannot be safely delivered would come as a shock to most geeks.

In the 1980s, the Richmond, California (an industrial North Bay town with urban problems, low income levels, and minority populations typical of an inner city), school district went bankrupt — but they had piles of unused donated computer equipment lying around. The head of Cisco half-jokes that Cisco's "take a router to school" program was successful, even when the schools in question didn't know what a router was (routers are devices that direct electronic messages on their proper pathways to their proper recipients). Somehow the schools found a way to make use of donated technology — for schools are grateful for anything they can get. It's a sad instantiation of cat–dead-ratness: You can bet that many of the schools that took on Cisco routers didn't have adequate telephone lines or proper wiring or teacher training or the network administrators these boxes really do require; routers do not, in terms of ease of installation, operate anything like an answering machine whose simplicity enables it to work anywhere there is a phone jack with touch-tone line. It's folks at the graduate-student or the $75/hour level that get and keep routers up and humming happily.

Cisco, in doing another dead-rat turn, is justifiably proud of its Cisco Network Academy, which founds network-technician vocational education in high schools. Voc-tech is a good thing, and it better addresses the international shortage of network administrators than not. However, since at least 80 percent of the routers on the Internet are manufactured by Cisco, the company is, in reality, getting future tech-support for cheap (whatever awful else can be said about public schools, it can't be argued that they don't deliver educational infrastructure and masses of students far more cheaply and easily than could be done any other way) — a generation trained with the Cisco way of networking. Pity poor Nortel, Cisco's major competitor. It's all about enlightened self-interest.

The point has been made often that donating computers (which quickly become obsolete, which require lots of training, which run hypnotic or boring software of debatable utility for kids) to schools is not such a Swell Thing in itself if other basics are lacking (fair compensation for good teaching; books and art supplies and musical instruments and lab equipment and proper teacher–student ratios); but a larger one perhaps has not. Although it is *certainly* not up to high tech to fix everything that is broken with public education, there really might be more community value in funding a storytelling hour at a local library than in donating a computer involving complex database operations that confuse patrons, vex librarians, and may not help people find what they need. Funding field trips to the tide pools at Pescadero may be of far greater value, pedagogically and developmentally, than throwing stale repetitive educational (or worse, "edutainment") software at kids. Conservatives rightfully complain that the liberal solution of throwing money at problems doesn't work; but neither does the technolibertarian solution of throwing technology at problems.

You can spot technology cats thinking about their dead rats everywhere. Since technologists believe so ardently in the value of the dead rats they've created and can point to jobs and wealth and export dollars created, they may feel they have already made their contribution to society. Unlike those who make their money from speculation (arbs and brokers, whether of currencies or square feet of office space), technologists feel they've created something concrete, so that no atonement (if that's what philanthropy is) need be made, no guilt money paid. Despite the fact that the net effect of much technology is to eliminate jobs without necessarily improving productivity, many technologists feel a sense of artisanal/good farmer self-justification, that they've done their share. T. J. Rodgers echoes this sentiment: To him, Cypress's biggest contribution to the community *has been* the creation of jobs — a good thing, no doubt about it. But is it enough?

THE VALUE OF MONEY, THE MEANING OF VALUE

Even more bedrock, beyond dead-rat-spotting, there is what the Marxists used to like to call one of the inherent contradictions of capitalism, a fundamental clash in ontology. Moore's Law and feature creep[42] put GM's planned obsolescence of the 1950s to shame. Nothing stands still in high tech, even if there's little appreciable benefit to moving on. In technoculture, everyone, aping the VCs, has an exit strategy. The rules of the game are that you cash out as quick as you can: If you acquire founders' stock in a company, you sell it as quickly as you legally can after the IPO, because who knows what tomorrow may bring and who cares if the company or its products lose value or go away altogether? And if these are the rules, what meaning can there be for community-building? How can corporations leverage off a notion of building things to last (community ties and involvement; longtime feel-good brand recognition) when this is at odds with the flickering phosphor-heart of Silicon Valley and its wealth-seeking/creating/destroying? How can companies justify such a move to boards of directors and stockholders in a New Economy so obsessed with quarter-by-quarter results? In which downsizing improves short-term cash flow but ravages long-term productivity through losses in customer satisfaction, gutted R&D, and retraining costs when restaffing needs to occur?

If the Good Technology Life Worth Living now is one where people have commitments to technology and not to companies, and if the technolibertarian ideal is to come and go like Michelangelo — hey Jude, how can philanthropy really be? If, as the Silicon Valley cliché goes, engineers will be able to change jobs without changing parking spots (that is, one company and the technology it's flogging is superseded by a newer company and a different technology, taking over the emptied-out corporate offices where

42 Feature creep refers to new releases and revisions of software that add ever more fancy and maddening functions, whether or not they are needed or desired or are buggy or incompatible.

the first company abandoned ship), what companies will even be around long enough to support the communities where they extract their wealth?

And you have to take note of the *flimsiness* of money in Silicon Valley. If your wealth is mostly in paper (that is, stock), and the company gets eclipsed through a fluke of market vagaries or changing fashions in technology, there goes the meaning out of your financial security. To pick one very obvious example: Netscape, the wonder-company of the World Wide Web, made its boy-wonder cofounder Marc Andreeson worth a little under half a billion dollars in its IPO; but within two years, Netscape was laying off hundreds of workers and posting a net loss in the fourth quarter of 1997 of $88.3 million. By 1999 it had been absorbed by AOL, and Andreeson had gone off to start an e-commerce-enabling venture, Loud.Cloud. But even with all this, it still would have been possible for Andreeson to have cashed in, say, $10 million and done something philanthropically Way New or Cool. That this didn't happen is a microcosm of the problem of giving in high tech: Any excuse will do.

Everyone knows, or knows of, lots of folks who happened to be working at the right company when it went public at the right time, so that money is not an issue in their lives for the indefinite future. But this makes the giving away of money problematic: Why should it be necessary, when there's so much of it around? Yet, in the winner-take-all/Casino Society that forms the backdrop to Silicon Valley, everyone also knows, or knows of, lots of other folks, just as talented and hardworking (or spacey or sneaky), whose startup tanked (as do nine out of ten startups), or never went public, or got bought out under terms where the value of their stock options would not even amount to compensation for overtime. You can slave away like the best-of-breed Iditarod sled dog and kill yourself for months on end waiting for your options to vest — and the deferred gratification that's being demanded of you is more than your life can bear or how long the company lasts. Worst of all, the company might not ever, ever, go public. Or it might get acquired, and only the VCs and a few of the founders get anything for their shares. Or by the time you can sell your shares, the company has passed out of technology and — more important — Wall Street fashion, so the shares are worth less than zero.

Thus, money is paradoxically there to be had in copious quantities, but it may never come your way in the righteous amounts that somehow seem to be everyone's due. It may never seem feasible to give it away when chance more than merit determines its presence or absence. But everyone wants to believe that brains and works, not grace, get them where they are. So if you're hard up, down on your luck, chronically ill, or born to better observe animal behavior or sculpt in clay than write JavaScript — then it's your own damned fault. There's perverse cold comfort in thinking this: better to feel the rules are fair and you can play to win by them than to feel the game is rigged by predestination or the aleatoric.

With the flakiness of high tech money comes a postmodern self-contradicting attitude toward it. *For sure,* money is a way of keeping score. But there's so much of it sloshing around, it can be forgotten that there are those who don't have it. What's more, money in high tech has a much fuzzier social meaning. Compared to the moves and mores of the nouveau riche in other rooms, with other voices (think of the museum-building, hospital-endowing, opera-patronizing ways of historic New York money; of arm-candy wives making the pages of *W* because of their appearances at couturier showings), well-to-do droids do not Dress Uptown. Many of them haven't exactly decided yet what to do with the money that they have made — except to have fun making new companies, building something, then running away.

Wanting to be involved in an endless stream of new companies is a desire indirectly rooted in anxiety, for having made it with a company once, there's the fear that you might never luck out again. Given the job insecurity and the shiftiness of the labor market (one-third of people in high tech are temporary workers. No benefits, no vacations, no stock options — and it's not just data-entry clerks, either) and the ruthless age bias[43] in high tech, there can be a lot of insecurity about the permanence of that money. Will its like ever come again? Will you be able to keep up technically as the trade-pidgin of high tech shifts, and shifts again, and most of what you know doesn't have that much commercial value anymore? The deep underlying principles won't change — but jobs will.

LESSON PLANS

Occasionally there are Found Moments that contain *all* the elements that make philanthropy in high tech so vaudevillian, and so mostly bogus. In an incident Sara Miles described in her October 1997 *San Francisco* magazine article, "The Digital Democrats," such a moment came about when the CEO of an Internet software company proposed some new software to be developed in order to be donated to schools. The CEO was Kim Polese, a photogenic blonde who formerly worked at Sun Microsystems. That she is an attractive woman matters because having such a *scenic* and *female* CEO in an industry that doesn't usually feature either has contributed to making Polese a spokeswoman for high tech way out of proportion to the less-than-financially wonderful performance of her company, Marimba.

What Polese proposed, to great applause, at an Al Gore–hosted Family Reunion confab (emphasis on education), was a piece

43 Even Guy Kawasaki, startup guru, now married, in his forties with two kids, says the startup game is for kids — meaning for those with the stamina and lack of need for stability that characterizes those in their twenties. And traditional ageism, of the kind where you may have a hard time getting hired once you're past fifty, is a very real problem that people don't want to talk about. Maybe if we don't mention it, it will all go away.

of vaporware[44] called Dashboard. Explicitly, Dashboard would enable parents to log daily onto their TV sets to get the latest stats on their kids (grades, attendance records, etc.), and if they chose, send notes back to their teachers. Implicitly, Dashboard would promote what's called push technology, the Internet technology Polese's company is based on. Push technology is modeled on traditional broadcast, consisting of sending stuff to people. As of late 1998, most folks using the Net would still rather "pull" and not be a recipient of push; that is, they would rather search for information. Sadly for Ms. Polese, once the world got past the you-can-make-a-million-as-long-as-the-lnternet-is-mentioncd-there-in-your-business-plan cuckoo days of 1995 and 1996, push technology and Marimba haven't been faring that well.

Does Polese, a graduate of Berkeley, really think that whatever might be awry or deficient in a school or a family would be remedied by Dashboard? Does a lack of measurable data rise to most people's minds as what's wrong with today's schools, or with parents MIA from their kids' schooling? But computers are good at collecting data! Never mind whether we need that data, or whether it conveys anything worth knowing. Parental negligence can obviously be fixed if Internet access is made easier, because making communications available online solves all communications problems! What a product like Dashboard *might* do, if it were ever programmed, is lead to the kind of privacy issues cypherpunks are worried about: a society where there is ever more surveillance and computer-retrievable information about people's private lives.

I don't mean to pick on poor Kim Polese; her seeing social problems mostly as marketing opportunities and her advanced case of cat–dead-ratness is no worse than most in high tech. But the lack of empathic imagination — or seeing such as irrelevant

44 Vaporware is a product that doesn't exist, and that might never come to exist, except for the air turbulence it creates from the hand*waving its marketers do on its behalf and the hot air they dispense.

— is as much about libertarian culture as about technology culture.

To focus a bit more on the libertarian and less on the techno, the brushing off of philanthropy by high tech rests on the presumption that people will always be well, will always be able to purchase what they need, will have easy access to any cultural artifact they value, will never be disabled, will always be able to work, will always have put enough money away, will have job skills still in demand, and will never need to rely on the freely available community-supported institutions not previously thought about, such as a community or Medicare-funded hospice for someone they love — or perish the thought, for themselves. It's an extension of the Valley's work-hard/play-hard ethic ("sleep is for the sick and weakly," was a button being sold at a technical conference for programmers). If you can't get by on little sleep, keep all hours all week, then barrel on up to the Sierras for a fun weekend of rock climbing, then roar back home arriving at 2am to start all over again, then you clearly aren't cut out for high tech's New Games of work and play.

If the libertarian fantasy is that we only participate in those freely chosen associations of our own liking and ignore the rest, then there's no need to preserve the commons — even out of enlightened self-interest. If you don't anticipate ever relying on it yourself, then there is no need to support it. Such a society doesn't even attempt to protect its weaker or less lucky or less commercially viable members, the very people who sometimes, in the long run, contribute the most. The list of penurious painters and musicians with health problems who have created the stuff we value and enjoy is way too long. The same is true of inventors as opposed to marketers. But then, how many people like this are very visible in Silicon Valley?

What's hard to tell, as we enter the new millennium, is if some very high-profile philanthropic gestures within the valley — the social ventures funds among them — signify a true change in high tech thinking or whether it's more window dressing. There's a new intimation that social structures are fraying and that something should be done about it. After all, how can the Valley continue to attract world-class engineers if the schools for their kids are so impoverished? No one knows whether such highly visible moves as the United Way of Santa Clara County bringing in ten Valley superstars (for example, VC John Doerr and Kathy Levison, president of E-trade) to kick-start fund-raising activities will come to matter, either in terms of raising money or influencing others in the Valley. Steve Kirsh, the guy who tried to get his friends to help bail out the United Way, has given tens of millions of dollars. But it's hard to tell whether such generous gestures are influencing the actions of a relatively small number of individuals while the great mass of high tech remains unchanged. The question that even people working within philanthropy in the Valley ask themselves is: Is what's being given in any way proportional to what's being made?

Realistically, almost no one, not Henry David Thoreau, much less Theodore Kaczynski, has ever really evaded relying on the social mesh to some extent. But in high tech there's a presumption of invulnerability (I don't need anything) and predictability (I will never need anything) that flies smack in the face of the certainty of human loss and suffering and, ultimately, interdependence. And if government is the designated Bad Actor of Last Resort, and traditional religious organizations say they don't have the capacity take up the increasing slack in an era of welfare reform, then who will support the community? And at a time when government spending on social and arts programs is falling away and corporate philanthropy overall is diminishing, what does it signify when high tech's way of being celebrates the exacerbation of these trends?

And high tech is supposed to be the way of our future.

CHAPTER FIVE

BUT HOW DID THIS HAPPEN?

ABOUT A WEEK after I attended the Second Bionomics Conference in the fall of 1994, I went to a memorial service in the Santa Cruz Mountains for the father of a friend. It was at a place called the Land of the Medicine Buddha; it's about what you'd think it would be like, a retreat devoted to the healing aspects of the Buddha, both personally and globally. I noticed that most of the people attending workshops there were white, female, age approximately thirty to fifty. Given the titles of the workshops, I speculate that they were there because they felt that things were awry in the world and they wanted to do something about it. Overhearing their conversations, I would venture to say that most of the attendees were college-educated, and they appeared to carry the markers of those who aren't worried about their phone and utilities being shut off any time soon. Their clothes were clean, in good repair, and fairly fashionable. Their speech was Standard American Middle Class. Their cars were fairly late-model and not notably bashed up.

What I was struck with was that the week before, I had been surrounded by a similar group of people: those who felt that things needed changing and were participating in a rather esoteric event in pursuit of that change. There was, of course, the huge difference in gender — the Bionomics Institute ever and always was a boys' club, and the Land of the Medicine Buddha was predictably mostly female and touchy-feely — but sincerity characterized both groups of folks, as well as rough equivalence in education and background.

The gender difference is telling, but it is really only a pointer, and not the point; thinking about the gender difference got me thinking about a larger issue, that of self-selection. Self-selection is a concept close in the semantic field to that of self-organization, so beloved of technolibertarians, so it's worth speculating on how self-selection operates in the making of technolibertarianism. I have stumbled on some clues — but none are conclusive, and many fall into the category of "yes, but" or "it ain't necessarily so."

I spent a few hours with a historian of technology employed by the Smithsonian Institution (boo hiss, a federally funded institution in the seat of our national government), an MIT grad, and every theory that either of us came up with to figure out whence the nexus of technology and libertarianism, the other shot down by saying, "But what about..." And trying to figure out why This happened, and not That, is necessarily an uncertain act. No one would suggest that there was a single prime mover that created the counterculture of the 1960s, or gave rise to the widening global outcry against slavery in the nineteenth century, or has made body piercing the current obnoxious-to-the-straights fashion statement.

DISEASE CENTERS

While it's obvious, it's worth restating that however unwittingly and unconsciously, we all do participate in the culture of our own times, calling down ideas that are floating in the troposphere. Today's high tech world came of age, post-Watergate and post-Vietnam, with all the antigovernment cynicism those cultural markers telegraph. Antigovernment attitudes revved up even more in the antigovernment anti-regulatory Reagan decade of the 1980s.

Another obvious shaping force is the vast sum of money that has poured into right-wing think tanks since the late '60s and early '70s. These think tanks have basically hijacked political discourse: Political terms of art in the United States are mostly of the right and far right, with a marginalized liberal constituent, often but not always from the Politically Correct Camp (which is *really* too bad). That these think tanks have such an effect on the zeitgeist is not that much of a surprise, as much of conservative philanthropy goes toward media projects. Poor befuddled lefties seem to spend less of their money trying to influence and more of their money trying to actually accomplish something. As a consequence, if the talk of the nation were imagined as a computer-screen desktop with icons and applications scattered around it, the conservative formfactor would appear to take up a lot of room. But these are stale insights, if no less true for their obviousness.

The reasons for the affinity between this generation of technologists and libertarianism are not as obvious they might appear. No one can really buy the explanation given to me by an earnest technolibertarian I ran into less than a year after my day at the Land of the Medicine Buddha. He and I were attending MacHack, the largest annual conference of third-party Apple developers. What this one-of-a-kind entrepreneur/college dropout/former Wall Street computer guy really believed is that libertarianism is the preferred political styling of today's with-it technologists simply because they are much smarter than anyone else. For it is true that programmers can be brilliant in their intuition for rule making and rule following and thus can assume they are brilliant in every other specific: It's the barbarism of specialization.

But this theory won't do; as we all know, there are all kinds of intelligences spread across the political spectrum and the range of human endeavor: That an art therapist is less likely to be libertarian than a C++ programmer does not mean that she is denser but that her mind works in different modes, and that her powers of imagination and empathy travel along different pathways than the guy Web-programming with Perl. Her gift for capturing a distinctive gesture in a few strokes of a watercolor brush, her instinctive understanding of what medium (clay, papier maché, pen and ink) might prove responsive to a troubled child might be just as baffling, at least natively, to the programmer as his aesthetic dismissal of spaghetti code would be to her.

Another technolibertarian, a longtime programmer of the sort with fringe interests in things such as nanotechnology, told me in all earnestness that the moment of libertarian conversion for technologists comes after the first time they witness a program doing maddeningly what they told it to do — but not what they wanted it to. This made them realize that the world wasn't controllable or fixable and therefore how could anyone have the means or brains to come up with rules and laws that would work or make sense. Wouldn't it be great if it were programmer humility and awe at the complexity of all things that led to technolibertarianism? Perhaps this moment of political technology-hubris-of-Saul becoming technology-humble-of-Paul really happened to this woman.

But *most* programmers I know are of the just-give-me-a-few-more-hours / days / lines-of-code-and-I'll-get-it-right / we'll-fix-that-in-the-next-release / no-problem-I-can-make-it-perfect clan; intellectual modesty and humility before the Murphy's-Law, ungraspable Zen nature of the universe are not qualities I would attribute to them. They *have* to believe they can make things work, and work correctly (even then, they *don't* work to most people's satisfaction) — or else they would be bedeviled by a nihilism, alienation, and cynicism typical of a character in a Huysmans novel or of a marketer who doesn't believe in the junk-for-consumers she is trying to flog.

With cause, many programmers are *proud* of the rule-based bounded universes they create; so if simple propositional logic were all that were operating in human affairs, then human affairs might very well be fixable through simple rules. But game theory, powerful as it is, can't explain all of human behavior. What constitutes as scoring points in the Game of Life for one person may not even rate for another.

In addition, dealing in rule-based universes can put you in a continual state of exasperation verging on rage at how messy and imperfect humans and their societies are. Anyone looking at our judicial system, particularly the criminal justice system, would have to write it off as an inconsistent corrupt mess, but there isn't one easy obvious fix. How maddening that there isn't a clear and easy correlation between considering human imperfection in all its variety and any obvious political (or for that matter, religious) philosophy. But just because you can see that much is wrong with the world, and that much should be changed in it, and that institutions everywhere suffer from stupidity and incompetence, does not necessarily imply that you are libertarian. Or socialist. Or Shaker.

There is no political philosophy that *necessarily* derives from an interest in and familiarity with technology. As far as I can tell, there is no political correlate to be drawn between those who subscribe to comp.risks — a USENET newsgroup moderated by the technically brilliant and socially conscious Peter Neumann, chief scientist at Stanford Research International (a long-standing Silicon Valley think tank) — and those regular readers of newsgroups on the Net who do not. The RISKS forum, as it is called, regularly documents all the ways software screws up and stumbles in major and sometimes life-threatening ways — breaches in security, breakdowns in military fail-safe gear, horrifying coding errors in medical equipment, and the like. RISKS is habituated by people as deep into technology as you could imagine, but it is not any more libertarian than any place else on the Net. In fact, the absolutely admired Neumann, while a fierce *civil* libertarian, is not remotely a *technolibertarian* in the sense of abhorring all regulation, holding as an article of faith that The Market Will

Provide, and abjuring participation in government panels, congressional hearings, and the like. He very much does participate in government (on panels, as an advisor), although he has the world-weariness of one who knows how seldom the Good Guys win. He knows how often regulation is badly or thoughtlessly enacted as much as he fears a world where there is no or little regulation.

Another apologist explained to me that the reason for the rise in technolibertarianism is that engineers are practical and like to fix things and get things right, so of course only the sensible political choice of libertarianism would fit. But given the disaster of drained wetlands (with their attendant flooding and ecosystem destruction) courtesy of the Army Corps of Engineers, the twenty-year mess created in trying to upgrade the FAA's air-traffic control systems, and the countless user-hostile, buggy, confusing chunks of software polluting the planet, it can't be argued that engineers are necessarily more practical or grounded in reality than, say, housewives, who have to keep a household and offspring functioning and maintained, 24/7. You always do have to be careful of explanations of political philosophy where one side is so clearly on the side of genius and Life Its Own Self, and the other, all that is foolish and hamstrung. It is not just in government where the Law of Unintended Consequences operates: if you have ever tried to upgrade your computer, you have seen that unwanted complex interactions occur — some of which even your $100+/hour computer consultant can't figure out.

THE POWER OF THE NET

The rise of the Net, simultaneous with the rise of microcomputers, was integral to the rise of technolibertarianism: the Net gave formerly isolated libertarians, then a small cultural minority, a place to find each other. On the Net they found solidarity and a better land: They were not alone. There, they were better able to mediate the struggle we all have — that of reconciling the need to prize our individuality with the need to interact well enough with others. Even one of the most famous recluses of our time, the Unabomber, had a need to be heard. The result was that libertarians felt less all alone in the world, and they created a highly vocal Net-wide libertarian culture. The Net became the meeting place for an anarchists' support group.

In 1994, *Self* magazine started an online gun-control forum on The Well (Whole Earth 'Lectronic Link), the electronic bulletin-board system, Internet gateway, and one of the first virtual communities. The Well, both in the actual physical location of its hardware and in the philosophical orientation of its early directors, is plunked right in the middle of tree-hugging, bleeding-heart-liberal, secular-humanist Northern California. I suspect *Self* and The Well assumed that there would arguments of all political persuasions; but, instead, participants' opinions ranged from mildly anti-gun-control to rabidly anti-gun-control.

This abiding, passionate, detestation of regulation, so out of whack with the opinions of the man and woman on the street in my own bioregion/demographic, showed how different a place the online/high tech world is from the terrestrial community to which it is nominally tethered — even an online world with countercultural roots as strong as those of The Well's. In 1999, on The Well, what with Columbine and other school shootings in the air, there were more gun-control advocates, and their presence there is also a signal of the mainstreaming of online culture from real-world culture. But to this day the gun-carriers vastly outgun the gun-decryers.

Mike Godwin, formerly online counsel for the EFF, said that "libertarianism (pro, con, and internal faction fights) is the primordial net-news discussion topic. Any time the debate shifts somewhere else, it must eventually return to this fuel source." In a decentralized community where tolerance and diversity are the norm (no one questions online special-interest clubrooms devoted to gecko husbandry or Wiccan nature-mysticism or space-colony development or...), it is damned peculiar that there has been, historically, a lot less space online devoted to political points of view other than the libertarian. Libertarians seem to have formed the single biggest plurality on the Net. You can count on them to show up in any even vaguely political online discussion. With time, cultures become self-perpetuating: A newcomer to the Net might either want to become part of the libertarian crowd, to be In with the In Crowd; or might shut up, if aligned with a different political persuasion, so as not to be bullied; or might be attracted to the Net precisely because its cacophony of singular voices suits people already predisposed to the libertarian point of view.

ASK NOT WHAT YOUR GOVERNMENT CAN DO FOR YOU

In searching for origins, you can't argue only from facts; motivations and feelings and social trends play an important role and are difficult to elucidate. There are plenty of inconvenient facts to support the contention that, libertarian fantasy to the contrary, government actually has been more of a benign than a malign influence in today's high tech metaverse (never mind its horridness and stupidity in other sectors of society) and that high tech companies actually do participate in government once they get to a certain size: if they export in any large amounts, they need the government. As one well-placed longtime Beltway insider pointed out to me, in the early '80s, the semiconductor guys came to DC because they were unhappy with how things were going abroad (they were feeling threatened by competition with Japan). Then in the late '80s, the hardware guys came running (more of the same). And by the early '90s, it was the software guys, up in arms about piracy and intellectual property outrages, mostly perpetrated by China. Home is the place that when you have to go there, they have to take you in.

I invoke the example of the Santa Clara Valley Manufacturers Association, an organization of decades' standing, which counts among its members the largest companies in the Valley, constituted specifically to find ways to work in better concert with local, regional, and state governments — and which is now working on initiatives to create infill moderate-income housing. Or, for that matter, ask venture-capitalist poster boy John Doerr and Al Gore if high tech and government don't find things to say to each other at the monthly Silicon Valley Technology Network meetings, where the once-and-future technology presidential candidate rubs up against arriviste technologists such as Halsey Minor, the mediagenic CEO of CNET, an Internet/New Media powerhouse. Endorsements and donations are sought; requests for legislative relief are made (charter schools, an end to stockholder lawsuits, and higher guest-worker visa quotas). And there are Republican and Democratic wings of Technet.

Another inconvenient fact is that in 2000, because of the money it's kicking out, high tech has become an irresistible lure to traditional parties and politicians. And high tech is responding: Who doesn't like receiving suitors? NetCoalition.com, a high tech lobbying group, is trying to bring Internet consciousness to Congress — which mostly entails a libertarian agenda of no tax on or regulation of the Internet (or anything else for that matter). For the first time, there is perceived political juice to be had in taking tours of Silicon Valley. Although I suspect all parties may profoundly misinterpret each other, obviously there is some sort of mutual fascination in play. Who knows what will happen when, as this attraction of opposites plays out, each makes the unfortunate discovery about who the Other *really* is?

BY THE PEOPLE, FOR THE PEOPLE

What do people inside the Beltway think about the guys in area codes, 415, 408, and 650? What have they observed about this community that is reputed to so despise them? Antagonists often have special insight into each other's ways of being. I spoke to a scientist who had worked for a long time in one of the great national labs, and who on fellowship had been rotated to DC to spend some time learning how congressional science policy works. He was shocked when he first got to town, to see how illogical and immoral and how like sausage-making the creation of laws and policy was. What he saw was horse trading and the influence of personalities, where he had been used to dealing with ideas. A staffer would explain that Mr. X over here had always been a good guy so we on the Hill support him this time, though we don't actually agree with his position, so that next time he'll do us a favor, and Ms. Y over there is generally a reliable narrator when analyzing legislative issues so we'll go along with her take on the policy, though we haven't done the analysis ourselves — and so it went. It finally hit him that politics is about *people,* and technology and science more about *ideas,* and the skillset in dealing with one doesn't often transfer well to dealing with the other.

Dammit, Jim, (remember Bones in the original *Star Trek* speaking up, agonized, for common sense? Nerds remember...) why *can't* the government issue more laws in beta![45] But actually, if you think about it, most laws *are* issued in beta. They get repealed, amended, updated, appealed to the courts. If there exists a model for how institutions evolve, the government is it. In everything from the amount of government information now available on the Web to environmental protection to the effects of Title IX of the Civil Rights Act, you can see how government changes and how it affects the society it is part of.

---

45 Alpha tests are in-house tests of new products; a few favored, experienced clients are given the next, or beta, versions of the software to test under run-time real-world conditions.

One fellow I spoke to who had long experience working with National Science Foundation funding of academic research projects further explained how political science and computer science are not miscible. His observation was that in computer science, as compared to other disciplines (physics, chemistry, biology), the best and brightest did *not* serve on the panels, did not circulate through DC for a year or so, either for the honor of doing so or out of a sense of civic duty, serving both country and professional peers. Nor did they have a sense, as many civic-minded professionals do, that putting in an appearance in Our Nation's Capital mattered.

To him, this went some way toward explaining the self-perpetuating antipathy / lack of understanding between government and high tech: High tech pacesetters / tastemakers don't spend any time dealing with policy, developing any sense of what government is other than an extraneous pest. Government service is not held in high regard in high tech circles. So the less estimable — in academic computer science, in industry — come to Washington, where, in turn, they aren't necessarily the best representatives of high tech and where, upon their return to hightechlandia, they also are not much listened to with their tales of the wonders they saw. A vicious circle it's called.

I identified another of these feedback loops with a negative outcome after talking to several guys in DC who had been on the circuit of private sector / science and technology policy / teaching, lather-rinse-repeat, for ten or twenty years. They came from *aerospace*, and when I asked them if they had any colleagues who came from *computing*, the answer was "no." And again "no." So no one from Our Town was going to Their Town (works both ways, depending on how you see Us and Them): all one place knew of the other was that they were barbarian hordes, and probably Bad People, and were not like us. Clearly, an experiment in international living is needed.

The lack of congress between DC and high tech is borne out by an article in the June 1998 issue of *IP: The Magazine of Law and Policy for High Technology*, a monthly supplement to the *San Francisco Recorder*, the daily newspaper of the Bay Area's legal profession. "Fortress California:...California's Tech Elite Remains Stubbornly Libertarian-And Mostly Disengaged," by lawyer George Kraw, described what he called the "Silicon Valley Lumpenpolitik" (that is, technolibertarians) and pointed out that "the Valley's lack of influence is partly explained by the relatively small number of tech industry executives who hold important positions in government — former Defense Secretary William Perry and current General Services Agency head David Barram being the exceptions rather than the rule."

He further touched on the embedded and invisible government support that high tech benefits from, but ignores or is simply ignorant of. Kraw quotes *New York Times* reporter Thomas Friedman in the April 18, 1998, edition of the newspaper:

> "The hidden hand of the global market would never work without the hidden fist," that fist being the American military and international institutions like the IMF and the UN. Another foreign policy guru, Robert Kagan of the Carnegie Endowment, told Friedman that people in Silicon Valley suffer from an ignorance of history that "leads them to ignore that this explosion of commerce and trade rests on a secure international system, which rests on those who have the power and desire to see that system preserved."

Kraw continues:

> An engagingly truthful executive explained to Friedman that he and his pals don't talk much about Iraq or the former Soviet Union or foreign wars. "We don't even care much about Washington. Money is extracted from Silicon Valley and then wasted by Washington. I want to talk about people who create wealth and jobs. I don't want to talk about unhealthy and unproductive

> people. If I don't care enough about the wealth-destroyers in my own country, why would I care about the wealth-destroyers in another country?"

Kraw's executive is not very different from the people polled in the CSU-SJ study:

> Discussion of political processes are striking in their absence. The workings of the market economy are viewed...as adequate... Government was widely blamed for its inefficiency and dampening effects on innovation, while entrepreneur-based private enterprise was celebrated. Faith in commerce was reflected in the belief that community could be defined as services delivered and that the electronic infrastructure must be marketed to the public so as to ensure sufficient support.

In other words, people in the Valley like to see themselves as victimized by the government, as struggling bold insurrectionists battling governmental oppressions.

> Smart Valley [a now-defunct Silicon Valley government-industry consortium that sounded great but didn't do a whole bunch] is presented as a "grassroots. organization, despite the preponderance of wealthy, powerful corporate members... Interviewees often spoke of Smart Valley as being comprised of outsiders who had been victimized by governmental sloth or over-regulation.

It's rather like second-generation Jews attempting to deny their ancestry by changing their noses and their names and pretending that coming from generations of inbred Talmudic scholasticism had nothing to do with being overachievers in the twentieth-century American professional class.

WHAT DREAMS ARE MADE OF

David Beers, in *Blue Sky Dream: A Memoir of America's Fall From Grace* (Doubleday, 1996), his elegiac memoir of growing up in the first wave of Silicon Valley (the post-World War II aerospace era, which laid down the grid in style, substance, housing, and industrial infrastructure of the '80s and '90s technoculture to come), spoke of how the early Valley offered

> cutting-edge work in the fields of electronics, aerospace, computers. The Pentagon and NASA contractors came with them... Indigenous contractors like Hewlett-Packard...boomed with the newcomers, prospering from the high technology synergy (rather than any real competition) created by federal spending in the area. When, in 1955, William Shockley's team came West...to refine his transistor, the Pentagon poured all the more money into the region, snapping up the miniaturized electronics for its missiles, planes, and computers. When other brilliant minds...replaced the transistor with the even lighter and tinier integrated circuit, the Pentagon redoubled its largesse. In 1967, for example, the military bought seven out of 10 of every such circuits made ...In other words, by 1967, the Valley of Heart's Delight had become a company town, and the company, in the final analysis, was the US Department of Defense.

This indirect but powerful government subsidy, embodied in defense-electronics contracting, manifested in other ways often forgotten. Beers also points out that

> the business of the Federal Housing Administration (FHA) was the insuring, with US Treasury funds, of bank loans for housing... The FHA reserved its...highest levels of insurance for the construction of detached single-family residences for entire neighborhoods of white, middle-income people... For those so favored, FHA insurance trimmed interest rates and drastically

> reduced down payments, making a...home a near risk-free investment for owner and builder alike.

Hence the hectare after hectare of affordable housing created for high tech millworkers, who are now two generations into living in them (of course, they ain't so affordable any more). There were extremely low-cost Veteran's Administration mortgages, in addition to the other suburban benefits of Fannie Mae and Ginnie Mae (the Federal National Mortgage Association and the Government National Mortgage Association), funneling money from banks all over the country to build new housing in former pruneyards.

But then, there's the wise comment a Washington, DC, insider made to me. A former white-collar prosecutor for the Department of Justice, now a solo practitioner cynically making an excellent living in the private sector by trading on the expertise he gained through working with the Feds, he knew nothing of the culture of high tech. But as a well-read boulevardier, he knew a lot about the history of the United States. When I explained to him what I knew of technolibertarianism, he nodded. "Sounds like the entire history of the West," he said. "Have the government bring in electricity, import water, pay for schools, impose some law and order — and then get the hell out." Yup.

And just to pick a *very* few government-funded computer innovations: The Dataphone, the first commercial modem, uses the data-transmission techniques originally developed for the SAGE air-defense network created in 1960. ASCII (American Standard Code for Information Interchange), produced by joint government-industry committee, is the standard way letters, numbers, and functions such as carriage returns are coded electronically (1963). The Arpanet, the mother of the Internet (1969), was funded by the Department of Defense's commitment to basic research. The Arpanet provided the underpinning Latin for the Romance languages of today's Internet.

High tech is most interested in itself, but the day-to-day government-provided services that have made high tech pleasant and possible are yet another set of facts inconvenient to the libertarian fantasy. There's the reliable energy source coming out of the wall socket: utilities have been highly regulated in this country for a long time, and the power grid usually works. And when Pacific Gas and Electric (the utility company in Northern California) screws up, the California Public Utility Commission gets on its butt for, say, more protective-maintenance tree-trimming near power-lines, and there is better emergency staffing of 800 numbers. Then there's tap water: federal, state, and local institutions (setting standards for purity) are involved in testing and maintaining the safety of it. When I lived in Charleston, South Carolina, a federal study came out documenting that the city's drinking water had the highest lead levels in the country. It was no surprise to me in that right-to-work, states-rights, next-to-no-environmental-regulation (a business-friendly climate!) place that the Feds cared more about the potability of drinking water than any institution in the Palmetto State. So when I got the water from my own kitchen tap tested, and it turned out it was way above the federal maximum, I *was* able to get my landlord to install a water filter (just don't tell the other tenants, he said). Where would I have been without those federal standards and the threat of their enforcement?

Kenneth Flamm is an economist and senior fellow in the Foreign Policy Studies Program at the Brookings Institution, one of the oldest and largest DC think tanks. He has published three books about the relationship between government and high tech under the Brookings imprint, the sort of books that are porcupiney with statistics and tabular data. Of the three, *Creating the Computer, Government, Industry, and High Technology* (1988) is the one I was told by just about everyone I interviewed in Washington, DC to take a look at.

The book spends a lot of time on the early history of the computer industry, the 1940s and 1950s when computers pretty much were like Stealth bombers today: fascinating, fragile, hypercomplex new technology only the government/military could afford to experiment with. Summing up the relationship between government and high tech, with some emphasis on the genuinely pioneering work in computing performed during World War II, Flamm concludes that there would have been computers without government/military assistance, but they would have come into existence decades later, if only because of the huge amount of risky investment their early development demanded. Computers had

> little obvious commercial payoff, enormous costs, and a solid consensus of scientific opinion that [they were] likely to fail... It is unclear how, having proved the feasibility of a large and complex system using an inherently unreliable set of components and techniques, a private business could have prevented competitors from seizing on its success to build similar complex systems.

Once computers began to become established commercial entities,

> the government role switched to one of sponsoring basic research and infrastructure and what might be called leading-edge technological projects in which R&D was divorced from the shorter-term commercial benefit... The expensive, high-performance experiment of today has often worked its way down into the everyday technology of tomorrow...
>
> The fundamental concepts for the design of a bread-and-butter business computer... are not terribly different from the designs of 1965... Architectural improvements have been made, and enormous improvements in component cost and performance have been achieved. Nevertheless, the latest computers embody concepts that have been floating around for decades... Even today...it is not difficult to identify the key pieces of technology that can be traced back to government-supported

> research projects. [The] networks...the fancy graphics, the mouse and graphics tablets, the modems — all have at least some root in expensive and exotic research projects funded by the tax-payer in past decades.

But again, let's not confuse facts with trends. Or libertarian religious faith that persists in spite of real-world evidence to the contrary. As UC-Berkeley city-planning professor Annalee Saxenian observed in her book *Regional Advantage*:

> The early entrepreneurs of Silicon Valley saw themselves as the pioneers of a new industry in a new region... This collective identity was strengthened by the homogeneity of Silicon Valley's founders... Virtually all were white men; most were in their early twenties. Many had studied engineering at Stanford or MIT, and most had no industrial experience. None had roots in the region; a surprising number...had grown up in small towns in the Midwest and shared a distrust for established East Coast institutions and attitudes. They repeatedly expressed their opposition to "established" or "old-line" industry and the "Eastern establishment."

Saxenian spends a lot of time emphasizing how cooperation and sharing, traits never very highly valued in the libertarian worldview, of both information and resources among competitors fostered the growth of Silicon Valley, as well as the total intermixing of work and social life, of nonstop socializing *about* work. Folks cooperated both in their professional capacities in their jobs and informally by maintaining social networks throughout all their job-hopping — with changes in jobs occurring no less frequently than every couple of years at most. Rugged unaffiliated individuals they weren't.

There was lots of collaboration between Stanford and industry, and even more between industry and the public education system, which are directly government-funded institutions. Not that great private research universities such as Stanford *don't* receive whole bunches of government money. But that's another story:

> The University of California at Berkeley...by the mid-1970s... was training almost as many electrical engineers as Stanford and MIT... In addition...the California state university and community college systems were also important — but often overlooked — -elements in Silicon Valley's technical infrastructure. By the 1970s San Jose State University trained as many engineers as Stanford or Berkeley and the region's six community colleges offered technical programs that were among the best in the nation. Foothill College in Los Altos Hills, for example, offered the nation's first two-year A.S. degree in semiconductor processing, and the mandate of Mission Community College in Santa Clara was to coordinate programs with the neighboring electronics complex. De Anza College in Cupertino similarly became known for its extensive electronics training programs and links with local firms.
>
> The community colleges were particularly responsive to the needs of local business: they contracted with local companies to teach private courses for their employees, even holding courses at company plants to enable employees to attend after hours...
>
> Paradoxically, however, while the region's engineers saw themselves as different from the rest of American business, they failed to recognize the importance of the networks [professional merged with social] they had created. Silicon Valley's entrepreneurs failed to recognize the connection between the institutions they had built and their commercial success. They saw themselves as the world did, as a new breed of technological pioneers, and they viewed their successes as independent of the region and its relationships...
>
> What appeared to both the actors and the outside world to be the outcome of individual entrepreneurial achievement and

> competitive markets was in fact the result of a complex, highly social process rooted in an industrial community. While they competed fiercely, Silicon Valley's producers were embedded in, and inseparable from, these social and technical networks.

TERATOGENIC

But enough of using fact shadow-puppets to do battle with technolibertarians. If the facts aren't on their side, they can still argue principles, for what matters is how people think of themselves and present themselves to the outside world in their everyday life. That is, how did the self-concept "I'm a libertarian and I'm OK!" rise and rise?

One of the libertarian critics to my *Mother Jones* essay raised the point that "just because you took the king's money once, does not mean you are forever beholden to the king," which is a good rebuttal to the argument that because the government did so much for the computer industry in the past, we should smile at the nice government of today. Technolibertarians are sick of being reminded that the Arpanet, precursor to the Internet, was a government-funded research project.

But the aspect of the Arpanet that gets overlooked, which Flamm touches on, and which is an indirect effect of it having been a government project, is that the Arpanet did not *have* to make money, create return on investment, or demonstrate clear commercial utility. That it became clear within a few years that people just loved sharing information, quick as a bunny, through the wonder of electronics — turned out to be an insight that thousands of people would be able to make money off in decades afterward. But the Arpanet was *sheltered* from commercial pressures; in fact, in its first fifteen years, commercial traffic was strictly forbidden on it. Venture capital would not have funded its revolution-for-the-hell-of-it. The guys who worked on it weren't necessarily thinking of its applicability to the Outside World, of markets, of quick payback. They had the time and space and freedom of a decade or more to argue and futz around and tinker and bicker for the joy of creating something they found fun and worthy, and ended up creating an institution of technology intersecting with people — the Net — that you can only admire.

Only the government could have had the resources to support such an exercise in supervised play. About the only other candidate might have been one of the great industrial R&D havens, such as Bell Labs — now long gone, alas, one of those frills sacrificed to competition in the new global economy. We want stockholder value, now, not pie-in-the-sky by-and-by!

Gestations when interrupted produce strange monsters; and some of the most interesting and complex organisms (elephants, people) have long gestation periods and prolonged vulnerable juvenile stages demanding profound protection. The Arpanet could not have become the Net without its long, untroubled childhood.

And I would argue that without such long-range temporary autonomous zones — that don't have to pay back investors, that are shielded from big nasty technology predators, and have room to fail, scatter, regroup, and try again — in the long run, fundamental innovation will disappear. And who can provide these time-out corners but the government?

Certainly not established high tech companies, which sacrifice most basic R&D more and more as the finance community/stockholders demand great returns every quarter. If there's money for research, it had better be for something applied, for a problem we're having right *now*. And there is certainly not research support for startups, for an obvious reason: They have to hit the ground running with a fungible idea.

Many people making money today in what is called high tech are really making money from the business case, the appeal to the institutional investor, the possibility of owning the dogfood.com space, where the value-proposition is primary and the technology is secondary. The ideal here is to enable the VCs and the founders to get their money out quickly, even if the company never turns a profit. This is clearly not a good environment for funding basic research.

As much as these carpetbaggers talk and walk like Silicon Valley hero-entrepreneurs, they are really more like speculators of any time and any place. And the entrenched libertarianism, and heedlessness of history that goes with the territory (if your goal is to try to keep generating new stuff, then you don't spend much time thinking about the past) suits them just fine.

PROGRAMMING IS A LOT LIKE LIFE

But maybe there is some kind of essentialist First Cause at work with computing, even if it's not any particular obvious triumph of the engineering genius. As a sweet, wise, smart, independently-wealthy-from-a-young-age-because-of-fundamental-communications-stuff-he-invented technolibertarian pal o' mine explained, computer science is a strange sort of science, because it's not really science but engineering. But unlike regular engineering, where you can see a bridge or a wastewater-treatment plant as a concrete bringing-to-life of your ideas, in computer science there are only 1s and 0s — electronic off and on pulses. But creating a *company* is a means to instantiate an idea, and the validation of the marketplace, the money that might be made from it, is more of a matter of *keeping score* and less the conventional valorization we all derive from money. All of which fits well with the technolibertarian idolatry of the market: It is the highest proof of the value of your ideas.

This is fine theory, as far as it goes; but, remember, entrepreneurialism existed before the microprocessor-based startup culture of the 1980s. Think of the startups that spun out of Route 128 in the 1970s, the Digital Equipment Corporation/"Soul of a New Machine" era. Indeed, you can go back to Hewlett and

Packard in the 1940s, paradigmatic garage-entrepreneurs whom nobody could dare label libertarian.

Brian Cantwell-Smith, a former principal scientist at Xerox PARC/former philosophy professor at Stanford, now professor of computer and cognitive science/adjunct professor of philosophy at Indiana University, has a complementary take on the science/engineering Moebius strip. Classical positivists (that is, scientists of the kind that have flourished in Western Europe for hundreds of years), whatever shortcomings and tunnel vision they may have possessed, had a fundamental humility in their spirit of inquiry. That is, they saw their job as figuring out better ways to understand the workings of the Divine Watchmaker. The truth was out there, somewhere, waiting to be found in the material universe.

In contrast, in computerland, reality is created from within; the object of worth is not waiting to be discovered. It is invention (that is, engineering), not discovery (that is, science), that is valued. This difference in orientation goes some distance toward explaining why the scientific community retains more of the vestiges of working for the Greater Good and satisfying the Inner Curious Child, whereas the computer community, which cants more toward engineering, looks more to the validation of the market and, hence, the cult of the entrepreneur and the individual. It's self-celebratory rather than interconnection-of-the-cosmos-celebratory.

I have heard it said so many times, by journalists and programmers and high tech PR employees and Sand Hill Road venture capitalists, that the contemporary technology-libertarian axis stems from the fact that the microcomputer industry was the *first* techno-economic culture that was not largely dependent on government contracts. From their beginnings, microcomputers were bought as much by businesses and consumers as they were by government — and so the microcomputer industry didn't have the symbiotic relationship with government that characterized some other industry sectors. There is much merit in this supposition; but recall the hugely intertwined relationship between government and computers outlined by Flamm and the hugely intertwined relationship between government and early Silicon Valley outlined by Beers. Until the early 1990s, the largest employers in the Valley were oldfangled military-industrial companies such as Lockheed. And it bears repeating yet again that government also generously funded university computer-science departments.

CLOSER TO THE MACHINE

So government, with the group effort that implies, and mixed personal/professional networks have been central to high tech's growth. Yet libertarians celebrate the cult of the individual, à la Ayn Rand, conveniently ignoring that most scientific and technological improvements are team efforts or are the results of gradual engineering improvements carried out over time. Most of the value in software comes through work done over time by many people, who create the upgrades, extensions, and other refinements. The era of the solo programmer making an impact is mostly long over.

The World Wide Web was simply one in a series of document-handling systems that came out of CERN (the European physics laboratory where basic technology for the Web was developed). The first release of Microsoft Windows (announced in 1983) went nowhere. It was a much later version, Windows 3.1, shipped in 1992, that took off commercially (more than a million advanced orders were place nationwide). A still later version, Windows 95 (1995), released more than ten years after the first version of Windows was announced, was the one that made marketing history.

Similarly, the underlying protocols of the Net were created over decades by the efforts of hundreds of people chipping in.

The Open Source computer movement — in which thousands of programmers from all over the world volunteer their efforts to augment and test public-domain software — is another example of group work in programming.

Yet it's very easy to sit at your computer and imagine yourself the Han Solo captain of your destiny — ignoring the thousands of work-years effectively put in by thousands of people to, say, develop the operating system (the fundamental software underpinnings of a computer) you are working with. The patches, the bug-fixes, the revisions, the distribution and marketing methods — even the materials-science work that went into making the case for your monitor.

So although programmers fancy themselves sky pilots, they are taking advantage of mass labor and social organization, whose handiwork is almost entirely invisible as they seek to create wealth where they sit. And the government's part in all this (R&D, for example) is similarly out of sight. A different political culture might look at a PC and see it as the pinnacle of communitarian striving, the proud handiwork of noteworthy gross tons of government and private-sector collaboration. And when startups are viewed without rose-(or mica-) libertarian-tinted glasses, it's easy to see how most of them are *collectivist* enterprises.

Personal computers themselves have been associated with revolutionary freedom for the individual since they came along in the early 1980s — although if you think about it, it's a little strange, rather like associating typewriters or oscilloscopes or garbage disposers with individuality. Personal computers are, after all, simply tools/dumb machines. The association with individuality is one Apple Computer has traded on for years. The company's famous "1984" television advertisement, shown only once during the 1984 Superbowl, presented the image of enslaved drones in quasi-religious obeisance to a nattering Orwellian Fearless Leader on a Big Screen; a youthful, athletic,

Technicolor young woman then sprinted into view, smashing the oppressive idol. The semiotics were all in a row: The mainframe people were colorless semi-chattel; the microcomputer people were free and brave and iconoclastic. Apple's 1999 ad campaign, "Think Different," featuring rugged individualists like Gandhi, was more of the same. Every culture has its Creation Myth; the personal computer industry has as one of its master narratives the story that The People came from the counterculture and were longing for freedom and, lo, the PC freed them up from the oppression of mainframes, the heavy hand of the corporate MIS department, the servitude of Your Father's Computer Company. PCs were all about power to the people. Never mind that these days portable computing turns out to be a way to keep people, wherever they go, more tethered than ever to their clients and their companies.

True, microcomputers freed programmers from dependence on a shared resource of a mainframe or a time-sharing minicomputer, where the presence of other humans was palpable. With that computing power sitting alone on your desktop, it's easy to imagine yourself as sole captain of your destiny, with no positive benefit to be derived from the intrusions of the outside world, of society at large. And if you find dealing with machines less baffling than dealing with the complex murkiness and illogicality of people, then there might be appeal in a worldview that states that the fewer societally imposed rules coming in from the outside, the better. It's human nature, and certainly the nature of humans in groups, but not computer nature, to operate in complex and not binary modes.

If you think about it, PC-based libertarianism can also be reframed as the mind-set of adolescents, with their deep wish for total rampaging autonomy and desire for simple, call-to-arms passionate politics, where Good and Bad are clearly delineated — taking for granted that someone else does the laundry and stocks the refrigerator. Please, Mom, I'd rather do it myself:

Yet these are the inheritors of the greatest government subsidy of technology and expansion in technical education the planet has ever seen. Remember the Space Race? Like ungrateful adolescent offspring of immigrants who have made it in the new country, technolibertarians take for granted the richness of the environment they have flourished in and resent the hell out of the constraints that bind them.

And, like privileged, spoiled teenagers everywhere, they haven't a clue what their existences would be like without the bounty that has been showered on them. But it's the teenager way — in fact it's human nature — to be annoyed with, to want to renounce, those to whom you are indebted. Ask any fifteen-year-old — or anyone who has not advanced beyond that age *psychologically*.

MACHINE DREAMS

So PCs make it easier to push human presence away. The bias away from humanity has lots of ramifications. For example, the engineer's lack of empathic imagination toward those who have greater affinity with people than machines could very well explain *why* computers and networks are still so damned hard to use and understand, so complex and inclined to strange malfunctions that they require way too much specialist knowledge to get them started and to keep them operating.

Perhaps it's the specific discomfort with people that makes intelligent agents and interactive entertainment such desired products-to-be in Silicon Valley. Intelligent agents are software organisms that filter and seek out information, doing their owners' bidding. The latest incarnation of this idea is an intelligent agent that will comparison shop for you on the Web, at e-commerce sites or auction sites. With interactive entertainment, consumers can choose one of several canned outcomes, instead of leaving the decision about what to leave in and what to leave out in a narrative up to the skills of a storyteller whose talents and gifts lie precisely in those areas.

In 1994, I attended a presentation at the San Francisco Exploratorium (a wonderful hands-on science museum, the brain-child of Frank Oppenheimer, J. Robert's brother) where videos from several high tech companies depicting the future were screened, among them, the famous *The Knowledge Navigator,* starring John Scully during his glory days at Apple. Other videos put together by Sun Microsystems, AT&T, and LSI Logic mapped out their vision of the good life and the promised land that technology would bring. Strangely enough, it was a *boring* world: A world where technology in general and software in particular has taken over all higher human brain functions (never mind that this won't be possible for generations to come, for a multiplicity of reasons) is one where people don't get to be creative, act on hunches, or, ultimately, get to use their instrumental intelligence. At best, people were reduced to cyber-kindergartners, cutting and pasting bits of information, collage-like, with their computers supplying the virtual equivalent of library paste. And what is really sad and strange, and shows how imaginatively impoverished high tech can be, is that many of those videos are now more than fifteen years old — yet they are the same visions of tomorrow that the rank-and-filers in the Valley trot out in 2000.

The happy land of a world serviced by agents and amused by content freed from dependency on another human's naggingly superior-but-elusive-and-irreducible aesthetic sense is a land of individuals isolated from the need for contact with other human beings and, relievedly, no longer reliant upon them.

Libertarianism would do nicely in this better place of the future, where there are no unpleasant dependencies on the quirkiness of humans. Self-reliance, and reliance on machine code, is the goal — since humans tend to be so irrational and are not reducible to any heuristic that can be easily hacked. Embedded in these techno-utopian daydreams is the fear, contempt, and devaluation of the functions of editing, evaluating, and making subjective assessments — functions that can truly be performed only by humans. Those whose livelihood consists of making such judgments (teachers, editors, librarians, film directors, middle-managers) are, in the deep unconscious heart of tech-weenies, best automated out of existence. Hence, the interest in educational software, distance learning, resumé-scanning programs, online narrowcast news services, interactive movies and games — and support for the Net but not for public libraries (except for computers with Net access in them).

Those who buy into these technolibertarian views not so much politically but philosophically don't understand that online library catalogs make some information hard to find just as much as they make certain very limited kinds of searches easier, that an experienced reference librarian (that is, a person, not a piece of software) can often help you find what you are looking for in a few minutes, whereas interrogating the machine might lead to hours of fruitless, pointless inquiry. A Bell Labs staffer I heard speak at a conference admitted that the best way he found to begin his researches was to go to the library and stare at all the books shelved in the topic areas he was interested in; since he didn't know exactly what he was looking for, and didn't know the field that well yet, seeing how the humans who had gone before him had grouped associated books was his mighty-fine heuristic. Nicholson Baker has written extensively on these issues in the *New Yorker*, as has San Francisco technology writer Cate T. Corcoran, in the online magazine *Salon*.

But as the CSU-SJ study participants put it, "Knowledge is viewed as data awaiting retrieval." This restrictive notion of reading as database query, of reading for information, may suit technolibertarians, but not the rest of us so well. When I interviewed the other Microsoft founder-billionaire, Paul Allen, for *Wired*, he trotted out the so-tired notion of the customizable newspaper, delivered electronically. I explained to him that most people read a newspaper differently, skimming to be surprised, reading it precisely because they are not sure what they would find. He was puzzled, poor dear, and didn't know what I was talking about. Just as nerds constantly ask me what something I've written is *about* (in other words, they want a key-word précis/abstract. All writing is conceived of as technical documentation).

In art, execution is everything. It's the way it's expressed, the implementation, that redeems *Anna Karenina* from being a Danielle Steele novel about adultery. And actually, any really *good* engineer intuitively understands this: As Jeff Braun, CEO of Maxis (the software company that brought you fun stuff like *Sim City*, the bestselling, rightfully loved computer-entertainment where you can spend hours creating, destroying, and changing the politics and ecology of a computer-simulated city), once said, "Ideas are cheap. Implementation is everything."

The technolibertarian worldview prefers Amazon.com over a locally owned real-world bookstore, where browsing and interaction with a knowledgeable human are part of the intrinsic appeal. Hey, I know which books on technology I want to buy, so what's the deal?

The notion of reading for pleasure, for whatever indirect data there is to be had in works that aren't so utilitarian (like, say, fiction), is utterly alien. Hey, if you don't like Amazon.com, there's always Fatbrain.com — the Net extension of Computer Literacy bookstores, where *all* you find is books on business and technology.

This model of all knowledge as retrievable data ignores the forty-plus years of failed experiments in artificial intelligence. Cognitive science keeps demonstrating that how we know and what we know are ever more mysteriously complex, that all different kinds of knowledge and understanding are interwoven in the human brain, and that none of it is easily articulated. In the CSU-SJ findings,

> one person described an on-line service for the entertainment industry… "What this did was put that on-line, so if they wanted to do screen tests they could do screen tests of ten to fifteen different people online. You could pull down a database, define what you are looking for with a word search, and according to the database, you would get back say fifteen sites that match and you could look at those sites."

Hmm, as if there could be a keyword descriptor for "interesting, offbeat" or "suggests Audrey Hepburn crossed with Sophia Loren" or "dangerous but vulnerable." So much of what we respond to and understand can't be articulated, is entirely suggestive and subjective. How do we know instantly by looking that it's a dog and not a cat, since none of us perform DNA testing in our everyday lives? Why is that shirt becoming and the other one unflattering? We know much of which we can't speak. Or explain. Or output into codable format.

The study touches on another aspect of this defaulting to code: "Striking here is the lack of attention to the sources of the data. Learners are not the producers of knowledge, only its consumers and manipulators. How data are generated, and how they are related to knowledge is unclear. Efficient retrieval is the main issue."

The technolibertarian worldview likes to pretend that there are not social decisions embedded in code, to pretend that technology is neutral. That by having to code or represent things in a certain way, representations of reality aren't twisted or minimized. A very simple example: The way different search engines on the World Wide Web find and rank different materials on the Web proves the differences that can exist in how information is coded and interpreted. You might not find what you are looking for if you can't come up with a search string that mediates between what you want and what the dumb search engine can find. And I won't even get into the problems of what is, and is not, available on the Web, or the quality or currency of what's available there. It's spooky to think of a generation of kids who are deluded into thinking that if something (an article, an idea, an author, a publication) isn't available on the Web, then it doesn't exist or doesn't have value. Human, Too Human. Not only is there bewilderment verging on mistrust with regard to many of those qualities considered most human; in philosophical technolibertarianism there is almost an embrace of the nonhuman. "All societies and most humans have some tendency toward the liminal — toward wanting to be taken out of ourselves by whatever narrow assortment of drugs our particular society deems acceptable: trance, dance, prayer, go-cart racing, bungee jumping, or playing the slots. But deep underneath much technolibertarian thought, and often going under the catchphrase of self-organization (what fascinating things can we learn about ourselves by observing other self-organizing complex social systems, such as beehives and ant farms?), appears a longing not just to be temporarily relieved of the burden of self but to be other than human. Recall former *Wired* executive editor Kevin Kelly's notion of the hive mind— the sort of simple organization behaviors exhibited by bees — as an ideal of social organization without pesky regulators.

Alas, we are not insects: We have more complex drives and desires and needs and perform far more complicated and ambiguous and multivalent tasks — often at odds with ourselves, each other, and potentially for the good of whichever hive we are acting on behalf of at the moment. Attendees of Bionomics conferences are fascinated by reports of the actual behaviors of ants as models of how economies can flourish with very simple rules — though ants are dumb, arguably feel no pain, and to take a hint from the existentialists, probably don't know or care if they are going to die. Similarly, there is a love of computer simulations of ant-farmish artificial-life beings (that is, computer models of organisms that exist only on a computer or computer network), whose fate, when observed over time, seems to prove that the poor will always be with us and that a tendency toward monopoly in unregulated systems is pretty damned inevitable. The Extropians, a fringeware technolibertarian cult — or rather, a group of radical optimists — believe in maximizing human potential by becoming transhuman: cryonics, uploading brain contents in computers, as much surgical enhancement as conceivable down here on Earth, and general reaching for the stars. As if being human were itself such an onerous burden that only machine modification could improve it. In reading those who cheered on Max More (philosopher founder of Extropy) while he and I engaged in a "Brain Tennis" debate (an online, point/counterpoint, "Jane, you ignorant slut" debate on *Hotwired, Wired* magazine's Web publication), I kept wondering why all these guys found being human something to be so eagerly transcended — to the point where I found myself eerily reminded of the positive side of ethnic studies and identity-self-help organizations: First you gotta wrestle with why you hate so much what you are (traditionally, being black or Jewish or a smart plain girl or gay or...). Why did these folks so hate being human that the fantasy of being transhuman so appealed? Hive insects and cyborgs are creatures not subject to the complexity and contradictions and vulnerabilities and despairs and defects of being human. Complexity and contradictions and vulnerabilities are universally acknowledged to be sad and scary — but are also the source of our genius and pleasure. Perhaps if we really could become more like machines, more algorithmic and less messy in our actions and emotions, we might very well need less government and less regulation.

But as we interact with more and more machines in our lives (ever been stuck in voicemail hell where you are dying to talk to a human being because your particular need doesn't fit any of the five choices?), we are more frantic and upset with how who we really are doesn't fit very well with these aliens, the machines, among us. As Stanley Bing wrote in his wickedly good satirical business novel *Lloyd: What Happened. A Novel of Business* (Crown, 1998),

> Like many improvements that had appeared on the scene recently, from cellular faxes to voice mail to personal electronic messaging, the increase in technological capability had not produced a resulting improvement in the quality of human life. It had just changed things in such a way as to make them unrecognizable.

The bias toward virtuality runs through the future dreams of participants in the CSU-SJ studies.

> New technology will permit users to experience much more, but this experience will be technologically mediated. It will be controlled by both its producer and consumer, and cleansed of the sloppiness and unpredictability-the inefficiency of life; it will be "virtualized."... Direct experience of life, with all its uncertainty and messiness, appears to be suspect. Face-to-face interactions with other people are eschewed in favor of electronically mediated interactions. Physical movement, too, is to be avoided, and electronic simulations provide a ready and convenient (i.e., efficient) substitute... [There is] the sense that the person need only interact with like-minded technical people and avoid cross-cultural and cross-class contact. One... clearly articulated this view:
>
> "I think what the information infrastructure does is that it allows me to do intellectual tasks without physical activity, which makes me more efficient, and anything you can think of that involves a form of a pen or something you have to write, well you shouldn't have to go somewhere to do it."

Perhaps there is a Stockholm Syndrome identifying-with-your-captor phenomenon going on: If you fit yourself into grooving well with the world of machines, the other parts become more gangly and vestigial and annoying and confusing and old and in the way. The Extropian path, though, is an extreme edge of high tech culture, and you have to be careful not to make drastic and silly conclusions about the mainstream from the interesting backwater eddies.

REARING ITS UGLY HEAD

Returning to the gender dimorphism of Bionomics versus the Land of the Medicine Buddha, I think it is more an effect than a cause; other traditionally male-dominated fields, such as physical chemistry or, say, neurosurgery, aren't particularly libertarian. Difference-feminist Carol Gilligan argues that women tend to be more concerned with relationships than abstract theories of justice, which means the relatively low value libertarians place on the social matrix implies that libertarianism is not a philosophy bound to be immensely attractive to women. This chain of intuition fits with what a longtime science-policy nice-guy I talked to in Washington, DC, said: In trying to figure out why *fewer* women were studying computer science now than ten years ago, he had a suspicion that many women were put off by the by-now default culture of libertarianism that characterizes even academic computer science departments. So it's the reverse of causality; it seems self-selection is opting women out of a discipline they could be very much at home in — guys having no exclusive franchise on thinking logically, paying attention to detail, solving puzzles, and wanting to make decent money.

When I gave a talk at the annual meeting of Computer Professionals for Social Responsibility (the small, ignored, mostly academic, though long-standing organization of those working in technology who think hard about its social consequences) in the fall of 1997, one of the audience members nodded agreement with much of what I had to say about technolibertarians — -and at the end, when I was taking questions from the floor, tossed off the joke, "But don't worry, it's a self-limiting problem because they don't reproduce." Laughter of recognition all around.

What we were all recognizing was how many of these guys (and they are far and away guys, though not exclusively) hadn't coupled off, hadn't had kids. There are plenty of exceptions, as there always are when you try to assign group characteristics to individual human beings; but it is eerie how many, particularly the *philosophical* as opposed to *political* technolibertarians, don't seem to have found a way to get themselves comfortable in that most fundamental interdependent human social connection: a relationship with a Loved Intimate. And almost nothing will throw you into thinking about being able to rely on decent schools and the wholesomeness of the food supply and the safety of in-front car seats and the notion of dependency itself as having a kid. Which is of course not to say that there aren't plenty of folks who eschew the Greater Community and resent the intrusion of the Damnable Government and homeschool their kids. However, many differently-abled-in-the-relationship-department technolibertarians could simply be making virtue out of necessity, and fancying themselves Cyberspace Texas Rangers Who Don't Need Nobody — intellectual superstructure for psychological aloneness.

In James Gibson's *Warrior Dreams,* the culture of the New Warrior is marked by a fear of dependency and a backlash toward the feminization of so much of the modern world (dammit, women are showing up everywhere and trying to do everything and generally getting under foot), and the fantasy of a society without baffling emotional demands and ambivalences is really appealing. Gibson quotes an editor in his book: "A story about human relationships moves much more slowly than a story about adventure and killing" (compare, say, Penelope Lively to Robert Ludlum). Similarly, a technolibertarian world of lots of churn and lots of action, death, and rebirth of companies and technologies can be seen as glorifying male emotion-porn (how many sci-fi novels have lots of battles/violent encounters with no real outcome) — and ignoring the human cost of all. Maybe technolibertarians are playing out their version of the zeitgeist, the same one that celebrates extreme sports and No Fear T-shirts, that seeks the adrenaline rush of battle simulation wherever it can be found.

BAD BOYS ARE SO MUCH MORE FUN

There is a cultural-studies theory, which I only semi-seriously make fun of, espousing that this generation of technologists, particularly the cypherpunks and cyberpunk camp-followers, have read too much Ayn Rand and too much Robert A. Heinlein — though not in his *Stranger in a Strange Land* mode. Ayn Rand and Heinlein are authors who in their work celebrate male prowess and defy conventional notions of affectionate attachment. They write books that are pure "Warrior Dreams" fodder.

Recall cypherpunk style, for these highly visible cyber-swashbucklers, the resistance fighters on the far outposts of the digital frontier, help shed light on the technological mainstream. Cypherpunkdom is a path to glory for those who in a much more benighted era might have been considered 98lb weaklings. What's also truly damned appealing about the cypherpunk phenom has been that it's mercifully antidotal toward all that is nauseatingly politically correct. Authentic cultural backlash at its finest. Yet as much as it is fun to induce interesting generalizations from exciting cypherpunk bad boys, they are not the entire story. Margins do inform the center, but they are not the center.

Something similar to this hyper-boy/lone-ranger undercurrent is at play with all the frontier imagery that gets thrown around when the tacticians and rhetoricians of cyberspace come together. The Wild West carries with it the Romance of the Great Outdoors. Everyone loves a cowboy, and many want to be one. Who wants to resist the promise of freedom and adventure?

Rave on, archetype of the Rugged Individual! But consider that most cowboys were actually hourly wage-workers, often for large outfits. They were more like office temps (with *really* bad working conditions) than bold cavaliers. Maybe the comparison isn't so off...

Being at the site where new fashions break out is part of what makes the sweet spot of a culture center compelling; it's why folks want to move to Paris and not be stuck in Mulhouse-and in discussions of business and technology, its force gets overlooked. Think of the astonishing originality in concept, and success in implementation, of *Wired* magazine, which made computers and communications sexy and glamorous and avant-garde. Pretty good for a field of human activity not too long ago considered by majority culture to be booorrriinngg and about as "with it" and culturally serious as, say, International Standards Organization proceedings on acceptable tolerances for machine tools. Now, every Hip Young Geek (or those, regardless of actual age or occupation, who would like to see themselves as such) wants to be in its pages — and the magazine's libertarian strut was part of its reflected sheen. Be a brave freedom-fighting entrepreneur and have a nine-year-old's fun of waving a pirate flag! At this point, it's hard to imagine a dashing techno-self-concept that *wouldn't* have libertarianism as part of its makeup, in no small part thanks to *Wired*. And for the business-porn magazines that have followed in its wake and the MBAs that have changed San Francisco as much as the 49ers did (a large percentage of Harvard Business School's class of 1999 came out to the Bay Area, whether or not they had a job lined up), glamour and technolibertarianism à la *Wired*, the first generation, suits.

So what *is* it out here, that all those MBAs want?

CLIMATE = DESTINY

Without getting into the silly rants about blood and soil and how geography influences culture that any sane person would try to avoid, it has to be speculated on how the anticommunitarian outlook is in some respects an outcropping of how suburban an industry high tech has been historically. The quintessential edge-city business, high tech celebrates people operating as monads, free agents who work in industrial parks and aspire, when they cash out in an IPO, to telecommute from horse country, puma country, or even from within the spare-bedroom-cum-home-office located in a million-dollar Eichler ranch house on a street somewhere close to El Camino Real. Never mind that most self-employed/startup/telecommuting Internet entrepreneurs are concentrated in New York, San Francisco, and Los Angeles, thriving on the grit/density/frisson/charge of urban areas.

Nevertheless, the monoculture of suburbs unhappily maps well onto the monoculture of high tech: Libertarianism might work really well in populations where folks have more or less the same education, drives, training, goals, orientation to the world, skillsets, cognitive blinders, and myopias. The wonderful, self-regulating world of the IETF (Internet Engineering Task Force), the voluntary standards group that determines the technology future of the Net, is an astonishingly glorious example of how the libertarian dream of how simple rules can work in a complex world (and until fairly recently, majorly funded by the National Science Foundation. There's that mortmain of ZOG again! You know, the Zionist Occupied Government that the militia people are always alerting us to).

But the world is not as tidy a place as the IETF, which consists of a thousand or so right-minded geeks who volunteer to think hard and do their best for that thing that they love, the Internet. In spite of the strong-minded differences of technical opinion in the IETF, the people who participate are obviously much more alike than not (civic-minded computer networkers) — and are working on a very bounded problem set. Simple rules work well here — but alas the Real World is a far messier, diverse, and confusing place, with all kinds of people with different intentions and levels of intelligence and things that they want and need and do; a more heterogeneous place requires a more complicated set of rules. Sadly, the world of the IETF would not map outward to the infinity and beyond of all the things politics and civic life is about, just as the housing covenants (what kind of roofline you are allowed) and retail signage restrictions (no neon) in a suburb wouldn't fly in a city. If everyone in the world were like some of the sweet, smart, self-disclosing, generous-of-spirit, ethical, thoughtful nerds I know, libertarianism would be the way to go. Unfortunately, most people, and most businesses, cannot be counted on to be so uniformly evolved.

Aside from the historical suburbanness of high tech, there may be something distinctive about Northern California that has made it such a technolibertarian hotbed. One of my computer scientist friends did feel there was something distinctive about Northern California high tech as opposed to that of Southern California. He remarked on how different the *social* climate was in the computer science departments at Cal Tech (where he got his Ph.D.) and at Berkeley (where he is a post-doc). He had the feeling at Cal Tech that there was a culture where, since everyone was brilliant and quirky and nerdy in similar ways, less-charming nerd behaviors were not tolerated. In other words, there was an ethos where folks generally were not encouraged in their I'm-so-brilliant-my-arrogance-and-asocial-qualities-are-excusable attitude. At Berkeley, he felt such behaviors were condoned, as a species of warpo Politically Correct hippie-individualism do-your-own-thing gone amok. A perfect incubator for libertarianism, perhaps.

But consider, too, that Silicon Valley *is* situated in Northern California, the fantasy of the discorporated transgeographical nature of cyberspace aside.[46] And what is the greater Bay Area but the site of what used to be called the human potential movement, the place that threw off Esalen and EST and all the rest. The New Age ethos holds that you create your own reality and that whatever happens to you is of your own choosing and that if bad stuff happens, it's karmically correct and entirely your own fault. These philosophies of human potential eschewed looking to what the Marxists used to like to call the objective conditions — that is, social, economic, or political forces — and they fit very well with a libertarian ethos. You have to wonder if there was a kind of trade route in ideas in the '70s and '80s where the divorced or unattached of Silicon Valley, after taking a weekend workshop or two, brought back to their day job some of these notions of the universe rewarding those who psychically manifest what they want properly. And if things don't come your way, it's because the cosmos — the divine marketplace — didn't deem you or your strivings worthy. It's perhaps not a coincidence that the successor to EST, called Landmark, describes its, uh, offerings and insights as *technologies*.

Whether or not Fritz Perls and Werner Erhard had anything to do with it, there really does seem to be a West Coast locus to technolibertarianism. When I talk to people from the high tech corridors of Boston and Northern Virginia, they shake their heads over what those goofy Berkeley-radical/sagebrush rebellion whacked-out Californians are up to once again. As a native Californian, I take umbrage at such simplistic dismissals (that's California, where all extremists and crazies are tolerated/originate; no, that's California, always in the cultural vanguard). But Mario Savio and James Watt are not who normally come to mind as technolibertarian cultural heroes in this largely Bays-Area

46 This is a fantasy increasingly at odds with reality as VCs continue to want to fund those companies that are within easy drive of their other companies and that they can staff with people and set up business relationships with enterprises they've worked with in their previous ventures

way of knowing.[47] It can't be as simple as being in a different time zone than DC, for the high tech culture of my childhood, the Southern California aerospace industry, was a four-hour flight away from our nation's capital, too.

Professional futurists like to call California the bellwether state. It is here, after all, that the antitax counterrevolution, manifested in Proposition 13, started in 1978. Its ethos — our kids have already gone through school, so why should we pay for yours — does, alas, provide a kind of backdrop for a libertarian political culture. But having lived in California before Prop 13 — and having attended its public schools for a time when they were among the best in the country, and remembering the spruce and well-stocked state of our public libraries and parks — it's hard to see how the passage of Prop 13 was a good thing. Perhaps those who have moved here since (as in most people working in high tech today) have not seen a time when things worked well because we paid, in the communitarian sense, to have them work well.

In another variant of her "dynamism versus stasis" argument, Virginia Postrel in the August 25, 1997, issue of *Forbes ASAP* — the quarterly add-on issue to *Forbes* (as slavering over perceived economic/technological winners and as nasty about perceived economic/technologic losers as a magazine of partisan *politics* would be) wrote a piece called "Resilience versus Anticipation." The essay was part of that issue's overall theme of "How the West Kicked Butt." And as was expected, the issue had all the de rigueur railing against bureaucracy and the corruptness of policy-making and the horrors of regulation you'd expect ("Feds Hate the Web. From the FCC to the IRS, Washington's war against the Web marches on"). The essay proclaimed how we in Silicon Valley are just The Best — as after all, we must be, for in a May 1998 poll of graduating MBAs, for the first time, San Francisco was where they most wanted to be.

47 Bays-Area includes Monterey Bay (to the south) in addition to San Francisco Bay. Santa Cruz is at the north tip of Monterey Bay.

Anyway, in her essay, among other explanations Postrel gives for the ascendancy of the *Sunset* magazine way of tech-work-life, she declares that it is "the California sun. Eventually all theories end up there, at the one thing that makes Silicon Valley unlike Boston, or Austin, or Seattle, the one thing they can never hope to copy: it's the weather."

Funny, there's also what I call the "why no great novel ever came out of Hawaii" theory, which has been propounded seriously by some folks who say you need radical changes of weather to create great literature. Think New England weather, or "It was a dark and stormy night" — though that was the opening for a novel in Bulwer-Lytton's nineteenth-century England.

Not that I don't love my native land with a grasping sappy pleasure; I do. But it rains half the year and some summers the fog never burns off and then there really isn't any summer. And it is a semi-desert; we worry about water in a constant background way that folks Back East can't imagine; worries of drought years are never far away. We worry when it doesn't rain, and it gets oppressive (or dangerous, as in flood years) when it keeps raining, week after week. And it's usually not East Coast cloudburst-thunderstorm-then-it-clears rain; it's an unremitting grayness worthy of bleak Northern European Gothic tales. Not to mention that many people in high tech don't have the opportunity to get outside enough to *notice* the weather.

Postrel also goes on to explain that California is "unstable," that is, prone to earthquakes, that "to live in earthquake country is to know, way back in the back of your mind, that your house, your car, your office could — at any moment — become your grave... That, too, makes Silicon Valley special."

To emphasize her point, Postrel quotes a guy named Art Hutchinson, a technology management consultant with Boston's Northeast Consulting Resources.

> "We'd love to live there-except for the earthquakes... But the risk of one great whomp and you're flattened on the 880? No...

> That feels very parallel to the risk profile people think about in business. If you're willing to move there, you've already accepted a certain subliminal level of risk."

It sounds so brave and heroic and dancing on the edge, that libertarian myth-making once again. And maybe it is true in ways I can't know. People from Back East seem to think and worry about earthquakes far more than the people who live in California do. They tend to ignore/not know that the site of the next Big One is as likely to be in Southern California as in Northern California, and more *Day of the Locust* than *Only the Paranoid Survive*. But somehow the image of Indiana Jones-style survival in the face of temblors — in a business metaphor kinda way — is much more compelling than when applied to a culture better known for its advances in technologies for cosmetic surgery and dumbing down mass media. But I tend to be skeptical of such arguments from the land anyway: They verge on the specious reasoning of the City College of New York professor Leonard Jeffries, who asserted that people of African descent were people of the sun — and hence warm and life-loving. Or the Aryan Volkish deep truths about the moral superiority that comes from being the icy People of the North.

You could in fact argue things just the other way around: Back East or in the Heart of the Country, where there is constant instability of weather, the *catastrophe*/Act of God that happens every year (it's called winter) should lead to there being a race of people who are instinctive chaos-wranglers/complexity-surfers and who go with the flow and know how to cope with the ever-changing flux of, of, of well, market conditions. Life. Whatever. I simply don't believe that every wanna-be film star or aeronautical engineer or Swiss winemaker who came to California in an earlier era to make his or her fortune was a risk-taker beyond any other immigrant to, say, Minnesota or Oregon or Argentina. And I don't think it's any different now — except that the high-frequency, high-amplitude buzz that emanates from Silicon

Valley seems to lend itself to this kind of myth-making.

So the sources of technolibertarianism remain a sweet mystery of life, as strange and singular as the feeling, after World War II, that European countries should begin to divest themselves of their colonies, or the late 1990s return of ghastly 1970s fashion. Some might blame it on an educational system that values money and skills-training over the teaching of humane values. But nobody can know; we can only marvel and be afraid.

CHAPTER SIX

THE THRILLING CONCLUSION

IT WASN'T UNTIL I was almost done with a week-long field trip to Washington, DC, in April 1997 that I realized how much I myself had drunk the Northern California technolibertarian Kool-Aid. I had made the trip not because I had any faith that there would be anyone useful to talk to but because logic dictated I should. No one in my circle could see the point either, but I didn't see how I could write about political culture and not go to the most explicitly political place in the country. At least, theoretically.

Initial signs were not promising. The lack of access and the stonewalling that folks always complain about with The Government I ran right into: I got nowhere trying to talk to the two congresspeople (Republican Tom Campbell/Peninsula and Democrat Zoe Lofgren/San Jose) I thought would have the most apposite things to say. I was dying to ask the members from Silicon Valley: How do you act as the elected government representative for a community that doesn't believe in government? I fared only a little better with my own representative, Sam Farr/Santa Cruz — I was rescheduled and jerked around so many times by his local staff and told I would only have five minutes to present my case (they couldn't seem to understand that I didn't have a case. What I wanted was to schedule some time for a *conversation*) that I finally gave up and went away, which was probably their intention. I can't imagine what I would have done if I had had a pressing personal problem, as opposed to a professional one. And I have to say, in all my years of banging around with my day job as a journalist, I have never found a bunch of folks so impossible to get through to. I've had far better luck with calling up architects, chemistry professors, and computer hackers out of the blue than with the people who are supposed to be working for me.

My god, it's all true, what they say about It, is what I was beginning to believe. But then my own networks kicked in and people knew people and so I went off to Babylon/Sodom/Gomorrah. And what I found was that, yes, there actually were all kinds of smart interesting people in DC. They might not be *in* the government — they tended to be in academia and nonprofits — but they made it their business to *influence* government. Which I suddenly remembered is how it works: People pound on different parts of the government, making it more or less responsive over time.

Once there, I was reminded that you don't *want* government to be a rapid-response SWAT team (except on the occasion of flood or fire). A certain ponderous backwardness provides a kind of stability, just as, assuming you want them to mostly remain solvent, you don't want insurance companies to be highly leveraged/margin-calls-run high-flyers. Institutional stability carries with it the curse of being behind the times and unresponsive. Being in and around high tech, so motorized and so now you're in/then you're out/onto the next thing, had raised my sensory threshold so high that I had forgotten that there are valid rhythms of work and life that don't operate like this. And actually, you don't *want* to have them operate like this, because laws and policy shouldn't have the half-lives of microprocessor generations.

So okay. That's the reality of governance. Witness the situation of the organic farmers in fifty states who asked the FDA to establish uniform standards for what "organic" meant in the spring of 1998. They wanted federal standards because they were finding it difficult, if not impossible, to meet all the different and at times contradictory criteria established in different states, which is a problem that regulations regarding interstate commerce can solve. Initially, it looked like the standards were gonna get hijacked by agribusiness (ah, the free market). In other words, genetically engineered and irradiated foodstuffs and use of sewage sludge (do you want the industrial by-products and household cleaners that go down the drain to be used as fertilizer?) were gonna be allowed, and their use not even labeled. Massive consumer outcry got these objectionable (objectionable to those who tend to care about organic food) loopholes dismissed.

The case of the organic farmers serves as a reminder of the nuts-and-bolts ways government can be useful — and that we live in the real world and not cyberspace. For most of us, unlike many of my geek friends, our homes and our lives are more than the place where we can recharge our laptops.

But this distinction gets lost. As the CSU-SJ study points out,

> The Valley might be seen instrumentally by many denizens as a place to work and not really live, but in doing so their lives are lived and a place is created. Its unique advantages are celebrated...but many products being developed there are intended to make space and time irrelevant. These claims are likely exaggerated, but to the extent that they are believed, they color...life.

Yet, even in Silicon Valley, people secretly know that nine-tenths of life consists of showing up. Dave Nagel, former higher-up at Apple who jumped ship during the Great Migrations from Apple of the last few years, is now president of AT&T Labs. In the May 11, 1998, issue of *The Industry Standard*, he was asked,

> Q: Do you think businesses need a presence in the Valley to be successful?
>
> A: For any business focused on next-generation networking and communications, being here is a near necessity. It's clear

> that the Valley has become the nexus where many of the industry-changing ideas get created and most get commercially tested. It's hard to imagine anywhere else with as active an intellectual and commercial stewpot.

In other words, in their heart of hearts, it's universally acknowledged that virtuality is bosh — except maybe for the hardcore coder-monkeys, HTML grunts, and other very specific high tech life-forms who can do what they do anywhere. Not that you can't do some work on airplanes or at the beach or from your Idaho redoubt; but even in Silicon Valley, you need to really be there.

Back in the late '80s, I attended a conference on Computer Supported Cooperative Work (CSCW), where scientists, both social and computer, explored how computers might enable work in groups. One of the speakers presented a paper demonstrating empirical evidence that in scientific work, people tend to talk to and work more closely with people next door than with the people on the next floor. And with those in the same building more so than those across campus. And with those at the same institution more with those at other institutions. I would venture to say that even with the rise of the Net, intellectual work remains social, as it always has been. Reality asserts itself in occasional fashion. So what is *real* in regard to technology?

WHAT IS REAL, AND WHAT IS NOT

In March of 1998, I participated in the launch event for Technorealism, the public unveiling of an eight-point document (please don't call it a manifesto), signed by twelve somewhat well-known technology writers, basically saying, chill, technology isn't all good or all bad, does have social consequences, and is embedded in the real world. The document (www.technorealism.org), and its attendant debut at Harvard Law School, got lots of press attention, way more than it warranted — and much of it surprisingly negative for so innocuous a statement of principles. Much of the negativity that emerged (in online conferences, lists, and publications, and in print) focused on what critics felt were the obviousness of the points ("Technologies are not neutral"; "The Internet is revolutionary but not utopian"). No sane person would find anything controversial about them anymore; we had all moved on since the techno-utopianism of a few years back, and weren't we TRs (technorealists) as behind the times as if we had courageously and daringly come out swinging for women's suffrage?

Technorealism point three ("The government has a role to play on the electronic frontier") was, according to the critics, typical of the TR tendency to lash out at enemies that didn't exist anymore — after all, no one bought that undiluted libertarian stuff of a few years back.

Could it be? Had the world moved on and I hadn't noticed? Perhaps more folks with a more mainstream political sensibility were participating in and writing about technoculture. After all, *Wired* had had a radical change of editorial board in January 1998, with the new editorial executives chosen by *Wired's* investors for their traditional editorial qualifications, rather than for their enthusiasm for the libertarian life. Coupled with the sale of the magazine in May 1998 to Condé Nast, its days as the *Daily Worker* for the libertarian technical elite were over.

Wouldn't it be great if it were all a bad dream people had woken up from? Or, as my mother would say about my wish that the incessant day-and-night libertarian drumming would stop — from your mouth to God's ears!

But the argument against this — that libertarianism was a charming excess of the recent past — was contained even in the slams TR was getting. In the online forum accompanying the release of the Technorealism document sponsored by the online magazine *Feed*, lo and behold, mirabile dictu, the libertarians came out in force, monopolizing the discussion, pounding their shoes on the table as they have been in the habit of doing for so long. Nope, things had not changed that much. The you-can-count-on-it libertarian presence in high tech is as persistent as the presence of pro-lifers at a Republican convention. It's there, and it's not going away any time soon — and can't be placed on any list of threatened or endangered species.

Over Halloween weekend in 1998, smack in the middle of the Microsoft/DOJ antitrust trial, Eric Raymond, an important figure in the open-source software movement, posted onto the Web a leaked in-house memo written by Microsoft program manager Vinod Valloppillil. The Halloween Document, as it came to be known, titillated anti-Microsoft partisans with its details of Microsoft's latest plans for world domination, specifically in the Linux/open-source software arena. But what went uncommented on was that both Raymond, the heroic Daniel Ellsberg–type programmer who posted the memo, and Valloppillil, Evil Empire functionary, were avowed libertarians. Raymond's libertarianism had already been well documented in *Salon*; with Valloppillil, all that was necessary was to go to the Microsoft engineer's vanity/personal Web site, www.vinod.com, and click on his "favorites" link. What popped up first thing was the topic heading "Libertarianism" ("Politically I'm a pretty hard-core libertarian"), along with brief but high praise for *Reason* magazine, the Cato Institute, and the Bionomics Institute (all with active Web links, of course.) It was rather like discovering that a liberal and a conservative senator had both acquired their law degrees from Yale: no news here.

Or witness the editorial written by a friend of mine, Richard Brandt, then the editor of *Upside*. "Telco Tar Pits" appeared in the May 20, 1998, online edition of the magazine and contained such classic technolibertarian refrains as the following:

> The FCC [is] dead... [Traditional telephone companies are] walking corpses. We're talking mangled and desiccated road-kill on the information highway here... Sure, some of them

> may actually adapt and survive... It's possible that some of the dinosaurs survived and became birds, too... So it's exciting to sit back, take it all in, and think about the enormity of the change we talk about, day in and day out... Joe Nacchio, CEO of QWEST, notes that telcos will not go into the dark night easily. "We live in the age of the dinosaurs. They move slowly, but they've got big goddamn feet."... The FCC is on the run, reevaluating its purpose in life, which is becoming the task of making deregulation happen... The bunch of dinosaurs have lived for the past century in a legal, regulated monopoly. Suddenly they come up against the giant Internet asteroid, deregulation's climate change and fleet-footed mammals. What do you think will happen? Nothing but the tar pits... Many will... die out in the change, and the strong will survive... The future look[s] like so much fun!

There's the borrowing from biology, with a heavy emphasis on natural selection; the love of ceaseless churn and change; the assumption that only the stupid and the virtue-deficient might object; a Robespierrian love of whatever is perceived to be tyrannicidal; a yumyumyum exultation over it all. Richard Richard Richard, when did you snag a supporting role in the 1998 Silicon Valley remake of *Invasion of the Body Snatchers*?

But then, it's been like this for a long time. Compare with this, from *Silicon Valley Fever: Growth of High-Technology Culture* (Everett Rogers and Judith Larsen, Basic Books, 1984), considered something of a reference text for understanding high tech:

> One wonders what kind of a national political leader a high-technologist would make. Likely...with a strong belief in free-market forces and faith in government policies that govern least. Most Silicon Valley tycoons are not concerned with issues of social inequality or injustice; to the entrepreneur, the poor and the weak in society are poor and weak because they are inferior. It is the poor and weak's fault that they are

> downtrodden, rather than the result of an unequal system. The engineer-entrepreneur believes in social evolution, the absolute correctness of competition, and in technological solutions to social problems. The engineer-politician lacks a liberal arts education, is suspicious of liberalism...
>
> As America moves forward as an information society, these values of competition, a faith in technology, and political conservatism are likely to become more widely shared and more widely held by the public...[leading to] increasing economic and political power for high-technology...and for the entrepreneurs who lead them.

Was ever thus. Sigh. So when I asked my friend Richard about his editorial, his response was telling:

> don't worry, i havent really turned that libertarian...i do worry about universal access with the death of the fee, which really does seem to be dying. i wrote an editorial once advocating universal access fees for internet access and got lots of flame mail...
>
> ...the libertarians have taken over silicon valley and most of tech, and it gets hard to resist them. but i believe the unfettered end of pure capitalism is something like dickens and as bad as unfettered socialism.
>
> the thing that's interesting to me is that so much of silval [Silicon Valley] is so hands off when it comes to any govt actions except anti-trust suits against microsoft. it's extraordinarily hypocritical.

Right. And so many technolibertarians of the extreme kind think the whole antitrust matter is merely the government exacting its extortionate Salt Tax; that is, Microsoft hasn't been tithing its share (to political parties, to highly paid lobbyists). That, at least, is wrong, because Microsoft certainly has. Engineers *like* things to be simple — never mind that even for them, these days their biggest problem is managing *complexity* in computer systems, a complexity that no single person can grasp.

I continue to have conversations with geeks of all ages and descriptions who come up with statements like, "I'm not libertarian, but I think the government interferes too much in our lives." Without looking for it, the language of new anarcho-biological freedom-fighting paradigms also continues to come my way. In the July 4, 1998, *Entropy Gradient Reversals* (www.rageboy.com), a rather in-your-face, confessional, at times profane, at times profound, at times funny occasional Web publication by Internet business consultant (and coauthor of *The Cluetrain Manifesto* [Perseus Books, 2000]), Christopher Locke says in all emergent-bionomical-insurrectionist fervor that,

> Command-and-control thinking throws cold water onto all that magic-mushroom enthusiasm... Workers at every level have had it with repressive companies [hmm, has Locke ever talked to people who work at Oracle?]... Debug on the fly, then iterate... Yeah it does [turn into anarchy] and you start instigating it. What I've always been interested in is revolution... I call it gonzo business management... These giant companies tend to look only over the tops of the trees at the other giants they consider their worthy competitors. Few bother to look at their feet. If they did,...more than a few would see their foundations being nibbled away by competitors many times smaller.

Meanwhile, the first porn movie with a cypherpunk story line and a cypherpunk male lead got produced, *Desdemona Affair*. What did writer/producer Randy French think cryptography, guns, and porn have in common? "Free choice." A 1999 issue of the *Sharper Image* catalogue (lots of gizmos and personal tech for the exec on the go) led off the ad copy for its high-tech wristwatch perpetually tuned to the US Atomic Clock with, "Libertarians may not rejoice, but the 'time' is whatever our government says it is." Something called Cyberfest '99, a Silicon Valley music rave/county fair, described itself as "250 mind-blowing acres of freedom." Guy Kawasaki, the original software evangelist for Apple, published a book in 1999 called *Rules for Revolutionaries* (HarperBusiness). The February 20, 2000, lead business story in the *San Francisco Examiner*, titled "The New, New Politics," explained that the Valley was getting shrewder politically, but still retained its "libertarian roots."

It really doesn't stop.

ENVOI

It's pointless to argue with what people feel, and this is the reason religion and politics are considered off-limits for polite dinner conversation: they touch too deeply on emotions and convictions that come from the soul rather than the prefrontal cortex. Rational argument in an irrational framework. So if people in Silicon Valley don't remember, to the best of their recollection, that there wouldn't be a Silicon Valley, or a microprocessor industry, without huge federal defense contracts, that there wouldn't be a Silicon Valley without what was once the best and best-funded public educational system in the country, that there wouldn't be a Silicon Valley without that peculiarly American mixed economy of free market and regulation that makes everyone and his maiden aunt want to immigrate here, both for quality of life and for the possibility of doing well, so be it.

It's been a strange venture, going after libertarians when I share so much of their fundamental orientation. What I most want is to be left alone; I don't have that will to power that would ever suggest that I know how to tell other people how to live their lives, a libertarian stance if there ever was one. I think victimless crimes such as prostitution and drug-use should be decriminalized but regulated. I think it would be terrific if there were to be a dual-track for pharmaceuticals and medical products in this country: one FDA approved, one NOT FDA approved, but both clearly regulated and *labeled* as such. But I have much less conviction that the free market and the private sector will protect the environment, my rights as a consumer, or the quality and quantity of books at the public library. I am not convinced that having a strengthened system of property rights will solve all; after all, who enforces those rights but the police? Somehow, I can't feature that more cops, or a private security force, are the answer to all that ails us in this chiliastic time. And I also don't think spending all one's days in lawsuits, to prosecute property trespasses that in other contexts would be considered violations of regulation/crimes, often offered as the libertarian alternative to regulation, is a productive or efficient rejoinder.

Still, it feels creepy and hollow to be defending government at a time when, as old New Lefty Barbara Ehrenreich says, we have government that is increasingly doing things *to* us and not *for* us.

So I am not calling for a series of town meetings where libertarians can be upbraided; nor am I proposing that they be rounded up and placed in detention camps. I don't have a ten-point five-year plan: I leave that to those who *do* have the will to power and who sincerely believe that if everyone just did as they told them, then everything would be fine.

And just as it's been said that the Republican right really doesn't understand that the countercultural revolution of the '60s is permanent (more open ideas about sexuality and gender, stronger identity politics, more comfort with a broader range of psychoactive substance use), the New Left of the '60s also doesn't seem to understand that the Reagan revolution of the '80s is permanent (Deregulate this! Phooey on government!). So my memories of a time when public services seemed to work and people felt some sort of connection with a commonweal that was more than saving taxpayer dollars and NIMBY are probably as useless as the memories of a White Russian of when she employed servants, as opposed to her sadly diminished present-day reality of being employed as one.

It's not just technolibertarians who do not want to pay for things they can't see — though how much of their blindness is willful, or based on ignorance, is hard to tell.

But I do believe that if you don't understand where you have come from, you can't well understand where you might end up. And I don't believe that a culture that presents itself as being the One True Way of the future, but which in so many ways embodies the worst of the past — where humane values and, ultimately, people count for less than machines — is one that is cause for rejoicing.

Afterword to the 2026 edition of *Cyberselfish*

Cyberselfish was written as a description of a subculture. It was never intended as a book of prophecy, but that sadly is what it has turned out to be. Social scientists and historians probably have a name for what happens when a minority culture becomes a majority one: what was written about here has become the dominant ideology of Silicon Valley leaders. The trends and ideas of this subculture coming into domination have had effects far worse than I could have imagined back when I was working on the project in the 1990s.

Happy days, *Cyberselfish* was fortunate enough to have been well and widely reviewed all over the world when it came out, but it did not sell well. No doubt the dot-com crash ("let's not think about those tech fools we got taken in by") followed by 9/11 turned attention elsewhere. Thus the book went out of print decades ago, only a few years after it was published.

There had been some glimmers of renewed interest in the title in 2025; prices on used-book platforms started creeping up from the longtime humiliating low of five dollars (where postage and handling were greater than the cost of the book itself) increasing within a few months to around ten dollars per copy—and then suddenly moving ever upward. Before *Cyberselfish* became totally unavailable, the asking price was two hundred dollars and higher. Graduate students from around the world reached out, asking if I could help because they could not afford collectible rare-book prices. There was nothing I could do for this new generation of readers.

Around the same time, in 2025, European academics started wanting to talk to me, as did some European media folks; I think the rise of Musk and DOGE were driving these outreach efforts.

In May of 2025, a meteor strike hit my LinkedIn page. Jonathan Sandhu, whom I had not heard of, then a stranger, posted a detailed appreciation of *Cyberselfish*. Inspired by a mentor of his, Steven Hertzberg, someone else I had no acquaintance with, Sandhu began his post:

> In 2000, Paulina Borsook published *Cyberselfish: A Critical Romp Through the Terribly Libertarian Culture of High Tech*. The title alone told you what you were in for: a scalpel through Silicon Valley's self-congratulatory delusions. She called the industry's bluff on its faux-rebel mythos, its anti-government fetish, its pathological allergy to the social contract. She mapped the libertarian ego trip before it bought a hoodie and launched a surveillance startup.
>
> And no one listened.
>
> The book dropped during the dot-com collapse. It vanished almost instantly. Not because she was wrong—but because she was too right, too early, and too unwilling to flatter the cathedral of code. The world rewarded those who said it all later, softer, or with credentials. And those people got book deals, fellowships, think tank gigs, tenured chairs, and keynote slots.
>
> Paulina got ignored.

And the post continued after that.

Sandhu's text went viral. Sometimes the algorithm gives, in contrast to all the times it takes away.

The post went on to show up in front of so many people who weren't acquainted with Sandhu or me or *Cyberselfish*. And a few of these newly acquainted with the work turned out to be critical to bringing it back from its state of suspended animation.

David Sierra bought a paperback and two hardcovers of *Cyberselfish* when these were still available for purchase in 2025. Among the many skills Sierra possesses are expertise with computer vision; after I asked him frantically if he could create a

PDF of the book, which was needed to help make the case for the book's revival to potential publishers, he did so within ten minutes(!). All electronic versions had long since been vaporized by Public Affairs, the now-Hachette-owned publisher of *Cyberselfish*; the book had been out of print for too long.

Another person the algorithm mysteriously led me to was Giovanni Lostumbo. Lostumbo would do many things on behalf of the revivification of *Cyberselfish,* such as search Substack to determine that starting in March 2025 there were more and more mentions of the book, still more proof of its reputational renaissance.

Lostumbo asked if I knew Gil Duran. "No, who's Gil Duran?" I was told Duran was working on a book named *The Nerd Reich.* I pinged Duran (whom Lostumbo was already in communication with); he had heard of *Cyberselfish* and we arranged to have lunch, where we then realized we were natural allies.

As a coincidence, shortly after that lunch, *Wired* published a piece that more or less said "How did these guys turn out to be such sociopathic louts?" Duran, who had been interviewed for the feature, was not quoted and *Cyberselfish* was not mentioned. Displeased, Duran wrote a long post on BlueSky to the effect of "*Cyberselfish* is really important and what writing about tech ought to be and the work has been unjustly forgotten. Let's help bring it back into print." Another case of where the algorithm giveth: Duran's post took off on BlueSky more so than anything else he had ever posted there and caught the attention of *New York Times* writer David Streitfeld.

Streitfeld was intrigued by the death and life of *Cyberselfish.* He and I talked and emailed for months and in the middle of this process, Duran had me appear on his podcast, aided by the work of his researcher/editor/producer Riley Robbins. The algos looked favorably upon this podcast episode as well, and within days, all copies of *Cyberselfish* had sold out globally. It then became only available in unauthorized editions or in the abridged audiobook from way back when: I had never been consulted about the abridgment.

The interaction with Streitfeld led to a feature appearing in the *Times* on Thanksgiving of 2025. That day, my agent, Stuart Krichevsky, emailed: "We always knew you were right." Publishers became interested in a reprint and thus *Cyberselfish* has been brought back to life from the Graveyard of Lost Works.

The following souls had the beat and kept it strong: David Temkin, Maria Bustillos, Kurt Taylor Gaubatz, Jeff Ubois, John Rieger, Jason Kehe. Each helped in his or her particular way to resurrect *Cyberselfish*.

It is unhappily worth mentioning that *Cyberselfish* was originally composed in a safer time. Freedom of expression wasn't so in jeopardy. Online and real-world harassment of people who hew to heterodox points of view hadn't become so intense and scary. I don't know that I would have had the courage to write *Cyberselfish* in 2026; I am just so grateful that what in effect is a twenty-fifth anniversary edition is now available.

That Damned Book a.k.a. TDB was the nickname I had long given *Cyberselfish*. It went through three publishers and threw me terribly in debt. A friend who bought TDB when it first came out remarked that it was truer in 2025 than when it was written. It seems there have always been larger forces at play in terms of the fate of *Cyberselfish*; rhetoric that's positioned for the future sounds a bit touched by the supernatural.

Paulina Borsook

ACKNOWLEDGMENTS

Undying gratitude and eternal thanx to:

Dan Lynch and Noel Chiappa. If all technolibertarians were like you two, I wish all the world could be technolibertarian.

Stuart Krichevsky, my agent, whose ferociously funny advocacy has never ceased to astonish and delight ever since I first lucked into it during my last semester in the Writing Division, School of the Arts, Columbia University in the City of New York. And to Paula Balzer, Stuart's former second-in-command, for her drollery and hand-holding.

Lisa Kaufman, editor extraordinaire, and all the other sweet smart humorous people at PublicAffairs. Long may you thrive as the publishers all authors would wish to have.

Kerry Lauerman and Sarah Pollock, formerly of Mother Jones, who, when all the rest of the world said "fie," believed that there was a story worth telling. Joey Anuff, Ana Marie Cox, and Carl Steadman, formerly of www.suck.com, for providing a run-time testbed for the ideas in this book. Amanda Griscom, Steven Johnson, and Stefanie Sayman at www.feedmag.com, who at a very critical moment, found some value in a very early prototype of the Bionomics chapter.

My Gentle Readers, who graciously agreed to read various portions of various drafts and have made valiant efforts to protect me from egregious errors of thought and fact. I am sure I have committed to print many gaffes in the making of TDB (That Damned Book), but that is not the fault of these very parfait gentlemen: Jon Callas, Peter Hero, Stefan Krempl, Paul Krugman, John Lazzaro, Larry Lessig, John Norman, and Alan Snitow. Very special thanks to Owen Thomas, amanuensis nonpareil.

The people who took me into their confidence and told me what they really thought, on condition that it remain off the record. Thank you for placing your trust in me.

The people who provided every possible assistance: crash-pads, mezzanine financing, use of their social and professional networks, suggestions of people to talk to and stuff to read, operation of crisis hotlines, access to their private intellectual capital, vocational assistance, housesitting, serendipity, and other things along the way too complicated to get into: Phil Agre, Steve Arbuss, Doug Barnes, John Perry Barlow, Tom Bell, Daniel Ben-Horin, Chip Berlet, Andy Blau, Richard Brandt, Chris Brantley, Glee Cady, Dan Carol, Jon Carroll, Jim Cook, Karen Coyle, George Davis, Gregory Dreicer, Larry Fields, Bronwyn Fryer, Kurt Gaubatz, Lawrence Gasman, Steve Gibson, James Glave, Mike Godwin, Marianne Goldberger, Jeff Goodell, Katie Hafner, Connie Hale, Christine and John Hollis, Emily Hoyer, Mike Huben, David Hudson, Mitch Kapor, the Kennedys next door, Tom Kosnik, Jon Lebkowsky, Judith Lewis, Jon Levine, Marina MacDougal, Susan McCarthy, Steve Martin, John Markoff, Vinnie Moscaritolo, Stanley Moss, David Noble, Sara O'Callaghan, Tori Orr, Andy Reinhardt, Scott Rosenberg, Corey Sandler, Nathan Shedroff, Jack Shulman, Rod Simpson, Dave Smallen, Dan Solomon, Kristen Spence, David Stanford, Mark Stephens, Lucy Suchman, Andrew Sullivan, Jeff Ubois, Ellen Ullman, Colin Ungaro, Beth Weise, Ed Weschler, Margaret Wertheim, John Perry Wiltgen (RIP), and Brian Zisk. To each of you, even if it's for reasons I wouldn't even know how to begin to explain, or for things you provided or set in motion years ago, I owe a debt I can never repay. Some of you may be surprised to find yourself on this list, but trust me, you were all part of the process of creating TDB.

Susan Sontag, whom I've never met, whose life and work have been an inspiration since before I hit puberty. In particular, "Illness as Metaphor" served as a model of what a book-length essay can be.

My neighbors in Santa Cruz, and their landlords, who served as a constant reminder during the writing of TDB of what's wrong with a worldview that's about property rights and nothing else.

Clive Matson, Doug Cruikshank, Phillip Lopate, John Battelle, and Louis Rossetto, who at different times and in different ways, encouraged me in the perhaps-mistaken belief that there was value to writing in a Martian way.

DISACKNOWLEDGMENTS

I must mention Jonathon Keats, because he asked to be listed here.

Printed and bound by CPI Group (UK) Ltd, Croydon, CR0 4YY
11/09/2026
02215520-0003